THE LAST BATTLE ON ENGLISH SOIL, PRESTON 1715

The book is dedicated to Liz, from Yorkshire.

The Last Battle on English Soil, Preston 1715

JONATHAN OATES
London Borough of Ealing Archives, UK

ASHGATE

© Jonathan Oates 2015

All rights reserved. No part of this publication may be reproduced, stored in a retrieval system or transmitted in any form or by any means, electronic, mechanical, photocopying, recording or otherwise without the prior permission of the publisher.

Jonathan Oates has asserted his right under the Copyright, Designs and Patents Act, 1988, to be identified as the author of this work.

Published by
Ashgate Publishing Limited
Wey Court East
Union Road
Farnham
Surrey, GU9 7PT
England

Ashgate Publishing Company
110 Cherry Street
Suite 3–1
Burlington, VT 05401–3818
USA

www.ashgate.com

British Library Cataloguing in Publication Data
A catalogue record for this book is available from the British Library

Library of Congress Cataloging-in-Publication Data
Oates, Jonathan.
　The last battle on English soil, Preston 1715 / by Jonathan Oates.
　　　pages cm
　Includes bibliographical references and index.
　ISBN 978–1–4724–4155–3 (hardcover : alkaline paper) – ISBN 978–1–4724–4156–0 (ebook) – ISBN 978–1–4724–4157–7 (ePub)
　1. Jacobite Rebellion, 1715 – Campaigns – England – Preston (Lancashire) 2. Preston (Lancashire, England) – History, Military – 18th century. 3. Jacobite Rebellion, 1715 – Campaigns – England, Northern. 4. Jacobite Rebellion, 1715 – Campaigns – Scotland – Lowlands. 5. England, Northern – History, Military – 18th century. 6. Lowlands (Scotland) – History, Military – 18th century. 7. Jacobite Rebellion, 1715 – Social aspects. I. Title.
　DA814.3.O25 2015
　941.07'1–dc23
　　　　　　　　　　　　　　　　　　　　　　　　　　　　　　　　2014048294

ISBN: 9781472441553 (hbk)
ISBN: 9781472441560 (ebk – PDF)
ISBN: 9781472441577 (ebk – ePUB)

Printed in the United Kingdom by Henry Ling Limited, at the Dorset Press, Dorchester, DT1 1HD

Contents

Acknowledgements   *vii*
List of Illustrations   *ix*

Introduction   1

1   Prelude to the Fifteen, 1688–1715   11

2   The Jacobite Insurrection in the North of England, October 1715   29

3   The North West of England, September – October 1715   55

4   The Jacobite March South, November 1715   71

5   The Opposing Sides   97

6   The Battle of Preston, 12–14 November 1715   123

7   The Aftermath of the Fifteen, 1715–1717   159

Postscript in 1745   187

Conclusion   189

Appendix 1: Jacobite Rioters   193
Appendix 2: Jacobite Prisoners   197
Appendix 3: British Army Casualties   217
Appendix 4: Civilian Losses   221

Selected Bibliography   *229*
Index   *239*

Acknowledgements

This book has its genesis in 2007, a year after the publication of a book I had written about the Jacobite invasion of North West England in 1745. It was written as a prequel, but one which considered the roles of the Jacobite army and the regular forces of the state, both military and judicial, both during and after the campaign. In the intervening years it has undergone numerous rewritings in order to increase our understanding of that campaign in England.

I would like to thank all those who have helped me with this book. These include Professor Daniel Szechi, Professor Bill Speck, John Nicholls MBE and Dr Eveline Cruickshanks, for having commented on the text. Don Higham and Ruth Costello have looked up documents relevant to Jacobite prisoners for me and my mother has assisted with research at Preston. Sir Bernard de Hoghton, Paul Howard Lang, John Nicholls and Towneley Hall have helped with a number of the illustrations seen here. Lancashire Record Office and the National Portrait Gallery, London, also assisted with the provision of illustrations. To the archive and library staff in London, Carlisle, Preston, Kendal and Chester, who fetched me numerous documents, without which this book would have been impossible, my thanks.

List of Illustrations

Illustrations between pages 122 and 123

1. Earl of Derwentwater. Author's collection.

2. Thomas Forster, MP. Courtesy of John Nicholls MBE.

3. Francis Atterbury. Author's collection.

4. Baron George Carpenter. Mezzotint by John Faber Jr, after Johan van Diest (1719 or after). NPG D11252. National Portrait Gallery, London.

5. Hoghton Tower. Courtesy of Sir Bernard de Hoghton.

6. Richard Towneley. Towneley Hall Museum.

7. Sir Charles Wills. Mezzotint by John Simon (published by Edward Cooper, after Michael Dahl, published circa 1700–1725). NPG D19943. National Portrait Gallery, London.

8. Map of the North of England. Author.

9. Map of the Battle of Preston. Lancashire Record Office.

10. Re-enactors: Redcoat soldiers, 2013. Author's photo.

11. Re-enactors: Jacobites, 2013. Author's photo.

Introduction

This is a book in which a battle looms large – the last battle fought on English soil, which was at Preston. It is, then, to a large extent a military history, about the officers and men and the little known and less understood battle in which they participated. Yet, in order to understand why and where the battle was fought, it is also highly relevant to explore the campaign which led to it, and it also concerns those civilians in the north-western counties who found themselves caught up in that campaign, that battle and its aftermath, for distinctions between combatant and non-combatant were not always clear-cut. So there are also elements of political, social and religious history interlaced with military matters.

There was a major military effort to overturn the newly established monarchy and government in Britain in 1715. However, it is a relatively overlooked episode in British history, which this book aims to shed light on, building on the work of recent scholars, especially Daniel Szechi's magisterial survey of the whole campaign and its aftermath.[1] In doing so, it reveals fresh insights on the Fifteen, and so is pertinent to both national history and local history. It also explores the effectiveness and remit of the early modern state as it operated at county level.

This relative neglect is not surprising. The Jacobite rebellion of 1715 is usually overshadowed by the better-known Jacobite campaign of 1745, as is oft remarked upon by the historians of the former.[2] There are very few books solely on the subject (four in the past century); this may be because of historians' traditional neglect of the topic or publishers' doubts about the viability of such a publication. Often it is treated as a cursory prelude to the better-known rebellion or the history of the British Army, or appears fleetingly in books about battlefields in England/Britain. In terms of more popular culture, there are no films set at the time of the Fifteen, nor, for Preston, are there any battlefield memorials and only a small display in the town museum; in all, the Forty Five reigns supreme.

---

[1] Daniel Szechi, *1715: The Great Jacobite Rebellion*, London: Yale University Press, 2006.

[2] John Baynes, *The Jacobite Rising of 1715* London: Cassell, 1970, 203–4.

Yet contemporaries saw the matter in a very different light. The number of men in Britain who supported the Jacobite cause by joining the Jacobite armies was far higher in 1715 than in 1745. This support was not just from the Stuarts' traditional heartland of Scotland, but from northern England, too, and from all sections of society. From the government's point of view, this was a very dangerous threat. The new king of a new and foreign dynasty, George I, had been on the throne for barely a year, and he and his government presided over a politically divided society. Furthermore, the armed forces had been reduced following the end of the War of the Spanish Succession (1702–13). It is arguable that this bid for the throne posed a greater danger than that of 1745, despite all the latter's apparent initial success.

A definition of what a Jacobite was is essential at the outset. It was a term which came from the Latin for James, Jacobus. In the context of this book, a Jacobite was someone who wished James Francis Edward Stuart, son of James II, to be restored to the thrones which had been lost by his father in 1688. He was known to his supporters as James VIII and III; to his enemies as the Pretender (and to history, generally, as the Old Pretender). The extent of the Jacobites' commitment was variable, ranging from drinking his health in private, to taking part in demonstrations in public, to participating in active conspiracies and even rising in arms to put James on the British throne.

As said, the study of Jacobitism and the Jacobite rebellions puts the '45 foremost. Studies of it, its battles and its leading participants, especially Charles Edward Stuart, are legion. The Fifteen is usually given short shrift as part of wider studies; a very necessary prologue but not worth a study in its own right. The last half-century has seen but three full-length studies.[3]

Several additional reasons can, perhaps, be put forward to explain this neglect. Firstly, the principal characters of the Forty Five – Charles Edward Stuart, Lord George Murray, the Duke of Cumberland and Flora MacDonald – tend to appear as larger-than-life heroes and villains, and most people react strongly towards them. The principals of the Fifteen – the Earl of Mar, James Stuart, Thomas Forster, Generals Argyle, Wills and Carpenter – seem less colourful, and uninspiring. With the exception of James Radcliffe, the third Earl of Derwentwater (1689–1716), they do not attract or repel as those of the Forty Five do. Derwentwater has been the subject of a number of books in the

---

[3] Christopher Sinclair-Stevenson, *Inglorious Rebellion: The Jacobite Risings of 1708, 1715 and 1719*, London, 1971; Michael Barthorp, *The Jacobite Rebellions, 1689–1745*, London: Osprey, 1982; John Roberts, *The Highland Wars: The Military Campaigns in Scotland of 1715 and 1745*, Polygon: Edinburgh, 2002; John Sadler, *Culloden: The Last Charge of the Highland Clans, 1746*, Stroud: Tempus, 2006.

nineteenth century, venerated as a Catholic hero and martyr.[4] The Forty Five included the dramatic Jacobite march to Derby, with London menaced, and then the long retreat to the decisive Battle of Culloden. The battles of Sherriffmuir and Preston in 1715 seem less colourful, and indecisive. The rebellion petered out in 1716; in 1746, there was a decisive battle. Culloden is commemorated by a visitor centre and battlefield monuments; Preston lacks these. Finally, some historians might cite the lack of source material; very few memoirs, newspapers, State Papers and correspondence, certainly when compared to 1745–46.

That said, there have been a number of full-length studies of the rebellion published from 1716. They all concentrated on Scotland, perhaps not unnaturally, because the bulk of the active military campaigning took place there; it was there that the Jacobites first openly rose in arms, and where they were at their numerical apex; it was to Scotland that their leader eventually arrived; and it was in Scotland that the last Jacobite units were dispersed in 1716. Relatively little space has been allocated to the English dimension of the struggle, and certainly not to that of the North West of England, where the rebellion's English dimension was resolved. It has not been ignored, but it has been under-examined and myths left unchallenged.[5] Nowhere is its military and political importance considered. As Szechi notes at the outset of his recent study, by his own admission a far from definitive work, 'Young scholars come hither; there is a great deal more work for you to do'.[6]

This book will seek to shed light on the campaign of the North West of England, the battle of Preston and its aftermath, examining the actions of numerous players in the conflict, inactive as well as those who were otherwise. It will also assess the importance of the battle as part of the overall campaign.

In order to do so, it is divided into seven chapters. Chapter 1 discusses the political flashpoints in the North West of England from the year following the accession of George I to the raising of the Jacobite standard at Braemar in

---

[4] William Gibson, *Dilston Hall*, 1850; Charles Bowden, *The Life of the Right Honourable James Radcliffe*, 1897.

[5] Anon., *A Compleat History of the Late Rebellion*, Dublin: Thos. Hume, 1716; Anon., *A Compleat History of the Late Rebellion*, London: W. Hinchliffe, 1716; Robert Patten, *The History of the Rebellion*, London: J. Warner, 1745; Peter Rae, *History of the Late Rebellion rais'd against ... King George by the friends of the Popish Pretender*, Dumfries, 1745; Samuel Hibbert-Ware, 'Lancashire Memorials of 1715', *Chetham Society*, 5, 1845; Alastair and Henrietta Tayler, *1715: The Story of the Rising*, London: Thomas Nelson and Sons, 1936; Baynes, *Jacobite Rising*; Szechi, *1715*; Margaret Sankey, *Jacobite Prisoners of the 1715 Rebellion: Preventing and Punishing Insurrection in Early Hanoverian Britain*, Aldershot: Ashgate, 2005.

[6] Szechi, *1715*, xiii.

September 1715. Rioting which took place in England, together with the rioters themselves, have been the subject of a nationwide study by Monod and of the study of the North of England by Oates (the latter also surveying responses to the said rioting).[7] Yet rioting was not the only phenomenon pertinent to what was to happen next; displays of loyalty to the government were not unknown, as well as grounds being laid there for a potential challenge against the new dynasty.

Chapter 2 is a narrative account of the progress of the Jacobite forces in the North East of England and the Borders of Scotland in October 1715, and of their enemies there. Parts of this period of the campaign are not unknown; all accounts of the Fifteen cover it since this is where the Jacobites first rose in revolt. The Rev. Robert Patten's *History* is a well-known source for the activity of the Jacobite forces at this time. Patten had been a Jacobite, and so was an eye-witness to these events.[8] Their ultimately unsuccessful marches have been little analysed, but the consensus has been that they were lacking in determination. Baynes wrote, 'the point cannot be overstressed that rebellions are activities which require immense vigour and drive to bring them to successful fruition; waiting is the tactic for the established army and not for the rebel'.[9]

More recently this longstanding consensus has been challenged, and the most detailed study of the Northumbrian Jacobites and their efforts has been by Leo Gooch.[10] He argues that the plan of campaign was well thought out, but that they were let down by the non-arrival of allies from abroad and by the decisive steps taken by their enemies. This is a very sympathetic account in contrast to the largely negative accounts by those historians writing after Patten. The counter-measures of their opponents, though, have been under-examined. Significant sources are the writings of leading Northumbrian Whigs such as John Johnson, the county's High Sheriff, and William Cotesworth, a Gateshead coal merchant, whose correspondence has survived and much has been published.[11] Archives of the War Office and Secretary of State (Scotland and Britain) also illuminate military activity at this time.[12]

---

[7] Paul Kleber Monod, *Jacobitism and the English People, 1689–1788*, Cambridge: Cambridge University Press, 1989, 173–94; J. Oates, 'Jacobitism and Popular Disturbances in Northern England, 1714–1719', *Northern History*, XLI:1, 2004.

[8] Patten, *History*.

[9] Baynes, *Jacobite Rising*, 90.

[10] Leo Gooch, *The Desperate Faction: The Jacobites of North East England, 1688–1746*, Hull: Hull University Press, 1995.

[11] Liddell, Henry, 'The Letters of Henry Liddell to William Cotesworth', ed. Joyce Ellis, Surtees Society, 197, 1987; Cowper, Mary, *Diary of Mary, Lady Cowper*, ed. Spencer Compton, London: John Murray, 1865.

[12] National Archives, SP44/116–20; WO 4/7 17, 5/20, 71/122, 116/1.

Chapter 3 is a discussion of the forces in the north-western counties of England in autumn 1715, both those sympathetic towards the Jacobite cause and those who were hostile towards them. Because histories of the Fifteen have focussed on the action of armies marching and not on those districts where they did not, activity in the north-western English counties in September and October has been overlooked. Yet they were the scene of active preparations on the part of those opposed to Jacobitism, for there was much hostility to the new government and dynasty there, given the district's recent history, as well as its political and religious sympathies.

Sources in the county record offices are crucial. The principal ones are Lancashire Record Office, Cheshire Archives and the four Record Offices for Cumbria. These contain, principally, the archives of the County Quarter Sessions, who ruled the localities in the eighteenth century. These include order books which detail what these authorities did in the time of acute crisis as in 1715. City order books contain similar information for activity there. They detail action taken against suspects and other security measures.

Lower down the administrative system were the parishes. Their archives include churchwardens' and, somewhat rarer, constables' accounts. Here payments are listed and many refer to unusual activity in response to the Jacobite incursion. Constables' accounts list payments referring to weapons and the militia; churchwardens' to ringing the church bells to denote their loyalties, or to hiding the church silver. These record offices sometimes contain letters and other papers of individuals writing at the time of events, but these are rare.

A valuable published source is the lieutenancy and quarter sessions records for this period for the county of Cumberland. Rupert Jarvis edited them and had them published in an excellent volume in 1954.[13] There is much here which records the activity of the Lords Lieutenant, the Justices of the Peace and the constables during the 1715 and 1745 Jacobite rebellions. These men were responsible for 'local government' in the counties, and one of their main tasks was to maintain law and order as far as possible with the limited means at their disposal.

Chapter 4 is a mixture of narrative and analysis. It outlines the Jacobite army's march through the north-western counties towards Preston, and the levels of support and opposition they encountered. One well-worn topic is of the strength of the posse of Cumberland, sent to oppose the Jacobites – most

---

[13] Rupert Jarvis, *The Jacobite Risings of 1715 and 1745 compiled from original documents in the possession of Cumberland County Council*, Cumberland: Cumberland County Council, 1954.

historians numbering it at over 10,000.[14] The only sceptical voice has been that of Rupert Jarvis, writing that 'these accounts all contain statements inherently improbable or absurd'.[15] Nor were the loyalist forces in Lancashire much better; according to Bruce Lenman they were 'thrown into some disarray by the sudden switch of the Jacobite forces from Newcastle to Lancashire' and it was 'considered that the loyalties of the bulk of the people were so dubious'.[16] One resilient myth, repeated as recently as 2005, surrounds the bravery of a Whig clergyman, the Rev. Samuel Peploe of Preston, who, when threatened in his church by an armed Jacobite, replied, 'Soldier, do your duty and I will do mine'.[17]

Chapter 5 is an examination of the Jacobites of the north-western counties and their opponents. One of the perennial issues of Jacobite history concerns the level of support that the cause enjoyed in England. Just as importantly, there is the question of how acceptable the Hanoverian dynasty was to the bulk of the population. Both these sides to the equation are crucial in explaining the outcome of the campaign. It is sometimes stated that the bulk of the Tories were supportive of the Jacobite cause, and with them, the Catholics and at least some of the Anglican clergy; whereas the Whigs and the Dissenters are seen as loyal adherents to George I. Yet how accurate is such a generalisation? Given that the Jacobite army marched through the North West, this was a test for the political allegiances of local people. Numbers bandied about as regards Jacobite strength are of importance because they are an obvious indicator. It is customary for those hostile towards the Jacobites to downplay their numbers and those more sympathetic to maximise them.

The part played by the Jacobites of the North West was thus essential. It has often been denigrated, even by sympathetic historians. One eminent historian even claimed that the rebellion of 1715 was restricted to Scotland![18] The Taylers referred to 'those elusive Jacobites of Lancashire, whose enthusiasm in 1715, as again in 1745, was chiefly confined to toasting the Stuart Prince and bore scarcely any real fruit in the way of military help'. The Taylers note in 1715 that there were 75 English gentlemen and nobles in total 'and only a few hundred

---

[14] Taylers, *1715: The Story of the Rising*, 82; Baynes, *Jacobite Rising*, 106; Leo Gooch, *The Desperate Faction: The Jacobites of North East England, 1688–1745*, Hull: Hull University Press, 79; Geoffrey Holmes and Daniel Szechi, *The Age of Oligarchy, England, 1722–1783*, Longman, 1993, 98; Ralph Arnold, *Northern Lights: The Story of the Lord Derwentwater*, London: Constable, 1959, 105.
[15] Jarvis, *The Jacobite Risings*, 99.
[16] Lenman, *The Jacobite Risings in Britain*, 125.
[17] Baynes, *Jacobite Rising*, 111; Sankey, *Jacobite Prisoners of the 1715*, 50n.
[18] John Plumb, *The First Four Georges*, London: Fontana, 1956, 46.

English'.[19] Gooch gives a total of 1,700 Jacobites in the Anglo-Scottish army in England on 3 November, but does not trouble about the Lancashire men.[20] As with the Taylers, Baynes relies on numbers of prisoners, giving the same numbers of officers, but with 388 other Englishmen. Sinclair-Stevenson agrees with Baynes, but gives an unsourced number of 1,200 Lancastrian recruits.[21] Monod estimates a total of 1,000 Englishmen; including at least 366 Lancastrians, 19 from Cumberland, 4 from Westmorland and 3 from Cheshire; excluding those who escaped (perhaps about 200–300).[22] Sadler states that the army's total strength, including the Scots, was under 2,400 men.[23]

Lenman notes the potential for Jacobite support in Lancashire: 'Here was a rich vein of potential support which the Jacobites hoped to mine. Nor were they totally unsuccessful in doing so'. He puts this down to the strong Catholicism of the county, to the hatred of local Dissent, and the strong interlinkage of gentry families there; at Preston there was 'a good deal of positive enthusiasm for the rebels' but 'without exception these gentlemen were Roman Catholics'. Yet he notes that the reality was limited, with only two recruits from Lancaster, and that the 'general response of the High Anglican Tories to the Jacobite rising was so apathetic as to constitute a decisive blow to the prospects of the rebels'.[24] According to Speck, 'some 1,600 recruits did come in, but it was observed that they were for the most part catholics and hardly any anglican tories were prepared to lift a finger for the pretender'.[25] Szechi concludes that 'the English half of the '15 went off like a damp squib'.[26]

As well as numbers, another key question concerns the military capacity of the Jacobite army and especially its leadership. Although Patten defends the activity of his master, the Jacobite general Thomas Forster, most historians have deemed him a coward and a fool. A typical assessment comes from Lenman, writing, 'Tom Forster was quite remarkably useless at everything, except saving his own skin.'[27] Yet in more recent times, this view has been questioned. Gooch writes, 'Forster's leadership should not be disparaged because of his failure to

---

[19] Taylers, *1715*, 80, 84.
[20] Gooch, *The Desperate Faction*, 79.
[21] Baynes, *Jacobite Rising*, 126, Sinclair-Stevenson, *Inglorious Rebellion*, 110, 112.
[22] Monod, *Jacobitism*, 321–2.
[23] Sadler, *Culloden*, 64, 65.
[24] Lenman, *The Jacobite Risings in Britain*, 123–5.
[25] William Speck, *Stability and Strife, England, 1714–1760*, London: Edward Arnold, 1977, 181.
[26] Szechi, *The Jacobites: Britain and Europe, 1688–1788*, Manchester: Manchester University Press, 1994, 75.
[27] Lenman, *Jacobite Risings*, 120.

bring off an operation he was neither qualified for nor intended to conduct'.[28] Yet Gooch failed to heed the criticisms levelled by contemporaries of Forster and does not examine Forster's role (or lack of it) during the battle.

This book also includes a military analysis of the generals and forces who were about to face each other in battle. Given that there is very little correspondence surviving from the victorious generals, this neglect is unsurprising, but there are other sources – those at the National Archives as referred to above, and part of a memoir of a junior officer – which help to explain the motivations of the commanding officers, leading to the battle of Preston.[29]

Chapter 6 is a detailed narrative of the battle of Preston and the events leading to the Jacobite surrender. The most thorough account of the battle to date has been by Baynes, but it suffers from a reliance on a limited number of published primary sources (chiefly those by Rae and Patten and those used in Hibbert-Ware's work). All other accounts are sketchy in comparison, though Szechi's is enriched by a fine diversity of source material.

Analysis of the battle's outcome is limited, with the majority of writers avoiding it almost entirely. More recently, there have been the radically diverse views of Gooch and Szechi. Gooch views the battle and the defeat of the rebellion as foregone conclusions and Forster as merely accepting reality against 'overwhelming odds' when he surrendered, after he had been let down by others.[30] Szechi disagrees. Unlike Gooch, he has utilised a number of anonymous but probably junior officers' accounts written shortly after the battle, which throw a different perspective on the fighting. He argues that the regulars were exhausted, demoralised after a day's lack of success, compared to the Jacobite rank and file who enjoyed high morale (unlike their leaders), and that an attempted escape 'offered them at least a fighting chance of both breaking out ... and inflicting a comprehensive defeat on a major government army'.[31]

The effectiveness of the armies at Preston is worth a re-evaluation. Did missed opportunities mean that the outcome could have been different? Was there incompetence on the part of the victorious generals? The military efforts of the regular army have gone largely unassessed, though one general's conduct has been severely criticised in recent years.[32]

---

[28] Gooch, *Desperate Faction*, 84.
[29] Charles Colville, 'Military Memoirs of Lieutenant General the Hon. Charles Colville', ed. J.O. Robson, *Journal of the Society for Army Historical Research*, XXV, 1947.
[30] Gooch, *Desperate Faction*, 84–5.
[31] Szechi, *1715*, 179.
[32] Szechi, *1715*, 196.

Contrary to popular opinion, in this instance, history has been largely written by the losers. This include four accounts by Scottish Lowlanders (the unpublished ones are probably two drafts by the same hand), the first of the published ones appearing in print in 1716, and the aforementioned *History* by Patten. The former mount a serious attack on the competence of Forster, who can do nothing right, while Patten defends the reputation of his erstwhile master at each turn. These Scottish accounts suggest that better leadership from Forster would have resulted in a glorious victory. Accounts supportive of the government in newspapers, in Rae's *History* and in soldiers' correspondence are sketchy indeed.[33]

The last chapter is an examination of the events taking place in the North West after the surrender at Preston, examining the behaviour of both victors and vanquished, including the process in which the numerous prisoners were dealt with in 1715–17.

Most histories of the campaign relegate the fates of the prisoners to a limited remit and one that is factually inaccurate. Much work has been done to rectify this by Margaret Sankey, who discusses the fate of the Jacobite prisoners throughout Britain and argues that the government aimed to show justice tempered by mercy towards its captured enemies, and so their lot, on the whole, was not severe by the standards of the time.[34] However, the omission of a crucial eye-witness report leads the account to be rosier than would otherwise have been the case.[35] The actions of the other participants in the campaign has been virtually ignored. The fates of both victors and vanquished will, therefore, be reconsidered herein.

Lastly, it should be noted that, although we know that the Hanoverian dynasty proved a resilient one and survived all the efforts of the Jacobites to supplant it, contemporaries did not have this knowledge. In fact, in the century before 1715, England had seen two monarchs overthrown, civil wars, republicanism, revolution and invasion. There was no way of telling that George I and his supporters would be permanent figures on the political landscape. England was famed for its chronic political instability at this time, and before we judge the actions of contemporaries we must remember that it was a very uncertain period and the outcome far from inevitable or foreseeable.

This new study of the Fifteen focuses solely on the North of England. Usually this is treated briefly within a consideration of the Fifteen, or, even more

---

[33] Rae, *History*.
[34] Sankey, *Jacobite Prisoners*.
[35] Henry Prescott, 'The Diary of Henry Prescott, LL.B., Deputy Registrar of Chester Diocese, II', ed. John Addy and Peter McNiven, *Record Society of Lancashire and Cheshire*, 132, 1994.

fleetingly, within a chapter or two as part of a wider study of Jacobitism or the Jacobite rebellions. This book puts the region, and its climactic battle, centre stage and exerts its importance in the history of the Jacobite campaigns and in the history of the Fifteen in particular. In doing so it also aims to challenge long-established myths, to critically consider the roles of both sides and non-combatants of varying political persuasion, and to assess the significance of this regional struggle and the battle within the framework of the campaign of 1715–16 and afterwards.

Chapter 1
Prelude to the Fifteen, 1688–1715

The period leading up to the Fifteen in the North West of England has not been studied in detail in its own right, and activity here has largely been confined to wider studies. Thus, there have been accounts of the Jacobite plotting in Lancashire in the 1690s.[1] Moving 20 years onwards, there have been studies of popular anti-Hanoverian disturbances, both on a national level and in the North of England.[2] Yet there was more to this in the political history of the north-western counties in the period leading up to rebellion in 1715.

Britain's last Catholic monarch, James II (1633–1701), fled England in December 1688 following the invasion of the Protestant William of Orange (1650–1702), who with his wife, James's eldest surviving daughter, Mary (1662–94), was crowned joint monarch in the following year. Responses in the North West of England to these tumultuous events were, as elsewhere, mixed. In December 1688, Chester Castle was held by those loyal to James, until his flight was confirmed, while elsewhere William's supporters threatened the garrison at Carlisle and others rode to join their fellows at Nottingham. No blood, however, was shed, although there were unfounded panics about disbanded Irish and Catholic soldiers intent on massacring the Protestant population.

James II had not given up his claim to the sovereignty of the three kingdoms, and in 1689 arrived in Ireland to continue the struggle from there. In Scotland, Viscount Dundee raised some of the Highland clans on his behalf. And in England, there were rumours about Catholic conspiracies. Furthermore, James II had the support of Louis XIV of France, the most powerful monarch in Europe.

Yet, despite initial successes, James's supporters were defeated in both Scotland and Ireland and the French invasion fleet was also ultimately beaten off. Jacobites in England, and in Lancashire in particular, were far from being cowed, however. In 1694, a number of the leading Catholic families in the county were implicated in a plot to restore James. Although they were found

---

[1] P. Hopkins, 'Real and Sham Plots in the 1690s', in E. Cruickshanks, ed., *Ideology and Conspiracy: Aspects of Jacobitism, 1689–1759*, Edinburgh: John Donald Publishers, 1982.

[2] N. Rogers, 'Riot and Popular Jacobitism in Early Modern England', in Cruickshanks, *Ideology and Conspiracy*; J. Oates, 'Jacobitism and Popular Disturbances in Northern England, 1714–1719', *Northern History*, XLI:1, 2004.

to be not guilty, the government's supporters were rattled. Peace broke out in Europe in 1697 and French support came briefly to an end.

However, the Protestant Succession was still in danger. William and Mary were childless. Their successor was Anne, James's younger daughter. Yet in 1700, the last of Anne's children died. Parliament passed the Act of Succession in 1701, which decreed that the succession should ignore the 57 closest blood claimants, as they were Catholic. Instead, the Crown should go to the granddaughter of James I, Sophia Dorothea, Dowager Electress of the Electorate of Hanover, a Protestant German duchy, and on her death, to her son, George Lewis (1660–1727).

In 1701, James II died in France and his son, James Francis Stuart (1688–1766), was recognised by both the Jacobites and the French as the rightful heir to the British thrones. William of Orange, William III since 1689, died in the following year, to be succeeded by Anne. In the same year there began the War of the Spanish Succession, which was to pit France and her allies against Britain and hers. In light of British-led victories against the French, there was an invasion attempt in 1708 by a French fleet, which took James Francis with them. Although the shores of Scotland were sighted, the weather and the Royal Navy deterred any landing and so the force turned for home.

The Treaty of Utrecht brought the war to an end in 1713. This was controversial, because a war-weary Britain deserted her allies in order to make peace. The Tories, who were in the ascendancy in government from 1711 to 1714, were at odds with the Whigs, who formed the opposition. The succession was another disputed issue. The Tories were disunited in that some believed that James Stuart, as son of James II, was the rightful monarch, while others preferred the Protestant George. The Whigs had the advantage of unity and gave their allegiance to the German Elector, and he, in return, favoured them.

Queen Anne died on 1 August 1714. The Stuart court in exile, although aware of Anne's long and lingering illness, were slow to act. Their supporters in government were not much better. Apparently some suggested proclaiming James in London, but this daring course of action was not followed. Instead, George's supporters took the initiative and proclaimed him as King of Great Britain on 1 August, without much trouble. Many noblemen and gentry signed the proclamation, including several from the North West, such as Charles Cholmondeley (1685–1756), an MP for Cheshire, James Lowther (c. 1673–1755), an MP for Cumberland, Christopher Musgrave (1688–1756), an MP for Carlisle, and John Bland (1691–1743), an MP for Lancashire. All these men save Lowther were Tories.[3]

---

[3] Rae, *History*, 60.

George arrived in England in late September and was greeted in Greenwich and then London by many of the country's senior politicians. One of these may have been Peter DeSitter, a London merchant, to whom Joseph Symson (1650–1731), a Kendal merchant, wrote on 30 August: 'I hope you will in a little time have the satisfaction to see our gracious Sovereign arrive safely at his palace of St James with the Princes his son and grandson to the unspeakable joy and comfort of all his good subjects'.[4]

His accession to the throne was met by a mixture of jubilation from his supporters and other responses from his enemies. The Bishop of Carlisle, William Nicolson (1650–1728), accompanied Thomas Pattinson, the Sheriff of Cumberland, to proclaim the new king at Carlisle on 4 August.[5] At Liverpool, the corporation greeted the news with celebrations. Cannon were fired, church bells were rung and there were bonfires in the streets. The corporation also called for punishment for the recent Tory ministers. Yet not everyone agreed with such activity. It seems that the curate of St Nicholas', Liverpool,

> headed about 450 mob who roar'd out the Church and Dr Sacheverell [an arch Tory], &c. and went with them down to the George in Water Street, where they swore and curs'd, threaten'd to break all the windows; and having placed his rectorship in a chair, they carry'd him about.[6]

There was also controversy in Ann Gibson's ale house in Whitehaven in late September. According to an informant:

> The sd Mr Lawson [collector of the Customs] importund; Mr John Golding to send for his fiddle, and when it was brought John Golding at the request of the Collector began to play the tune of the King shall injoy his own again. Thomas Luttridge, merchant, said it was a Jacobite tune.

Lawson replied, 'It's a very good tune', and had it played again. When one Dr Briggs objected, Lawson assaulted him. The Whigs present said that the tune implied that the lawful king had been deprived of his rights.[7]

Lancashire Jacobites, including Thomas Tyldesley (1657–1715), celebrated the Queen's death with a feast in anticipation of the arrival of James as king.

---

[4] Symson, *Letter Books*, 279.
[5] William Nicolson, 'Diaries of William Nicolson', ed. Bishop of Barrow in Furness, *CWASSSJ*, V (1905), 1.
[6] *The Post Boy*, 3004, 7–10 Aug. 1714; *VCH Lancashire*, IV, 28.
[7] British Library Additional Manuscripts, 38507, f128r.

There were also numerous Jacobite drinking clubs in Lancashire and Cheshire, such as the Ardwick Corporation, founded in 1714, the Rochdale corporation, founded in 1712, and the Walton-le-Dale corporation, which had its origins in 1701. At these places, like-minded men met to discuss politics, among other matters.[8]

Most, though, seemed not to be opposed to the new king. Dissenters supported him for religious reasons. William Stout (1665–1752), a Quaker merchant of Lancaster, wrote in his memoirs:

> Upon his entring upon Councill, he [George I] declared that he would maintain the toleration of Protestant Dissenters as by law settled; which gave great satisfaction to all well wishers of the nation's true intrest.[9]

Likewise, James Clegg (1679–1755), a Dissenting minister, wrote:

> I returnd that night to Macclesfield, and next day home where consulting with Mr Middleton we causd King George to be proclaimed in our Town. I never knew the nation in a more dead calm than during the time of the Queen's death and the Kings coming over.[10]

Some people were apparently so little interested in politics that they did not refer to it. Nicholas Blundell (1668–1727), a Catholic squire of Little Crosby, Lancashire, did not even mention the succession, let alone comment upon it. For him, what was important at this time was cutting the corn, settling the accounts, and seeing his friends and neighbours.[11]

Carlisle Corporation greeted the news of George's accession and his coronation with some enthusiasm. In the first instance, public money was spent on five gallons of ale, two dozen barrels of wine and four dozen pipes, in order to feast the populace. Two tar barrels were bought in order to illuminate the festivities. For the coronation, £11 2s 6d was spent on similar purchases. Nicolson recorded attending the bonfires there with his son and daughters, and also noted that there was a firework display.[12] In fact, it was from Carlisle that a

---

[8] Colin Haydon, *Anti-Catholicism in Eighteenth Century England, c. 1714–1780*, Manchester: Manchester University Press, 1993, 79; Peter Lole, 'A Digest of Jacobite Clubs', *Royal Stuart Society Papers* (2002).
[9] Stout, 'Autobiography', 172.
[10] Clegg, 'Diary', III, 920.
[11] Blundell, 'Great Diurnall', 107.
[12] Cumbria Archives (Carlisle) Ca 4/4; 'Nicolson's Diaries', V, 2.

loyal address towards the new monarch was first sent, signed by Pattinson, the county gentry and the clergy, and arriving in London in late August.[13]

There were similar demonstrations of loyalty in Chester. The new king was proclaimed on 4 August, Henry Prescott (1649–1719), Tory Deputy Registrar of Chester writing with some equivocation, 'The solemnity of the proclamacion proceeds, a melancholy pomp of Joy. I see it from the palace where I first drink King Georg his Health'.[14] According to Prescott, on 20 October, 'great applicacion is made to celebrate his Majesties Coronacion this day solemniz'ed'.[15] As late as 20 January, Prescott could record, 'The Bells very early awake the Town ... A Thanksgiving is strictly kept for His Majesties peaceable accession to the Crown'.[16]

Elsewhere, throughout the North West, as with the rest of the kingdom, loyal addresses were sent to the new king. This, of course, was commonplace after the accession of a new monarch, and may signify little.[17] They were sent from Liverpool, Kendal and Carlisle.[18] There was a rumour that William Farrington, High Sheriff of Lancashire, had refused to proclaim King George, but this was probably incorrect, for the King was proclaimed in a number of places throughout the county.[19]

Furthermore there seems to have been no outburst of rioting in the North West. Mrs Savage, a Dissenting minister's wife, of Cheshire, wrote:

> The Coronation of King George was observed throughout ye Nation wth great solemnity, Bells and Bonfires, illuminations, &c. great reason to rejoice yt we have a Protestant on ye Throne who we trust will seek ye welfare & peace of our English Israel. My earnest prayer for him is a wise & considerative heart & may his throne be established in righteousness.[20]

Yet rioting did occur elsewhere in England on the King's coronation day, chiefly in the southern counties.

George I favoured the Whigs, which was unsurprising; they had always supported his cause and had attacked the Treaty of Utrecht. Conversely, the

---

[13] Jarvis, *Jacobite Risings*, 22.
[14] Prescott, 'Diary' II, 399.
[15] Prescott, 'Diary' II, 411.
[16] Prescott, 'Diary' II, 424–5.
[17] *The London Gazette*, 5260, 14–18 Sept. – 5273, 30 Oct. – 1 Nov. 1714.
[18] Rae, *History*, 103.
[19] *The Post Boy*, 3016, 4–7 Sept. 1714.
[20] Bodleian Library, MS Eng. Misc e331, 20.

Tories had been responsible for this treaty and some of their members favoured a Stuart restoration. Yet he did offer some Tories high office, and it was not his fault that only the Earl of Nottingham accepted. The new government, then, was headed by Whigs, replacing their Tory predecessors, James Stanhope (1673–1721) and Viscount Townshend (1674–1738) being the two secretaries of State. The armed forces were once more headed by the Duke of Marlborough; his Tory predecessor, the Duke of Ormonde, was dismissed. Whigs took power in the counties. The Whig Edward Stanley (1664–1732), 10th Earl of Derby, was appointed to the vacant post of Lord Lieutenant of Lancashire and the Earl of Carlisle was restored to his lieutenancy of the two most north-westerly counties. Many of the recently appointed Tory JPs in Cumberland were dismissed and replaced by reliable Whigs. Other north-western Tories lost out: Sir Henry Bunbury (c. 1678–1733), an MP for Chester, was dismissed from his post in the Irish Customs and James Barrymore (1667–1748), of Cheshire, soon to be an MP for Wigan, was dismissed from his colonelcy. However, many Tory JPs retained their posts – in Cheshire they included Peter Legh (1669–1744), Barrymore, Bunbury, Sir George Warburton (1675–1743) and Sir Richard Grosvenor (1689–1732). No Cheshire JP lost his post at this time. It would appear that there were few changes, if any, among the Lancashire JPs, though the Lord Lieutenant 'often pressed the court to have the commissions of peace changed but could never get it done'. In part this could have been because the Chancellor of the Duchy of Lancaster was Lord Aylesbury, 'a high Tory and suspected very justly of affection to the Pretender's interest'.[21]

These changes were, naturally, controversial. Symson approved of them, writing on 13 September:

> If the clemency of our good King spare those moles and caterpillars, who during the last distracted reign were so hellishly busy and eager to undermine and devour our happy constitution, I hope our most merciful deliverer will take from them the power of exercising their mischievous faculties for the future or the faculties themselves.[22]

Not all agreed with this assessment. Prescott was horrified, writing in his diary in September of 'the great and shocking alterations on the side of the Whigs' and that 'the King's recepcion of the Whig lords and rejection of Ormond,

---

[21] Romney Sedgwick, *The History of Parliament: The Commons, 1715–1754*, I, London: HMSO, 1970, 440, 507, 557; The National Archives, C234/5; Dudley Ryder, *The Dairy of Dudley Ryder, 1715–1716*, ed. William Matthews, London: Methuen, 1939, 176.

[22] Symson, *Letter Books*, 279.

Oxford and Bromley [three leading Tory ministers] with his partiality is a melancholy Entertainment'.[23] He later wrote, 'To those who reduce their thoughts to the last raign and consider the partial proceedings in this, melancholy prospects are presented'.[24]

Yet the Jacobites overseas did little at first to capitalise on this discontent. James Stuart penned a proclamation at Plombières to protest against the accession of George I, but little else. As one supporter wrote, correctly, 'I feare your majesty's measures cannot be ready, and I very much feare Hanovre, the Whiggs, Ld Churchill and the Treasurer have taken their measures'.[25] It was not until the end of November that the following resolution was made: 'That the King [James Stuart] is firmly resolved to goe himself in person to them as soon as he can'; yet 'a little time must be allowed for getting together what is necessary, especially for raising money and for taking measures with friends in England, without which little good is to be expected'.[26]

Parliament was dissolved, as always happened after the accession of a new monarch, in January 1715. A Tory pamphlet, *The Englishman's Advice to the Freeholders of England*, was widely distributed and declared by the Whigs to be treason. Prescott read a copy and declared it to be 'bold and smart'.[27] Polling took place throughout the country. As ever, this was accompanied with violence in some instances. Ralph Ashton, a Lancashire JP, accused the Whig Sir Henry Hoghton (1679–1768), an MP for Preston, of hiring a mob of between 50 to 60 men, in order to damage the property, amounting to £2 11s, of a rival in Preston.[28] There was controversy at the Cheshire and Chester elections, too, Prescott writing that 'both are carry'd on with warmth'.[29] The Whiggish Symson had great hopes for the elections, writing on 29 January, 'Our neighbouring elections we have grounds to hope will [be] better than formerly. It behoves all honest men to be stir them in whereon the Protestant religion and the welfare of Britain so much depends'.[30]

Generally speaking, though, the elections were favourable towards the Whigs and they secured a decisive majority in the Commons. This was partly

---

[23] Prescott, 'Diary', II, 407.
[24] Prescott, 'Diary', II, 411.
[25] *Historical Manuscripts Commission*, Calendar of the Stuart Papers, I, London: HMSO, 1902, 333.
[26] *HMC*, Stuart Papers, I, 336.
[27] Prescott, 'Diary', II, 426.
[28] Manchester Central Library, L1/21/4/21; L1/42/1/10.
[29] Prescott, 'Diary', II, 428–9.
[30] Symson, *Letter Books*, 292–3.

because they had the influence of the Crown behind them, but perhaps also because of the concern among some of the electorate that the Tories were supportive of a Catholic Stuart restoration, whereas George was staunchly Protestant. In the North West, though, the results were not dramatic. Of the 14 constituencies, only 3 saw contests; Chester, Cheshire and Clitheroe. Of the 28 MPs who sat after the election, 17 had previously occupied the same seats.[31] The actions of the new government were not universally popular. Prescott wrote on 25 March, 'The contents and tendency of the King's speech are the common talk and matter of suspicion'.[32]

This proved to be but a lull in the storm. Violent outbursts occurred in May and June 1715 throughout England, and this time the North West was no exception. The first indication was at Warrington on 5 May. James Stuart was proclaimed as James III there three times in the morning of that day by 'a considerable number of disguised persons'.[33] This may have been a mere ripple of protest on apparently becalmed waters. Yet on 28 May, George I's supporters in that town celebrated the new king's birthday, as did other Whigs throughout Britain. They lit a bonfire and put candles in their windows in order to illuminate them. Furthermore, some of these Whigs, the Dissenters among them, 'inadvertently, made some Reflections upon the Church [of England], which were soon aggravated to that height, that the two Parties came to blows'. There was another Jacobite demonstration on this day, too; this time in Manchester.[34] The Jacobites were more numerous than their opponents and gained the upper hand. They then extinguished the Whig bonfire, scattered its remnants and smashed those windows which were lit up.[35] In Chester, Prescott noted merely, 'The King's birthday rememberd in the Bells, little els'.[36]

However, there was to be even more violence in Manchester in the next few days. This was one of the most significant riots in England in 1715. Townshend wrote of it in no uncertain terms:

> The King has receiv'd several accounts that the tumultuousness and Disorderly proceedings at Manchester have not only continued there for many days without any check to the great terror and Damage of many of His Loyal and Dutifull

---

[31] Sedgwick, *Commons*, I, 202–3, 269.
[32] Prescott, 'Diary', II, 433–4.
[33] *The Flying Post*, 3660, 18–21 June 1715.
[34] Anon., *History of all the Mobs and Insurrections in Great Britain from William the Conqueror to the Present Time*, London, 1715, 56–7.
[35] *The Flying Post*, 3660, 18–21 June 1715.
[36] Prescott, 'Diary', II, 444.

Subjects, but have also grown more daring and dangerous by spreading further into the Neighbourhood.[37]

There was a newly built Dissenting chapel in Cross Street, Manchester, the first ever built in the town. It attracted the attention of those opposed to Protestant Dissent on 1 June, and they took out three or four pews and burnt them. Emboldened by this early success, they continued their destructive work on 5–6 June, when the windows were smashed. Three days after this latest visit, a crowd of about 300 to 400 men reappeared before the chapel, drums beating and in a reasonably orderly fashion. They destroyed the internal furnishings. On 10 June they took slates off the roof and began to break part of the walls. On the following day it was reported that 'they are resolved to continue till they level the whole within the ground'. Even gravestones were not left undisturbed. Yet the congregation continued to use the chapel, and on 12 June, during a service, it was attacked again. Internal pillars were then pulled down and the whole structure was at risk of total collapse. Only then did the rioters leave it alone for fear of injuring themselves.[38]

It was not just the chapel that was the target of the mob. The rioters also verbally harassed their enemies, 'insulting all the honest men in their way'. Anyone who would not join them in drinking James's health was 'affronted'.[39]

Following this destruction, there were further attacks on the Dissenters. On 14 June, those in Manchester were told that their private property would be attacked, too. Unsurprisingly, as a sympathetic newspaper observed, 'the honest part of the town are in the utmost consternation and distress'. Some fled and others planned their escape routes.[40] Others, though, fought back and during one clash, the Dissenters were fired upon. Their assailant's gun failed to go off, and he and his companions were soundly thrashed after having their weapons seized.[41]

The crowd went further afield in search of their prey. Meeting-houses at Blakeley and Green Acres were damaged. Those at Monton and Stand were reached on 20 June and that at Plat on 22 June. The Monton chapel was destroyed; others suffered lesser damage. At Stand and Plat, the rioters encountered such resistance that they were forced to retreat. There were even rumours that they might march

---

[37] TNA, State Papers 44/116, 306–7.
[38] *The Flying Post*, 3660, 18–21 June 1715; TNA, PL28/1, 230.
[39] *The Flying Post*, 3660, 18–21 June 1715.
[40] *The Flying Post*, 3660, 18–21 June 1715.
[41] *The Flying Post*, 3667, 5–7 July 1715.

into Yorkshire to continue their trail of destruction.[42] Concern among Dissenters continued until mid-July at least. According to Prescott, writing on 11 July, 'the Town [Chester] in some commocion, about a panick Fear or rather false suggestion of the Dissenters, that their meeting House was threaten'd'.[43]

Although no Chester Dissenting chapel was attacked, there was an attack on one elsewhere in the county. This was at Congleton between 11 and 12 at night on 21 July. Several unknown people broke into the Presbyterians' meeting house and 'broke the Greatest of the Glass Windows belonging to the said meeting house & pilled down the most part of the stalls and pews therein with the pulpit and carried out the same & burnt a great pile of them'. There may also have been disturbances in Stockport, with rioters attacking the Presbyterian chapel and annoying the loyalist Rev. William Nicholas at the Vicarage there.[44]

Apart from the purely destructive element, there was also an element of theatre in these riots. The rioters at Warrington and Manchester had carried green boughs, symbolic of the Restoration of Charles II in 1660 and also of a hoped-for second Stuart restoration in the near future. Some rioters wore women's clothes as a disguise.[45] The mob drank the health of James Stuart at both Warrington and Manchester. They also shouted 'Down with the Rump', an allusion to the Whig government of 1708, which lasted but three years. At Manchester, the mob proclaimed James Stuart as James III. At Warrington on 10 June, James's birthday, the church bells were rung and a bonfire lit to celebrate the day.[46]

It is noteworthy that the destructive mob in Manchester was allowed to proceed with a minimum of interruption. Although the mob was allegedly made up of 'chiefly ... poor workmen', they numbered, at Manchester, between 500 and 600 men. They were wholly plebeian, from 23 different known occupations, including husbandmen, labourers, weavers and fustian cutters. Almost all were from Manchester, with a few from neighbouring Salford (a list appears in Appendix 1). They were led by Thomas Sydall, a blacksmith, who cried 'God damn King George' and was referred to by his enemies as 'Colonel

---

[42] *The Flying Post*, 3670, 12–14 July 1715; *Calendar of Treasury Books*, 2, 1717, London, 1957, 187.
[43] Prescott, 'Diary', II, 451.
[44] TNA, CHES 24/152/3; Peter Walkden, 'Correspondence of the Rev. Peter Walkden, ed. James Bromley, LCHS, 7, 1884, 31–2.
[45] *The Flying Post*, 3667, 5–7 July 1715.
[46] *The Flying Post*, 3660, 18–21 June 1715.

of the Mob at Manchester' and 'a notorious offendr & of great esteem there amongst the disaffected'.[47]

It was reported that one of the rioters said, 'Let us consult J. Va–l–n before we proceed further'. This man may have been a local magistrate, who may also have called a man a rogue because he drank the King's health instead of James Stuart's. A number of gentlemen in Manchester had gathered at the King's Head inn, where they drank Jacobite healths. They also 'plentifully' subsisted the rioters, too.[48] Major John Wyvill wrote that Mr Baladine, a Manchester magistrate, was a 'sad Church Dog', for winking at the riots.[49] The clergy, too, did not discourage the rioters. The Rev. Richard Wroe (d. 1718), Warden of the Collegiate Church of Manchester, 'could not be prevail'd upon but any entreaty to declaim against such riotous proceedings'. His enemies termed him 'the drum Ecclesiastick' and encouraged the Tory doctrine of passive resistance.[50] Some seem to condone these riots. Prescott noted, 'Mr Pigot from Manchester comes and entertains us with the Humors of the Manchester Mobb on the Church side'.[51] This should not lead us to the conclusion that the rioters were merely the tools of the Jacobite gentry; the latter encouraged them, certainly, but they did not initiate the destruction.

Yet the rioters did not have it all their own way. As we have noted, Dissenters were not passive in face of persecution. Warrington Whigs soon stopped the bell ringing on 10 June. On 28 May, Manchester constables and others had suppressed the Jacobite disturbances there at least at that time.[52]

Shock was the reaction of Mrs Savage, writing in early June:

> This week brings tidings of much disturbance by ye Jacobite mob great outrages in London, Oxford, York, Manchester. Fire kindled in some meeting houses, &c &c God in mercy I trust will set bounds to their rage, as he does to ye pious waves, hitherto shal ye come and no further ... We hear more tidings of ye rashness of ye mob in many places ye meeting house in Manchester quite demolished.[53]

---

[47] *The Flying Post*, 3672, 16–19 July 1715; TNA, PL28/1, Lancashire Record Office, GJ1/2/10, 522–3, BL Stowe MSS 750, f157r.
[48] *The Flying Post*, 3670, 12–14 July; 3667, 5–7 July 1715.
[49] Anon., *A True and Exact Copy* ... Manchester, 1715, 2–3.
[50] *The Flying Post*, 3667, 5–7 July 1715.
[51] Prescott, 'Diary', II, 445.
[52] *The Flying Post*, 3660, 18–21 June 1715; Anon., *History of all the mobs*, 57.
[53] Bod. Lib. Ms Eng. Misc e331, 48, 50.

Timothy Cragg, a Lancashire yeoman, wrote, 'About this time there was a great uneasiness in the nation and many Presbyterian Meeting houses pulled down in several parts of the nation. It was reported that several were killed about it'.[54] There is no confirmation about fatalities, however.

By late June the government began to react against these disorders. Townshend wrote to Ralph Ashton that troops would be employed 'at Request of the Sheriff, JP or other civil magistrate' to help 'extinguish this turbulent and outrageous spirit', which was 'insolent, illegal and treasonable' and 'destructive to all government and of so dangerous consequence to the peace and tranquillity of his [the King's] good and loving subjects'.[55] Thus William Pulteney (1684–1757), the Secretary at War, ordered the two troops of Cobham's dragoons who were currently stationed at Doncaster, to ride to Manchester, 'where they are to return until further orders'.[56]

Wyvill was in command of the troops, who arrived in Manchester on 24 June. The soldiers were greeted with hostile cries of 'Down with the Rump'. On another occasion, a group of soldiers, walking through the town, were molested by a crowd, but when other soldiers arrived and charged, the crowd retreated; some received 'a good cudgelling and broken heads'. Later the crowd offered to fight the soldiers, if the latter laid down their arms. However, calm eventually descended. Wyvill told Townshend that his men had 'struck a great Damp among the Tories'.[57] Whigs reported, 'We are tolerably Easy and Quiet'. Those Dissenters who had fled Manchester returned and dismissed the guards whom they had hired to protect themselves and their goods.[58] Wyvill was told by Townshend on 19 July that the King was 'very well satisfied with your prudent conduct'.[59]

After the troops had arrived, the civil magistrates could begin their investigations. Several Lancashire JPs had been told by Townshend on 25 June to do so. They arrived in the town on 29 June and immediately set to work, and Townshend wrote on 5 July to commend them for their zeal. The Earl of Warrington was congratulated on 'securing a chief leader of the Rioters at Manchester'.[60] Five of the ringleaders, including Sydall, were identified and were

---

[54] Shairp, Walter and Craggs, 'Jacobites and Jacobins: Two Eighteenth Century Perspectives. The Memoir of Walter Shairp, The Story of the Liverpool Regiment during the Jacobite Rebellion of 1745 and The Writings of the Craggs Family of Wyresdale', ed. Jonathan Oates and Katrina Navickas, *RSLC*, 3rd series, 25, 2006, 54–5.
[55] TNA, SP44/116, 307.
[56] TNA, WO 5/20, 65.
[57] Anon., *Exact Copy*, 2–3.
[58] *The Flying Post*, 3667, 5–7 July 1715.
[59] TNA, SP44/116, 325.
[60] TNA, SP44/16, 310, 313–14; SP44/118, 8; *The Daily Courant* 4273, 5 July 1715.

condemned to spend time in the stocks in Lancaster. Yet they did not want for sympathisers, for 'no person was allowed to fling anything at them'.[61] Sydall and his fellows were sent to the county gaol at Lancaster Castle, doubtless to await further trial, and Sydall remained there until released by fellow Jacobites in early November 1715.[62]

There was some dissension among the soldiery, too. Wyvill complained to Townshend that one Lieutenant Colonel Holley arrived on 29 July and had attempted to supersede him in command. Wyvill threatened to have Holley arrested, but first sought Townshend's commands.[63] Cornet Sadler was arrested for 'speaking seditious and scandalous words' against the King.[64] A trooper was gaoled for shouting the Jacobite cry 'Down with the Rump'. Yet when the crowd offered to set him free, he refused to accompany them.[65]

It must be remembered, of course, that most towns in the North West were wholly immune from any kind of Jacobite disturbance whatsoever. None was reported anywhere in Cumberland and Westmorland. Symson makes no reference to any such disturbance.[66] It was further noted:

> During the late mobs those preludes to the late Rebellion, it was not in the power of the enemies of the Government to raise any tumult there [at Preston], which must in a good measure be attributed to the Reverend Mr Peploe, the parson of the Town, who ... had the honesty and fortitude to declare on all proper occasions as well from the pulpit as in his conversation, that nothing humanly speaking could secure our Religion and our Laws but the succession of the Crown as settled in the most illustrious House of Hanover and who since His Majesty's accession to the Throne has shewn as eminent a zeal for His Royal person and Government.[67]

There were certainly signs of loyalty to King George in the churches in Nicolson's diocese, too. The bells of St Andrew's Church, Penrith, were rung for the King's birthday on 28 May, with four shillings given to the ringers, and no controversy

---

[61] E.L. Edmunds, *The Life and Memorials of the late W.R. Baker*, London: William Tweedle, 1865, 22; Peter Clarke, 'Journal of Several Occurrences from 2nd November 1715 in the Insurrection Begun in Scotland and concluded at Preston in Lancashire', in *Miscellany of the Scottish Historical Society*, vol. 1, Edinburgh: T and A Constable, 1893, 518.
[62] Patten, *History*, 78.
[63] HMC, Manuscripts of the Marquess of Townshend, London: HMSO, 1887, 159.
[64] TNA, SP44/116, 346.
[65] *The Flying Post*, 3660, 18–20 June 1715.
[66] Symson, *Letter Books*, 311–18.
[67] P. Purcell, 'The Jacobite Rising of 1715 and the English Catholics', *English Historical Review*, 1929, 423.

is recorded.[68] At Wigan, the events of 29 May were ambiguous. Prescott noted, 'This day is remembered here in a great Bonfire, ringing the Bells, drinking to Monarchy and Episcopacy in a course solemnity in dull ale by the Bonfire'.[69] Nor were there any riots in Chester, Preston or Lancaster, and there was only one in Liverpool, and that in 1714. It is possible that relations between Whigs and Tories were less violent in these places, or that one side had enough authority to prevent any disturbances by their enemies. Certainly, there was conflict already in Manchester, as Edmund Harrold, a wigmaker there, noted: 'These troublesome times of Rioting, drinking & swearing & foreswearing party against party so that charitys driven into corners and dare not appear barefaced this seditious rage'.[70]

These disturbances came to an end in late June, probably because troops were beginning to be stationed in towns which had seen Jacobite disturbances. The rioters, too, may have expended all their energies and did not wish to continue. In any case, once existing local chapels had been destroyed, it was difficult to do much more, especially if they had to work for a daily wage. However, if anyone thought that the troubles were over and peace was to return, they were in for an unpleasant shock. Some already saw straws in the wind. Prescott referred to 'the whetting of swords in the North' on 17 December, and on 3 June he noted of a discussion:

> the doubtfull prospect of affairs, the present state of the Government, the Common Genius and inclination of the Nation to another Revolucion, are the subjects which carry us to 10 at night.[71]

Nationally, in the summer, three of the principal Tories were attacked by the Whigs. The Duke of Ormonde fled abroad to avoid impeachment, as did Viscount Bolingbroke – both to join the Jacobite court. The Earl of Oxford remained to face the music and was incarcerated in the Tower. For the Tories these were unhappy times, and their sympathisers in the counties were alarmed for themselves, too. As Prescott wrote, 'The News is of ill portent'.[72]

Since 1688, the exiled Stuart court had been granted asylum in France by Louis XIV. Here James Francis and his supporters discussed plans for a restoration. Yet leaks were frequent as security was lax. George I's astute 'Resident' in Paris was the Earl of Stair, who had been feeding his royal master information about

---

[68] CRO, (C) PR110/75.
[69] Prescott, 'Diary', II, 444.
[70] Chetham's Library, MUN.A.2.137, Edmund Harrold's Diary, 10 July 1715.
[71] Prescott, 'Diary', II, 420, 445.
[72] Prescott, 'Diary', II, 448.

Jacobite plans. On 20 July, the following dramatic news was announced to the House of Commons:

> That he had certain Advices, that attempts were preparing by the Pretender from abroad, and are carrying on at home, by a restless Party in his Faction's Favour.

A number of steps were soon taken by the Government to strengthen the country's defences; after all, following the peace of 1713, the armed forces had been reduced to low levels, as usual after any major conflict. On 22 July, Sir George Byng's fleet was to patrol the seas around Britain; an Act was passed to increase the number of seamen serving in the Royal Navy. Troops were concentrated at Portsmouth and also in London, where the militia and trained bands were summoned. There was a purge of officers felt to be politically unreliable. Commissions were given in order that new regiments could be formed; in all, these were 13 regiments of dragoons (2,574 men) and eight battalions of infantry (3,440 men). Guards regiments were also strengthened. All officers were ordered to return to their posts and half-pay officers were told to be in readiness for service. Officers from Frank's Regiment were sent to Chester and officers from General Elliot's and General Evans's Regiments were despatched to Carlisle, in order to help train the militia and volunteer forces there.[73]

It was fortunate for the new dynasty that most of the Continent was at peace (except in northern Europe). There were discussions with friendly foreign powers for assistance. Holland had, under the terms of the Barrier Treaty, promised to provide 6,000 men in case the Protestant succession was in danger. On 4 August, the Dutch agreed to this request and began negotiations in earnest. Emperor Charles VI also offered troops, but these were declined.[74]

At home, steps were taken against potential Jacobites. Orders in Council of 20 July were given to the lords lieutenant, including those in the north-western counties. They were ordered to put into effect the laws against Catholics. Magistrates were told that they could order searches of the property of anyone who was suspected, and any horses they had valued at over £5 and any weapons other than those needed for self-defence could be confiscated for the duration of the emergency – unless the owners swore oaths of loyalty to the King and the Protestant succession. Finally, the Riot Act was passed, enabling magistrates to command a mob to disperse or be forced to do so.[75]

---

[73] Rae, *History*, 169–72; *The London Gazette*, 5367, 24–7 September 1715.
[74] Rae, *History*, 172–3.
[75] Rae, *History*, 169–74.

The County Militia were also summoned into being. Those orders which were sent to Carlisle were transmitted six days later to Hugh Simpson, clerk of the peace to the county of Cumberland. Carlisle signed commissions for the militia captains, but left the commissions for the other officers blank, in order that they might be filled in by the captains themselves. He requested that Simpson send copies of the letter to the deputy lieutenants and the JPs.[76]

Anti-Catholic laws were certainly enforced in Lancashire. Blundell recorded in his diary on 18 August that 'Henry Valentine the High Constable serched here for Horses, Armes and Gunpowder'.[77] It is unlikely that this was the only Catholic premises searched in the county. In Cheshire, Hugh Cholmondely (1662–1725), the Lord Lieutenant, was thanked by Townshend on 27 July for his prompt activity.[78]

Prescott was shocked and highly critical of these developments. He wrote on 26 June, 'the Ministry so alarmd that they are providing an Act for the further security of His Majesties person and extinguishing the Hopes of the Pretender'. A month later, he wrote, 'The News of the Army to bee raised, a new oath to be form'd for the clergy, and the yet suspected recess of the Duke of Ormond, are the common matters of discourse and mortficaion'.[79] Loyalty to George I was far from unanimous, as Prescott noted on 1 August 1715, when referring to celebrations for the first anniversary of the King's reign: 'see few Illuminacions but in the windows of the Mayor, Recorder and Whigs'.[80]

There was considerable discussion at the Stuart Court as to when and where the attempted Jacobite restoration should take place. In fact, for all the discussion which passed at St Germain, the decision was taken by John Erskine (1675–1732), Earl of Mar, a prominent Scots politician, who had travelled to London in August and took a boat to Scotland via Newcastle. He had the Stuart banner unfurled at Braemar on 6 September and soon attracted several thousand followers from among the Highland clans. They took Perth from the loyalists without a fight and established themselves in this important Scottish city. Total Jacobite strength in early November has been estimated at about 15,000 men – the largest number that ever rose in favour of the Stuarts, and far more than were ever out in the Forty Five – although they were never all gathered in one place. The outnumbered regular forces were stationed at Stirling in order to prevent

---

[76] Jarvis, *Jacobite Risings*, 143–9.
[77] Blundell, 'Diurnall', 144.
[78] TNA, SP44/117, 211.
[79] Prescott, 'Diary', II, 449; 454.
[80] Prescott, 'Diary', II, 455.

their marching south. They were soon, however, to be commanded by the Duke of Argyle (1680–1743), a veteran soldier.[81]

Initially the Jacobites planned to focus their efforts in England on the North East, but decided to switch their aim towards the South West, though none of their allies in the North East seem to have been alerted to this. There were certainly rumours of Jacobite activity in the South West, and there had been a number of riots in Devon and Dorset earlier in the year. Oxford was a haven of Jacobite activity, too. But the government was aware of this. Troops were sent to Bristol, Bath and Oxford; Jacobites were rounded up. Ships arriving at Liverpool from France with Stair's passport were to be searched.[82] Elsewhere, the government decided to arrest other English Jacobites in order to deprive the Jacobites of leadership. These included a number of MPs and peers. Only two of them were from the North West. One was Edward Harvey (1658–1736), MP for Clitheroe, whose correspondence with the former French ambassador in London and with Ormonde appeared treasonable. He was arrested and tried to commit suicide, but failed.[83] Another MP to be arrested was Bland, who was taken to London on 26 September by a King's Messenger, 'as [the perpetrator of] dangerous and treasonable practices against His Majesty and Government'. Peter Legh of Lyme was also taken up.[84] With these arrests, the government felt so confident that Townshend and Stanhope were said, on 24 September, to be 'out of all apprehension of any attempt upon England'.[85] Two days earlier, there was a rumour in Edinburgh that the Jacobites had landed at Liverpool, which encouraged the Scottish Jacobites.[86] This was false. However, the government's conviction that England was now secure from the Jacobite threat was a trifle premature.

---

[81] Rae, *History*, 188–9, 191, 218–21; Szechi, *1715*, 121.
[82] Rae, *History*, 214–17; Rupert Jarvis, *Customs Letter Books*, 6.
[83] Sedgwick, *History*, I, 115.
[84] Sedgwick, *History*, I, 468; TNA, SP44/118, 30, 39.
[85] *HMC*, Townshend, 174.
[86] TNA, SP54/8, 52.

Chapter 2

The Jacobite Insurrection in the North of England, October 1715

The outline of the Jacobite campaign in the North of England and the borders of Scotland have been narrated by John Baynes and other historians.[1] Until Gooch, though, the Jacobites' efforts, ultimately unsuccessful, underwent severe criticism, Baynes concluding, 'The story of the rising in northern England and the Borders has elements of farce in it which make it difficult to take seriously'.[2] Gooch was the first to mount a significant defence of their actions, arguing that they were let down by potential allies at home and abroad, and did all that was asked of them.[3] Szechi adds a cautionary note that the Jacobites, having been thwarted, had no secondary plan.[4] Most of these writings have concentrated on the Jacobites, though works by Oates discuss the efforts of their enemies, both civil and military.[5]

Traditionally historians have attributed the rising in the North East to religious and economic motivations. It was stated that those in rebellion were facing economic collapse and that armed insurrection was a desperate gamble to restore their fortunes by restoring them to political power; or, that the Catholics among the Jacobites were equally in economic extremis due to the penalties imposed upon them by the government because of their religion. The final push for rebellion was the government's efforts to arrest a number of leading Northumbrian nobility and gentry; but for the latter, they might have remained at home.[6] More recent explanations have been put forward by Gooch, stressing genuine Jacobotism as their motivation, stating that a rising in Northumberland was to have been supported by forces from abroad and would enable a strong position to be established at Newcastle.

---

[1] Baynes, *Jacobite Rising*, 83–104.
[2] Baynes, *Jacobite Rising*, 204; Lenman, *Jacobite Risings*, 123.
[3] Gooch, *Desperate Faction*, 83–5.
[4] Szechi, *1715*, 171.
[5] Oates, 'Responses in Newcastle to the Jacobite Rebellions of 1715 and 1745', *Archaeologia Aeliana*, 5th series, 2003.
[6] Lenman, *Jacobite Rising*, 116–19.

Encouraged by the numerous anti-Hanoverian and Whig demonstrations throughout England since the accession of George I, James was ready and willing to make preparations to regain the thrones which he saw as rightly his. His secretary was the exiled English Tory, the Viscount Bolingbroke, and he was responsible for Jacobite strategy. In July 1715 he decided that the northeast coast was the best place for a Jacobite descent, preferably with arms, officers and men from the Swedish and/or French armies. Overtures were made to both courts, who were hostile to George I. Charles XII of Sweden was an aggressive warrior and anti-Hanoverian, but his forces were hard pressed by those of Denmark and Russia, so none could be spared.[7]

The court of Louis XIV seemed more sympathetic. Arms, money and ships were promised. According to Rae, 'the Rebels were forming their bloody project, and, not without Grounds, conceived great Hopes of a powerful Assistance from Lewis XIV'.[8] Twelve ships, to be guarded by frigates, were loaded with arms and ammunition at Le Havre and St Malo. These included 12,000 muskets and bayonets, 18,000 swords, 68 cannon and 4,000 barrels of gunpowder. There were 120 gunners, and 1,861 volunteer officers and men from the French army.[9]

The Northumberland coast was certainly vulnerable to an overseas incursion, having been raided by French ships in 1691. It was distant from the centre of power and the only regular troops stationed there were the small garrisons at Berwick and Holy Island. It would be some time before their enemies could march there to try to repel them. But also, there were a number of sympathetic Catholic and Tory gentry and nobility there who could assist with a Jacobite landing with horses, men and other resources; and it was near to Scotland, from where Jacobite support could be expected. Early notice was, however, essential, 'And when the King's friends here know that he is in a condition to make this provision he shall be informed of the particular places wither they may be sent and of the persons who may be instructed in the receiving them'. The beginning of October was deemed the optimum time for a descent.[10]

However, that autumn there was a change of plan. James and Bolingbroke decided in early October that 'Mr Campion and Mr Courteney repair immediately to the West of England; and that they give notice to the King's friends in those parts of His Majesty's resolution to land somewhere near Plymouth'. The Duke of Ormonde, another exiled Jacobite peer, was to arrive

---

[7] *HMC*, Stuart Papers, I, 528–35.
[8] Rae, *History*, 191.
[9] Rae, *History*, 221–2.
[10] *HMC*, Stuart Papers, I, 522–3.

prior to James. Ironically, this was where the Duke of Monmouth landed in 1685 and William of Orange did likewise in 1688.[11]

By this time, support from France was less likely; Louis XIV had died, and though the regency was prepared to overlook ships being laden with arms and money, under pressure (backed with naval power) from the Earl of Stair, it was forced to prevent their departure from Le Havre. It is presumed that north-eastern Jacobites were unaware of this and expected support from abroad and so had, unknowingly, become very isolated. Co-ordination and communication were poor, as had been the case with the unsuccessful two-pronged rebellion in 1685.

The North of England, then, harboured numerous potential Jacobite conspirators. Since unsuccessful conspirators do not keep letters or diaries or write memoirs, their actions prior to open rebellion must be a matter for speculation. That there had been plans and discussions is undoubted. Patten wrote, 'There had been Measures concerted in London by the Pretender's Friends some time before the Insurrection in Northumberland broke out'.[12] The three principals were three army officers, Captains John Shafto, John Hunter of North Tyne and Robert Talbot, an Irishman once in the service of France. In August 1715 they took ship from London to Newcastle to prepare their allies to rise against King George. Patten wrote:

> it is very reasonable to suppose a design of this consequence could not be carried on by the Measures concerted, the Parties furnished, prepared and brought together in a Posture fit to appear in Arms against the Government, without long Debates, frequent Correspondences, carrying and receiving of Letters, Orders &c and abundance of People employed to concert Measures, and ripen up Things to the Height they afterwards were brought to.[13]

The principal agents in distributing messages which could not be risked in the post were Colonel Henry Oxburgh, Messrs Nicholas and Charles Wogan, James Talbot, and, in the second league, Messrs Clifton and Beaumont of Nottinghamshire and the Rev. Buxton of Derbyshire. Another was Richard Gascoigne, who had served in the Spanish army as a volunteer and was involved in the planning of the Jacobite rising in the South West. They and their servants were armed and on horseback and rode around the counties, pretending to be genuine tourists.[14] One part of the plot in the North East was the seizure of

---

[11] *HMC*, Stuart Papers, I, 532–3.
[12] Patten, *History*, 16.
[13] Patten, *History*, 16.
[14] Patten, *History*, 17; BL., Add. Mss, 38851, ff.74r–76r.

Newcastle and Tynemouth Castle.[15] The Northumbrian Jacobites may also have met Mar in August when he took a boat there en route from London to Scotland.[16]

The government was aware of conspiracies taking place and decided to nip them in the bud by arresting the principal suspects among the nobility and gentry. Warrants were sent out by King's Messengers to effect the same.[17] Six members of Parliament, including Forster, had warrants published against them on 22 September.[18] These Messengers arrived at Durham at the end of September.[19]

Another leading Jacobite was the Earl of Derwentwater, of whom Sir Robert Walpole (1676–1745) later wrote, 'yet to my knowledge, he had been tampering with people to persuade them to rise in favour of the Pretender six months before he appeared in arms'.[20] A warrant was issued for his arrest, too, though it seems there was a leak from the Secretary's office.[21] A Newcastle upholsterer told Derwentwater about this threat of arrest. He went to the house of a certain JP near Dilston, but then went to the house of Richard Lambert. Meanwhile, Forster decided to evade arrest, too. Eventually he arrived at the home of Fenwick of Bywell. The Messengers arrived within half a mile of Bywell, but stopped to seek the aid of a constable. This delay allowed Forster to escape them.[22] Certainly by 6 October his whereabouts were unknown, as were his intentions, for William Cotesworth (1670–1725), a leading Whig of Gateshead, was asked, 'They [government ministers] desire you will inform them iff T.F. be gon over to Lord M[ar]'.[23]

The Jacobites decided that they must act to prevent themselves being taken to London for questioning. The recent arrest of Jacobite MP Sir William Wyndham was also a blow to their morale; 'it was a feeling cold blow to all the Party, especially to the Northumberland Rebels'. Derwentwater bought his horses, which had been confiscated by a JP. They decided to meet on 6 October and messages were despatched to all relevant parties. Forster and 20 others met at Greenriggs. Believing it was an inconvenient rendezvous, they gathered at the Waterfalls Hill, which allowed them to see anyone approaching, either friend or foe. Earlier that day, Derwentwater had left Dilston Hall with his friends and

---

[15] Henry Liddell, 'Liddell–Cotesworth Letters', *Surtees Society*, CXCVII, ed. J.M. Ellis, 1987, 180.
[16] Rae, *History*, 188.
[17] Patten, *History*, 17.
[18] Liddell, 'Correspondence', 179.
[19] Patten, *History*, 17.
[20] Walpole, *The Life and Memoirs of the Administration of Sir Robert Walpole*, I, ed. William Coxe, London, 1798, 72.
[21] Patten, *History*, 48.
[22] Patten, *History*, 17–18.
[23] Liddell, 'Letters', 182.

servants, mounted on coach horses and armed. They rode to Corbridge, swords drawn, then to Thomas Errington's seat, Beaufront, where other Jacobite gentry met them. Eventually they all met at Waterfalls Hill, to the number of 60. After a discussion, they rode to Plainfield on the River Coquet. Others joined and they stayed at Rothbury, a small market town, that night.[24] While at Rothbury Forster wrote to Mar, requesting assistance in the form of troops from his command; this was received five days later. Forster was confident, believing their numbers would swell, and 'that next Day they would be Seven hundred Horse, and very soon a great many more'.[25]

Yet as this was happening, the government was deciding on the steps needed to counteract any Jacobite rising. On 29 September, cavalry horses had been taken from grass; and on 1 October, William Pulteney instructed the army to have their regiments 'in a readiness to take the field'.[26] On 6 October, Townshend wrote to the Earl of Scarbrough, the elderly Lord Lieutenant of Northumberland and Durham: '[Newcastle] is a town of so much importance, that His Majesty hopes you will take the best precautions you can to secure it'.[27]

Henry Liddell in London told Cotesworth that the government sought his opinion on

> the state of Northumberland with your opinion of what force would be necessary to prevent any disturbance in that or your county [Durham], as also what would be requisite to secure the peace off your corporation ... if anything to be don in relation to the troops, send word and itt will be complied with.[28]

On the 7th the Jacobites rode to Warkworth, another small market town on the coast, picking up additional supporters en route. They stayed at Lesbury Common, just outside the town, for a few days, on the 8th being joined by William, fourth Baron Widdrington (1677–1743), another Catholic Northumbrian peer, with 20 followers.[29] It was here that they sent Robert Lisle to Newcastle to spy for them.[30] On the Sunday Forster styled himself as general for the first time. Mr Buxton asked the Rev. Henry Ion of St Lawrence's church,

---

[24] Patten, *History*, 223, 18–19.
[25] Rae, *History*, 439.
[26] TNA, WO4/17, 205, 209.
[27] TNA, SP44/118, 334.
[28] Liddell, 'Letters', 182.
[29] Patten, *History*, 19.
[30] Mary Cowper, *Diary of Mary, Lady Cowper*, ed. Spencer Compton, London: John Murray, 1865, 185.

Warkworth, to take the Sunday service, but he refused, for this would mean him being obliged 'to pray for the Pretender as King and in the Litany for Mary the Queen Mother, and all the dutiful branches of the Royal Family and to omit the names of King George, the Prince and Princess'. Buxton preached instead, as Ion went to Newcastle to give information about the Jacobite progress to their enemies. It was at Warkworth that James was first proclaimed King. This was carried out by Forster, in disguise, with a trumpeter as his assistant.[31]

On 9 October, Forster wrote to Mar again, informing him that, though their numbers were still small, he remained confident of receiving additional support very soon, telling him that they would be joined by the Lowland Jacobites on the next day. The plan then was to march straight to Newcastle, 'which they were sure of, and getting good Numbers of the best Foot in the north of England to join them'. He advised Mar to attack Argyle, before the latter could be reinforced, and assured him that communications between Argyle and London would now be severed.[32]

True to this plan, the Jacobite forces marched north to Alnwick and then southwards to Morpeth on 14 October. At Felton Bridge they were joined by 70 Scots horsemen, known as the Merse Troop, under the Hon. James Hume's command. By now they were 300 strong:

> all Horse, for they would entertain no Foot, else their Numbers would have been very large, but as they neither had nor could provide Arms for those they had mounted, they gave the Common People good words and told them they would soon be furnished with Arms and Ammunition, and then they would list Regiments to form an Army.[33]

Taking potential foot soldiers would have added little positive to their enterprise and have slowed their movement considerably.

One episode which casts the first equivocal light on the Jacobite leadership comes from this period. An officer from the Merse Troop found that Felton Bridge was being approached by their enemy. He stated that he found Forster and Widdrington in bed. Forster's initial response to this, allegedly, was that this danger was impossible because he believed no one could advance there without his knowledge. When pressed, Widdrington sent the officer some

---

[31] Patten, *History*, 19–20.
[32] Rae, *History*, 441.
[33] Patten, *History*, 20–21.

reinforcements, to deal with what was probably a false alarm.[34] Yet Patten does not mention this incident at all.

It seems that the Jacobites intended to take control of Newcastle. Newcastle was the wealthiest and most populous town in the North of England and a key centre of the coal trade. It was also of great strategic importance and was not garrisoned. It was certainly a great prize and Forster hoped to have surprised the town and so take it without any opposition, perhaps with assistance from fellow Jacobites within the town.[35] Certainly their enemies believed the Jacobites had Newcastle as their goal. John Johnson, Sheriff of Northumberland, thought that the town was what 'they so much aim at, expecting a great many friends at their Entrance' and was concerned that artillery would be used 'to batter the walls of this Town with'.[36]

The Whigs were prepared. By 8 October at the latest, the town's gates had been barricaded. The County Militia had been ordered on 1 October to muster on the 11th, and this was brought forward to the 9th by Johnson. He also summoned the posse comitatus into being 'to prevent the Rebels further strolling into this Country'. This numbered 250 men on 9 October and 407 on the 10th. Lisle was arrested shortly after he entered Newcastle by Pandon Gate on the orders of Alderman Matthew White, thus denying Forster inside information and communication, and Lisle told Johnson and White who was gathered together at Rothbury. Cannon at North Shields Fort were brought to Newcastle by 10 keel boats. After taking these preparations, Johnson was confident: 'I don't question but we shall keep them out here till such Times as we get further Assistance, most people in the Town being better inclined than thought of'.[37]

This confidence was well placed. On 9–12 October Sir Charles Hotham's battalion of infantry arrived at Newcastle from Yorkshire (on 6 October they had been ordered to march from York to Berwick, but by 14 October were ordered to remain at Newcastle). Colonel George Liddell mustered over 1,200 militia, divided into horse (two troops) and foot militia (six companies) on Gateshead Fell. Yet they were probably not well armed; 'Arms for horse are very much wanted'.[38] Some weapons, 94 guns and 31 swords, were provided by Joseph Crisap, armourer.[39] The militia of Durham was marched to Gateshead on 11 October. Cotesworth wrote, 'We got the Town of Newcastle put into a State

---

[34] *A Letter about the Occurrences in the Way to, and at Preston*, Edinburgh, 1718, 1–2.
[35] Patten, *History*, 22.
[36] Cowper, *Diary*, 185–6.
[37] Cowper, *Diary*, 185–6.
[38] Cowper, *Diary*, 187; TNA, WO4/17, 222, 231.
[39] TNA, SP35/5, f179.

of holding out against 2,000 men, if they come without a Train [of artillery]'.[40] There was even discussion whether the posse and militia should march toward the Jacobites at Warkworth, but this idea was not pursued.[41]

The Whigs also had an extensive spy network to learn what they could about the Jacobites and distribute this information to allies in Scotland and London. As early as September, Cotesworth and Sir George Warrender, Provost of Edinburgh, had set up a network of agents.[42]

The Durham Militia sent patrols to watch the Jacobites. Johnson could write on 15 October, 'wee had intelligence that by our spies that the enemy had entered Morpeth'. He had also sent his clerk and two bailiffs to watch the Jacobites at Rothbury.[43]

Elsewhere, on 11 October, three dragoon colonels were summoned to meet Pulteney in London and to march their troops northwards; two to march via Derby, Leeds, Northallerton and Durham to Newcastle.[44] They seem to have begun on the following day, and a letter of the 13th from Townshend to Pulteney stated, 'forthwith despatch another express to the regiments that are marching towards Newcastle with repeated orders to hasten their march with the utmost expedition'.[45]

On 14 October, Lieutenant General George Carpenter (1657–1732) was ordered to take command of those troops ordered northwards: Molesworth's dragoons, Cobham's dragoons, Churchill's dragoons and Hotham's foot. His orders were aggressive: 'march into Northumberland and the Borders of Scotland and without loss of time ... repair to those parts and march with these our forces or such part of them as you judge sufficient and attack the Rebells wherever you find them.'[46] He left London on 15 October and arrived in Newcastle three days later.[47]

It was not all plain sailing, however. Whigs were critical of Scarbrough. Liddell wrote, 'I am surpriz'd that your Lord Lieutenant did not send you down armes'.[48] Johnson thought that Scarbrough's giving the militia 14 days' notice

---

[40] Northumberland Record Office, ZCE2/10.
[41] Cowper, *Diary*, 186–87.
[42] George Warrender, 'Warrender Letters: 1715', ed. William Dickson, *Scottish Historical Society*, 3rd series, 25, 1935, 98–9.
[43] HRO, D/EP F195.
[44] TNA, WO4/17, 227–8, 4/7, 235.
[45] TNA, SP44/118, 61.
[46] TNA, SP44/117, 114.
[47] Patten, *History*, 25.
[48] Liddell, 'Letters', 183.

to appear in arms was far too slow; it resulted in passing the initiative to the Jacobites and led to Newcastle being vulnerable to a Jacobite thrust.[49]

There were also concerns expressed about the keelmen of Newcastle (men who rowed boats with coal to the ships in the Tyne). Liddell wrote, 'Pray how stand your keelmen affected?'[50] The keelmen had often rioted, had struck in economic disputes and many were employed by Jacobite nobility and gentry; Sir William Blackett (1690–1728), a Tory MP for Newcastle and a coal owner, in particular.[51] These concerns were mostly unfounded. Thomas Sabourne, a Newcastle tailor, later related, that he 'did by ye interest he personally had with ye keelmen and their ministers procure a promise to rise for ye Diffence of ye Prest Government'.[52] They armed themselves, and 700 were allegedly ready to defend the town if necessary.[53]

Another concern was that the common people might support the Jacobites. In October 1714 a celebration of George I's accession led to a riot in Newcastle.[54] On the same occasion, White had his windows broken. A year later, on 5 October, George Levistone called William Robinson 'a Rogue and a Knave if he did not take the part of the Earl of Mar and his men and if the Scotch came here he would joyn them'. Later that month John Hewlison was heard saying, 'God damn King George' before drawing his sword.[55] These actions may well have been those of a minority, but probably gave the Whigs concern about the allegiances of the population if it came to a trial of strength.

Others from whom support was expected did not rise to the occasion, as Liddell noted: 'The High Sheriff wrote to me last post that Robert Lawson off Chirton refus'd to appear or so much as send a horse to the posse comitatus upon his summons'.[56] The Lord Lieutenant himself was criticised for being too tardy in his orders relating to the militia, and Cotesworth noted, 'He is very hearty in his duties but for want of health and vigour things are not done with ye dispatch that is necessary for matters of this nature'.[57]

The Whigs were not content to stay on the defensive. Cotesworth and Scarbrough discussed using the militia cavalry along with Cobham's dragoons,

---

[49] Cowper, *Diary*, 185.
[50] Liddell, 'Letters', 183.
[51] Gooch, *Desperate Faction*, 43.
[52] HRO, D/EP F195 f4.
[53] *Daily Courant*, 4360, 16 Oct. 1715.
[54] James Clavering, 'Some Clavering Correspondence', ed. Edward Hughes, *Archaeologia Aeliana*, XXXIV, 1956, 21.
[55] Tyne and Wear Archive Service, QS/NC/1/3.
[56] Liddell, 'Letters', 189.
[57] HRO, D/EP F195.

once they arrived, to 'drive the Rebels into the Sea, for they lie down by the Sea-side'. Cotesworth was no armchair warrior but asserted that if 20 of his country men came along, he would, too. He thought that such a forward move 'is the Way to strike Terror into all the Enemies of happy Constitution and Government'.[58] Liddell agreed with such a proposal; 'while the lye undisturb'd in the open countrey, itt gives incouragement to people to join them dayly and is a president for other countyes to rise in hopes of a like success'.[59]

The Jacobites were not wrong to believe that they had sympathisers within Newcastle. There were certainly hopes that the High Church would be supportive. Cotesworth noted, 'no doubt there was but too good a Disposition in some People to it'.[60] The town corporation was not viewed by the government's supporters as being entirely reliable. Liddell wrote, about the despatch of arms to the town, 'lett us consider into whose hands they should be putt for distributing. I should think that your good neighbours should not have that left in the least to their disposall'. He added that if the town was left without any military presence, the gates would be shut behind them.[61] However, these suspicions proved unfounded. Thomas Yorke, no friend of the corporation, wrote, 'I doubt not their resolution to maintain ye town under ye present establishment will be a disappointment to ye rebels who might have grounds to expect from ye former behaviour yt they would deliver ye town up to them'.[62] Cotesworth concluded, 'It is thought they desgynes hither but they will meet a warm reception ... many in the Town that seemed not well pleased with the government are become very zealous, no more Whig and Tory, but papist and Protestant'.[63]

Yet, though Newcastle seemed secure against the Jacobites, they had some success at this time. Lancelot and Mark Errington seized the little fort at Holy Island from the handful of troops there on 10 October, under Forster's orders. Yet their triumph was short-lived and was unsupported. Colonel Laton, the Governor of Berwick, sent 30 troops and 50 volunteers to retake the fort, which they did by wading over when the water was at low tide, on 12 October. Lancelot Errington was wounded and he and his nephew were captured.[64]

This was an important act because

---

[58] Cowper, *Diary*, 187.
[59] Liddell, 'Letters', 186.
[60] Cowper, *Diary*, 187.
[61] Liddell, 'Letters', 187, 188.
[62] Durham University Library Archives and Special Collections, Clavering Correspondence, 9.
[63] NRO, ZCE10/2.
[64] Patten, *History*, 21.

> The Design of taking this Fort was, to give Signals to any ships that seem'd to make the Cost to land Soldiers; for by the Assurances they had from Friends beyond the Sea, they expected them to land on the Coast with Supplies of Arms and Officers, but they never came till they were gone for Scotland, and then two ships appear'd off at Sea, and made their Signal, but having no Answer from the Shore made sail northward.[65]

We do not know what the content of these ships was, but had they contained money, arms and officers, they could have made an important contribution towards the Jacobites' military efforts. Yet Forster and his colleagues evidently thought they had waited in one place for long enough. As has been said, communication between the Jacobites within Britain and abroad was poor and often proved, as here, another nail in the campaign's coffin (the interior lines possessed by the government and its allies were one of its advantages).

It was not certain what the Jacobites' next move would be. John Sibbitt, Mayor of Berwick, wrote on 14 October, 'The Rebels in Northumberland are yet at Warkworth, I suppose they may endeavour to joyn on our Border'.[66]

Meanwhile the Jacobites were at Morpeth, arriving by 15 October, 12 miles to the north of Newcastle. Unaware of developments inimical to their cause in Newcastle, they were in an optimistic mood, 'promising themselves great things at Newcastle'. Gentlemen continued to join them, but country people, lacking horses, were still being turned away. Buxton, now herald as well as clergyman, proclaimed James as King. The Jacobites also took one Thomas Gibson, a blacksmith, at Felton Bridge. Gibson was believed to have been a spy. However, at this point they realised that Newcastle would not simply open its gates to them and let them in.[67]

Yet disappointment was not total. The Jacobites marched south-west to Hexham, a distance of 14 miles. They then gathered on a moor three miles to the east, nearer to Newcastle and halted:

> this was Design, as it was thought, to go to Newcastle for the Surprise of that Town, which as above, they hoped to have done sooner: It is certain that they had a great many Friends there: and it was reported amongst them that Sir William Blackett would join them. If all that was Said of this Gentleman's Conduct was true, they were not in the wrong to have some Dependence upon his Assistance.[68]

---

[65] Patten, *History*, 21–2.
[66] TNA, SP54/9/47.
[67] Patten, *History*, 22.
[68] Patten, *History*, 22–3.

Blackett was a figure of suspicion among the Whigs, too. Cotesworth wrote, 'I have taken a good deal of Pains to have Sir W. Blackett secured from going over to the Enemy. T. Wilkinson is now with him at Wallington. I do not think it advisable that he be seized till we are in a more quiet or secure State'.[69] Yet not all shared these concerns. Liddell noted them, but commented, 'I can't imagin a man off his noble fortune would run a risque more than probable off loosing all'.[70] Liddell was correct. Blackett did not want to commit to either side and evaded both by going to his uncle's house in Yorkshire, where he was advised to lie low until the crisis was over. In January 1716, Blackett kissed the King's hand to signify his loyalty.[71]

It was uncertain what the Jacobites should do next. Newcastle, their goal, was unobtainable. Foreign aid was not forthcoming. Their numbers were relatively small and hardly battleworthy. They presumably became aware that regular troops were now garrisoning Newcastle and might act aggressively against them. They could not, therefore, stand still. One possibility was that they could march to Lancashire. This was a fear among Whigs. Johnson wrote, 'We … are afraid the Rebels will march into Lancashire and quit this Country before we can give them Battle'.[72] While at Hexham and Dilston the Jacobites took horses and arms from Whigs, but otherwise their conduct was good, as even their enemies admitted: 'They plunder none as yet'. Charles Radcliffe, Derwentwater's younger brother, was assiduously recruiting; one man later stated that they were to 'fight for ye Church of England' and another that recruits were given horses and pistols.[73]

They also, as in Warkworth, had Buxton ask the minister of the church at Hexham, St Andrew's, formerly the Abbey, to read the prayers and name James III/VIII as King. Patten records, 'The Minister modestly declined it (for there was no speaking boldly to them)'. The Minister was presumably George Ritschell (1657–1717), curate since the death of the previous incumbent, his father, in 1683. However, 'Mr Richardson had promised to join the Rebels, and there are strong presumptions there to believe that as a Matter of Fact'. Patten describes Richardson as curate, so presumably Ritschell was meant.[74]

They also drew up around the cross in the market place where James III was proclaimed and affixed a copy of the proclamation to the cross. It was not removed by the townspeople for some time. This could have been because the

---

[69] Cowper, *Diary*, 187–8.
[70] Liddell, 'Letters', 183–4.
[71] Liddell, 'Letters', 219.
[72] Cowper, *Diary*, 188.
[73] Cowper, *Diary*, 188; TNA, KB8/66.
[74] Patten, *History*, 26.

bailiff and clerk were supportive of the principles of the lord of the manor, Blackett, and so discouraged its removal.[75]

It was at Hexham that the Jacobites learnt that a force of Lowland Horse under William Gordon, sixth Viscount Kenmure, had ridden into England to join them, and Forster wrote to them. He also wrote to Mar to ask for Scottish infantry. On receiving a reply a few days later and realising that Newcastle was defended and, on 18 October, that the regulars there were planning to march out to attack them, it seemed that joining forces was the best move, as well as removing themselves from immediate danger. They left Hexham for Rothbury on 19 October.[76]

Kenmure, together with other Lowland nobility – William Maxwell (1676–1744), fifth Earl of Nithsdale, Robert Dalzell (c. 1687–1737), fifth Earl of Carnworth, and George Seton (c. 1679–1749), fifth Earl of Winton – had been encouraged by Mar to raise the Jacobite standard south of the River Forth, after having been involved in active plotting since August.[77] As with the leading English Jacobites, their rising may have been prompted by the government's pre-emptive action against them. At the end of August, an Act to further encourage loyalty was passed. All four of these peers, among others, were summoned to appear at Edinburgh and be bailed for good conduct. Needless to say, none did so.[78] The standard was eventually raised on 12 October at Moffat in Annandale. The flag had the Scottish arms in gold on a blue background on one side. On the other was a thistle and the following text: 'Nemo me impune lacesset'. The standard had pennants of white, on which were written, 'For our Wronged King' and 'For our Lives and Liberties'.[79] According to enemies, they numbered either 153 or 200 men.[80]

On the following day they marched to Dumfries, in order to surprise it. However, as in the case of Newcastle, they were beaten to their goal. William Johnstone (1664–1721), first Marquis of Annandale and Lord Lieutenant of Dumfriesshire, had arrived there the previous day and 'concerted such Measures as made that Design abortive'.[81] A Lowlander later claimed that Kenmure 'had not the Courage to maque the town'.[82]

---

[75] Patten, *History*, 26.
[76] Patten, *History*, 26, 28; Rae, *History*, 243.
[77] Rae, *History*, 188.
[78] Rae, *History*, 211.
[79] Patten, *History*, 26–7.
[80] Rae, *History*, 252; Cowper, *Diary*, 188.
[81] Patten, *History*, 27.
[82] Blair Castle, Atholl Papers, Box 45/12/77.

After much dispute, they marched away, towards Lochmaben. On the 14th, the standard was unfurled and James proclaimed King. They then marched to Ecclefechan, and on the 15th to Langholm and then towards Hawick. It was when they were within two miles of the latter that they had a message from Forster delivered by Robert Douglas. This suggested that they should meet the Northumbrian Jacobites at Rothbury. This they agreed to, and by nightfall of 15 October were at Jedburgh. En route they heard news that Jacobite forces had crossed the Forth, that Argyle planned to attack them and that their advance guard had been ambushed. Only the former was true, but it put the force into some alarm. On arrival at Jedburgh, James was proclaimed.[83]

On the 16th they were at Rothbury. Mr Burnet of Carlipps was from there sent to Hexham with a message for Forster, asking whether they should wait for him there or should advance to meet him at Hexham. Forster's reply, that his force would join them, quickly arrived. Making a long march, Forster's forces arrived there on the night of 19 October. On the 20th the combined force marched to Wooler, resting there for the next day. This was when the Rev. Robert Patten, curate of Allendale, Northumberland, and a number of Scottish keelmen, joined them. Other good news was from Mr Errington to tell them that Mackintosh's Jacobite force from Scotland was marching southwards.[84]

The march of the combined force of English and Lowland Jacobites took them out of England and across the border, on 21 October, towards Kelso. En route they captured a Mr Selby and seized a number of horses. On assembling before the town, they were informed by townsmen that, though the town had been barricaded, Sir William Bennet of Grubbett and his militia, who had erected the barricades, had left and so the place was defenceless. Crossing the Tweed, they entered the town by the south side. Presently Colonel William Mackintosh (c. 1657–1743) of Borlum (known as 'Brigadier') arrived at the north side to the sound of bagpipes. Yet the Scots were 'extremely fatigued' by long marches. Even so, they were an impressive sight, led by their brigadier.[85]

Mackintosh had had a number of creditable achievements to date. He had taken the unguarded Inverness in the previous month with 500 men before marching south to join Mar in early October. Mar had then ordered him to take about 2,500 men to cross the Forth, despite the presence of enemy warships. On the night of 11 October they crossed, arriving at Haddington, but about 1,000 men had to turn back and 40 were made prisoner. This force was an immediate

---

[83] Patten, *History*, 27–8.
[84] Patten, *History*, 28–9.
[85] Patten, *History*, 30.

threat to Edinburgh, undefended as it was by regular troops. The Duke of Argyle swiftly learnt what was happening and led a force of cavalry and mounted infantry from Stirling to the Scottish capital. With news also of the militia in the city and the approach of the regulars, Mackintosh did not press his attack home and retreated to Leith, where they stayed on 13–14 October.[86]

The Jacobites took up defensive positions at the old fort at Leith. Since Argyle lacked artillery, this was a formidable position, as Argyle realised when he marched against it with his cavalry, infantry and militia on the following day. He did not attack, but retired to Edinburgh. His enemies knew the danger they could be in, so left Leith at nightfall. Mackintosh communicated with Mar, to tell him his news. The Jacobites then marched to Seton House, making this seat their new headquarters. On 17–18 October they received orders to march into Northumberland and a deputation informing them about the rising in Northumberland and the Lowlands. Forster also sent them a message inviting them to join him at Kelso, which would have reinforced messages sent from Mar to do so. They marched southwards, reaching Longformacus, 17 miles from Seton House, by 19 October. They marched on the 20th to Duns and on the 22nd to Kelso.[87]

At Kelso on Sunday, 23 October, Kenmure was now in command of the combined Jacobite forces in the Lowlands. He instructed that all the men attend Sunday service at the great Kirk (the parish church which had once been part of the Abbey) as opposed to the Episcopal meeting house. Buxton read the prayers and Patten read the sermon based on the text 'The Right of the First Born is his'. In the afternoon, a Scots Non-Juror clergyman, William Irvine, preached there. These services were well attended and well received.[88]

On 24 October, the Scots gathered in the churchyard before marching to the marketplace, with flags flying, drums beating and bagpipes playing. Once the lords and gentlemen were standing in the centre, there was silence. A trumpet was sounded and Seaton Barnes, claiming to be the Earl of Dunfermline, proclaimed King James. Then Mar's manifesto was read. It stated that all owed allegiance to James III and VIII, and the Union of 1707 was denounced. Finally, soldiers in the regular army were offered money to desert. Once the manifesto was read, 'the People with loud Acclamations shouted No Union! No Malt tax! No Salt Tax!'[89]

The Jacobites stayed at Kelso for several days. They spent the time in extracting what resources they could from the town and its surroundings. These

---

[86] Patten, *History*, 7–8.
[87] Patten, *History*, 13–14.
[88] Patten, *History*, 30–31.
[89] Patten, *History*, 34–7.

included the excise, customs and other taxes collected and held locally. Weapons and ammunition were also sought. Some had been left by the retreating militia of Sir William Bennett, such as 'some small pieces of Cannon of different Sizes and Shapes which formerly belonged at Hume Castle, and had been employed in former ages in that Stronghold against the English'. A few swords were found in the church, and a little gunpowder was also taken. The cavalry foraged in the locality and took hay from a seat of the Duke of Roxburghe.[90]

One report stated, 'The Rebels remain about Kelso under very great Extremities; they spoil Houses, and chiefly take all the pewter to melt down for bullets'; the Highlanders were 'in a very poor condition' and some were deserting.[91] They were also slack in security arrangements; one Jacobite later recalled arriving at Kelso on 23 October without anyone asking about who he and his men were.[92]

A message from Mar arrived, taken by Dr Arthur, and one was given to him to return to the sender. The contents of the latter are unknown. In all, the Jacobites had a good fighting force: 'they were more in Number at that time, and better Armed Men than at any other time after'. There were five troops of Lowland horse, six regiments of Scots infantry, five troops of English horse and two small groupings of gentlemen volunteers on horseback. Patten stated there were 1,400 men, but the real figure was probably nearer 2,000.[93]

Meanwhile, all of Carpenter's forces had arrived at Newcastle. Carpenter made sure of where the Jacobites were, for as he wrote, 'I have constant spyes out'.[94] On the 21st he could confidently state that the Jacobites had marched to Scotland, 'so I am impatient to follow them ... Had the troops of the Royal Regiment [Cobham's] been here two days sooner they might have confounded the Rebells at Hexam'. He wondered if the Jacobites were planning to attack Argyle at Stirling.[95] In fact, Argyle had his deputy, Major General Joseph Wightman, write on 24 October, to urge Carpenter 'to follow the Rebels into Scotland, who now lye at Kelso ... The most materiall part of the service at this time, is to cover this city [Edinburgh]'.[96]

---

[90] Patten, *History*, 37–8.
[91] *St. James' Evening Post*, 65, 27–9 Oct. 1715.
[92] *Weekly Journal*, 10 March 1716.
[93] Patten, *History*, 39–51.
[94] TNA, SP54/9, 63A.
[95] TNA, SP54/9, 63A.
[96] TNA, SP54/9, 83.

On 25 October he marched his forces northwards towards Kelso, seeking an engagement.[97] They had been despatched in haste, however, and lacked all their equipment. The ships carrying most of the soldiers' uniforms and bayonets for the infantry had not arrived and so, as Johnson wrote, 'they'll be obliged to march without them'.[98] The intentions of the Jacobites were unknown. Johnson was convinced he knew, writing, 'They design to press the Duke of Argyle's Camp on this side whilst Lord Mar does the Like on the other'.[99]

A spy noted that the Jacobites had 800 horsemen, half of whom were well armed. Then there were 1,300 infantry, of whom 400 to 500 were fit for service but the remainder were 'good for nothing'. Morale was thought to be low; 'they were in the utmost consternation on learning of your approach'.[100]

On Thursday, 27 October, the Jacobites faced an important decision. They learnt that General Carpenter with his four regiments had arrived at Wooler that day (though he may only have been at Alnwick, reaching Wooler on the following day), intending to attack them at Kelso on the following day. Kenmure, as commander while the army was in Scotland, called a council of war to decide what to do next. Winton 'press'd them earnestly to march away to the West of Scotland, but the English opposed and prevailed against that wiser Opinion'. It was then argued

> to pass the Tweed, and attack the King's Troops, taking the Advantage of the weakness and Weariness of General Carpenter's Men, who were indeed extremely fatigued, and were not above 500 Men in Number, whereof to Regiments of Dragoons were new raised and had never seen any Service.[101]

Charles Radcliffe, younger brother to Derwentwater, was in favour of such an attack.[102]

Patten commented:

> This also was Soldier-like Advice, and which, if they had agreed to, in all Probability they might have worsted them, considering how they were fatigued and not half

---

[97] TNA, SP54/9, 63a.
[98] Cowper, *Diary*, 189.
[99] Cowper, *Diary*, 189.
[100] BL.Add. Mss. 37993, 26.
[101] Patten, *History*, 51.
[102] Charles Radcliffe, *A Genuine and Impartial Account of the remarkable Life and Vicissitudes of fortune of Charles Radcliffe Esq.*, ed. Gerard Penrice, London, 1746, 30.

the Number the Rebels were. But there was a Fate attended all their Councils, for they could never agree to any one thing that tended to their Advantage.[103]

A Lowlander wrote, 'Our Generall refused to fight Carpenter'. Apparently it was claimed that Forster refused to fight at that moment 'till they were joyn'd with a better Body of Horse'.[104] The real issue was that the English and Scots leaders were divided; neither had a strong inclination to go to the country of the other. They may also have had differing goals, with the Scots wanting to break the recent Union of 1707, which may not have been a priority with the English. Such disagreements would continue to dog the Jacobites throughout the campaign, always at key moments. To maintain unity and avoiding their little army from diverging, the line of least resistance was taken.

A successful battle against the regulars would result in a great fillip in morale; it would provide horses and arms for the Jacobites, encourage potential supporters, and allow Newcastle to be taken, with all the strategic and economic gains that would entail. Government morale would have fallen, and it would have been a major success for the Jacobite cause.

However, it is not entirely certain whether the decision was as clear-cut as this suggests. All military action entails risk, and so armies often avoided conflict unless victory was highly probable. Battle would result in the loss of men and might well end in defeat. A Jacobite force had been routed by enemy cavalry at Cromdale in 1690. .[105] Adam Cockburn (c. 1656–1735), Lord Justice Clerk, assumed that this was evidence of 'how much the rebels are afraid of regular troops'.[106] Colonel Hotham concluded, 'We have found by experience they will not stand regular troops though not one third of their number'.[107] The officers of the regular forces clearly had a low opinion of the fighting capacities of their enemies.

Another option was outlined by Winton:

> He was always forward for Action, but never for the March into England; and he ceased not to thwart the Scheme which the Northumberland Gentlemen laid down for marching into England, not so much from the Certainty, which as he said, there was of their being over power'd, as from the greater opportunity, which, as he insisted, there was of doing Service to their Cause in Scotland; in

---

[103] Patten, *History*, 51.
[104] BC, Atholl Papers, 45/12/77.
[105] Barthorp, *The Jacobite Risings*, 5.
[106] TNA, SP54/9, 99.
[107] BL Stowe, 748, f108r.

order to which, he argued with and pressed them back into Scotland and leaving Edinburgh and Stirling to their Fate, to go and join the Western Clans, attacking in their way the Town of Dumfries, and Glasgow, and other Places, and then open a communication with the Earl of Mar and his Forces. Which Advice, if followed, in all probability would have tended to their great Advantage, the King's Forces then being so small.[108]

A Lowlander tended to agree, though suggesting one plan was to attack Argyle via Dalkeith and to take Glasgow. He wrote, 'Had this proposal been presented it had been well for us and the country, but we were deluded by lies and fair promises'.[109] This might well have been the best course of action, because they could have added to Mar's numbers or have taken loyalist towns, such as Glasgow, and have threatened Edinburgh or Stirling, at the latter of which Argyle's little army would have found themselves increasingly beleaguered. It was also arguably the least dangerous. Indeed, Jean de Robethon, one of George I's confidantes, wrote, 'they give out that they are to march back and make another attempt upon Edinburgh Castle'.[110]

This, too, was not agreed upon. Cockburne wrote, three days later, of the argument: 'the English were positive they should march into England, the Highlanders refused to goe, saying they would be all knocked on the head'.[111] Instead, a compromise was reached, to march along the borders, in a south-westerly direction, leaving the option open of marching either into Lancashire or against Dumfries and into the western part of the Lowlands.

The reasoning for this split on nationalistic grounds was probably twofold. Firstly, the English had leadership in England and the Scottish in Scotland, and therefore it was natural that each should be biased towards its own best interests as to command. This compromise led to a fatally divided command. Secondly, the English rank and file probably had no liking to go into Scotland, perhaps seen as an alien and savage land (in 1745 an English Jacobite said he would rather hang than go to Scotland), and likewise the Scots rankers thought England equally inhospitable and foreign. A united command might have resolved this disfunctionality, but this is what the Jacobite army lacked. Yet it might have led to a split which would have fatally weakened their force and allowed it to have been picked off by Carpenters' dragoons and other loyalists. One witness stated that the decision was taken to fight Carpenter, but was

---

[108] Patten, *History*, 39–40.
[109] TNA, SP54/9/107.
[110] BL. Add. Mss. 37993, 23.
[111] TNA, SP54/9/48.

rescinded on the following day, and a spirit of compromise and a tendency to take the best short-term solution prevailed.[112] Mackintosh astutely observed, 'The longer they deferred an Engagement the stronger the Opposition they were like to have met with'.[113]

However, the force left Kelso later in the day and marched to Jedburgh, in four columns: one of the Scots infantry, one of the Scots cavalry and two of English.[114] It was not a happy experience, dodging a fight. On the march a party of the Jacobites was mistaken for Carpenter's men. Captain Nicholas Wogan rode with a patrol to ascertain who this party was. They, too, wondered who his men were. Wogan fired his pistol and caused an alarm. But this was short-lived, and the cause of the confusion soon discovered. The cavalry arrived at Jedburgh without further incident. But then they heard news that the infantry, who were inevitably trailing behind the cavalry and had not yet reached the town, had been attacked by Carpenter's force; 'This put them in the utmost Consternation'. They went to investigate. While this was happening, Patten noticed the diverse looks among the leaders: 'I did then behold a great paleness in some faces, and as much Fire and Resolution in others'. There was another alarm that day when a party of men who had taken a different route into the town appeared.[115] This would suggest that morale was low and cohesion limited, for retreating from a foe does not raise spirits.

While at Jedburgh, the Merse Troop had been asked to scout out the regulars' camp. They found the men were scattered in billets in numerous hamlets: Hounam, Mindrum, Town Yetholm and Kirk Yetholm. They were also foraging for food. Finally, their 'horses were jaded, and their foot men raw and undisciplined'. At the subsequent Jacobite Council of War, 'the reasonableness of attacking the enemy was urged by some brave and wise men, but the overture was rejected upon the consideration, that we expected a better opportunity when joined by a greater force'.[116]

The Jacobites stayed two days at Jedburgh and left on the 29 October. Again, a decision on the route had to be taken, with Carpenter's force three days' march away. The English gentlemen were 'earnestly pressing' to re-cross the border and march into England. John Hunter was sent with a patrol to North Tynedale to arrange for quarters there for the rest of the army. But some of the Scots 'began a Mutiny' because they 'could not be persuaded to cross the Borders'. Persuasion

---

[112] *Weekly Journal*, 10 March 1716.
[113] Rae, *History*, 269n.
[114] *Weekly Journal*, 10 March 1716.
[115] Paten, History, 52.
[116] *A Letter*, 3.

was to no avail. Thus Hunter's men were recalled and the army marched to Hawick. The Scots still believed that they were intended for England, and on this march they separated themselves from the main force and took up positions in a hill, declaring that 'they would fight if they would lead them on to the Enemy, but they would not go to England'. They agreed with Winton's advice given at Kelso that they should march to the West of Scotland and join their allies there.[117] Apparently, the Scots even 'threatened to fire on the Horse, who were obliged to comply with the Foot'.[118]

It was a tense time. The only man they allowed near them was Winton. Allegedly, he had previously told them that if they went to England they would be massacred or sold into slavery (after all, the Scottish invasions of England in 1648 and 1651 had led to disaster). After two hours of negotiation they agreed to carry on marching together while they remained in Scotland but would desert if otherwise. So the march to Hawick continued. There was another false alarm that midnight when a party of horsemen were taken for enemies and the infantry formed up as if to fight. The error was rectified before blood was shed.[119]

There was, apparently, another opportunity to fight Carpenter: 'We were resolved to fight in that strong ground, but one thing is to be noted that our Generals courage was so great that they never durst took any body in the face and altered their resolutions every half hower'.[120]

Next day was Sunday, 30 October, and they marched to Langholm, another small market town. At night time a part of the 400 cavalry led by Carnwath was sent to Ecclefechan in order to blockade Dumfries as a prelude to the main army's taking the town. They advanced to within three miles of the town. This was a wealthy place, on major trade routes. It was also lightly defended by only militia, and was without fortifications. Its capture would yield arms, money and supplies and provide a base for a march to either Glasgow or England.[121] An anonymous Lowlander wrote that 'from which we might have ... got armes and ammunition', but as 'on other occasions, our generals' hearts failed them'.[122]

Although the main body of the army began to march to Dumfries, they only marched two miles from Langholm before an express arrived to declare that there was dissension between the Scots and English leaders. Thus the opportunity was not taken, one commentator suggesting that the fear that Carpenter was so close

[117] Patten, *History*, 53.
[118] TNA, SP54/9/98.
[119] Patten, *History*, 54.
[120] BC, Atholl Papers, 45/12/77.
[121] Patten, *History*, 55–6.
[122] TNA, SP54/9/107.

at hand resulted in this decision;[123] 'But all these arguments were in vain, the English gentlemen were positive for an attempt upon their own Country'. Their argument was that they had letters from 'their Friends in Lancashire, inviting them thither, and assuring them that there would be a general Insurrection upon their appearing, that 20000 Men would immediately join them and promising them Mountains'. This was so vehemently made that it proved decisive. Those men sent to Ecclefechan were retracted and ordered to ride to Langton to join them.[124] A Lowlander later wrote, 'we were flattered into England with a number of pleas & fair promises ... but all their promises came to nothing'.[125] How easy would it have been to have taken the town? Rae argued that its defences were strong and its civilian defenders resolute. On 30 October the magistrates had caused trenches to be dug and a redoubt constructed. There were seven companies of militia and armed countrymen from the surrounding districts. Cannon were mounted.[126] Robert Corbett of Dumfries was confident, writing that he and his townspeople 'made all the disposition possible to give them a warm reception'. Annandale thought morale was high; 'our people at Dumfries and ain all that county are very hartie'.[127] As with Monmouth and Bristol in 1685, the rebelling force was reluctant to take on even a civilian force defending a town.

Again, the same clash of opinions surfaced as on 27 October. The English wanted to be back in England and believed they would find additional support in the north-western counties, among people whom they knew, rather than in the relatively alien Scotland. Furthermore, to avoid advancing towards Dumfries meant avoiding conflict; again, the line of least resistance was taken; risks were avoided. Such could not continue forever, but as long as a decision could be postponed, it was.

The Scots halted, uncertain about the arguments offered above. About 300 to 700 left the army (probably mostly Highland infantry) rather 'than to go forward to certain Destruction'. Their leaders tried 'All imaginable Means' to prevent them, but to no avail. Winton and his troop also left, convinced that they were likewise marching to ruin (having split up into smaller parties, the deserters were mostly taken by militia and loyalists in the Lowlands). They later returned, still unhappy. Winton was certainly further antagonised by the ending of the calling of the councils of war, which had hitherto made decisions for the

---

[123] *Weekly Journal*, 10 March 1716.
[124] Patten, *History*, 56.
[125] BC, Atholl Papers, 45/12/77.
[126] Rae, *History*, 182, 274–5.
[127] TNA, SP54/10/13, 14B.

army. He was further slighted by not having quarters fit for a nobleman and retreated mentally by talking of his former experiences.[128]

Whig commentators soon heard of these desertions and saw them as signs that the Jacobite army was at the point of collapse. Annandale wrote on 3 November, 'the Horse both Scots and English were gon in great disorder back to England, 700 of the Highlanders are in a manner deserted, 200 are made prisoners in the church if Lammington by the country people'. Robert Corbett wrote likewise, that the Jacobites were 'in all appearance in a desperat & disordered condition'.[129]

The Scots were not wholly against the march into England. Mackintosh was recorded as stating, 'Why the devil not go into England, where there's both meat, men and money? Those who are deserting us are but the rascality of my men [another observer thought they were his best]'. Winton was less enthusiastic, but stoically observed:

> It shall never be said in history to any of the generation that the Earl of Winton broke off from or deserted King James' interest, and his country's good. You or any man shall have liberty to cut these [his ears] out of my head if we do not all repent it.[130]

When the Jacobites had arrived at Langholm, they decided to abandon the two cannon they had brought from Kelso, having nailed them up so they were unfit for service. They then marched to Longtown, which 'was a very long and fatiguing March'. They learnt that a party led by Brigadier Stanwix had been there seeking intelligence of their numbers and motions, but retired on the Jacobites' approach. The Ecclefechan party returned, and on 1 November the army finally arrived in England at Brampton. The Jacobites proclaimed their King, claimed the excise and customs revenues, and paid the Scots a wage of six pence per day.[131]

It was here that Forster became commander of the army as he opened the letter from Mar dated 21 October. Kenmure also had a letter from Mar, written at Perth on the same date. Mar desired news about the campaign south of Perth. He had no advice to give, having no knowledge of affairs in England. Finally, he wished them luck: 'Success attend you'. Having marched from Kelso to Brampton, a distance of 70 miles, in five days, they halted at Brampton for rest.[132]

---

[128] Patten, *History*, 56–7.
[129] TNA, SP54/10/13, 14b.
[130] *A Letter*, 4.
[131] Patten, *History*, 57–8.
[132] Patten, *History*, 58–63.

At the same time, Carpenter had called off the pursuit. He had marched to Yetholm on 29 October and was at Jedburgh the next day. Here he was joined by a Mr Cranstoun and 120 militia cavalry, who helped guide his forces through terrain unknown to them. He rested his men there for a day, most of whose infantry were now mounted on horses lent by the gentry.[133] Cockburne looked forward to hearing about a successful encounter, writing:

> Lieutenant General Carpenter has made such speedy marches that last night he lay within eight or nine miles of them, his following them so close even to the fatiguing a little his troops will be of great consequence, I hope by my next your lordship shall hear that body is disperst to the utter damping of all the rest of the Rebels.[134]

Annandale was also in hopes of an early victory, that he would 'make a good account of them in a verie little tyme'.[135] He learnt the Jacobites had been at Hawick and had marched to Langholm. On 1 November, however, his forces marched back to Newcastle, via Hexham, returning to the former on 4 November.[136]

This was in part because his men were far from Newcastle and he was concerned that the Jacobites might make a dash for this crucial town. It may also have been because of the difficulty of the terrain and the risk of exhausting his men and horses. It did mean that the Jacobites were far from any significant force of regular troops. At this time, too, the militia of both Northumberland and Durham had been dismissed.[137] Meanwhile, reinforcements were on their way. On 31 October, Major General Charles Wills was given command of three regiments of dragoons (Wynn's, Honeywood's and Newton's), Pitt's horse, and three battalions of infantry (Fanes, Sabine's and Preston's) in the Midlands.[138]

The Jacobites had failed to secure Newcastle, but given the defence put up by Cotesworth, Johnson and others, and the arrival of regular troops, this was never practical. Secondly, support from abroad never materialised. Given the aggression of their opponents, the Jacobites had to retreat to Kelso. Thereafter, divided leadership ruled out decisive action. This continued until the end of

---

[133] Rae, *History*, 273.
[134] TNA, SP54/9, 98.
[135] TNA, SP54/10, 13.
[136] Jonathan Oates, 'Responses in North East England to the Jacobite Rebellions of 1715 and 1745', Reading University PhD Thesis, 2001, 74.
[137] Liddell, 'Letters', 197–8.
[138] TNA, WO4/17, p. 257.

October and resulted in mass desertion among the Scots. On the other hand, Carpenter had not succeeded in his primary task of bringing the Jacobites to battle and defeating them. In this 'peaceful' phase of the campaign, no one is noted as being killed; one of the Erringtons was wounded, as were three children, by accident, by a Jacobite in Kelso.[139]

The first phase of the campaign could have gone better for the Jacobites, it is true, but their army, though reduced from its peak, was intact and undefeated and was advancing into the North West of England, in the expectation of further support and success. Their regular opponents were some distance away and unable to confront them. Yet they were not without their weaknesses. There had been two opportunities in the final week of October for the Jacobites to have attacked Carpenter's outnumbered and possibly exhausted men, and only one in four regiments were veterans. In both cases the opportunity was not taken. The case for aggression is strong with the benefit of hindsight, but perhaps less so without it. Commanders often did not seek battle because it was risky and even if successful could result in severe losses for the victor, blunting further offensive capacity. Furthermore, civilian generals such as Kenmure and Forster may have wanted to avoid large-scale bloodshed if at all possible; after all, a monarchy had been restored in 1660 and another overturned in 1688 with a minimum of violence (at least in England). Yet rebellions are dangerous and difficult undertakings, and once the sword has been drawn it cannot easily be resheathed with safety. Once opportunities pass, others must be sought. The Jacobite leaders, or at least some of them, believed the North West of England would supply mass support and so create these new opportunities.

---

[139] Patten, *History*, 21, 38.

Chapter 3

The North West of England, September – October 1715

The state of northern England before the Jacobite army marched through it in November 1715 is a relatively little studied subject. Rupert Jarvis examined the topic of the militia in Westmorland and Jonathan Oates has published a short paper surveying responses towards the Jacobites in the northern English counties.[1] Yet there was much activity on the part of the county authorities, both ecclesiastical and secular, in the face of news of a Jacobite incursion. Concerns about local Jacobites as well as external enemies were considerable. Similarly, the Jacobites were in high hopes of garnering support from Lancashire. These expectations, and actions taken in light of them, will now be considered.

The Jacobite army which was about to march through the North West of England had high hopes of gaining support from its allies there. It had been claimed that 20,000 men would enlist, but there were other estimates. One report claimed that 1,000 would join in Lancashire and another 4,000 from Manchester (overlooking the fact that this town's total population was only about 8,000 at the time).[2] Apparently, in September, Widdrington and other Catholic gentry had paid a visit to Lancashire and consulted with the peer's son-in-law, Richard Towneley (1687–1735), of Towneley Hall, near Burnley, who promised an enthusiastic welcome and the addition of 20,000 men once the army arrived in the county.[3]

Others thought so, too, on both sides of the struggle. Mar, in July, wrote as to a suitable place for the Jacobites to begin their attempt on the throne, 'If on the West sea, some place in Lancastershire [sic]'. When discussing places which would offer strong support, he referred to Lancashire among them.[4] It was not only the

---

[1] R.C. Jarvis, *Collected Papers on the Jacobite Risings*, Manchester: Manchester University Press, 1971, I; Oates, 'Responses', *Northern History*, 2006.
[2] *Political State*, X, 1715, 161, 163.
[3] Hibbert-Ware, 'Memorials', 27.
[4] *HMC*, Stuart Papers, I, 521–2.

Jacobites who thought thus, but Townshend did, too, writing that the Jacobites 'reckon themselves sure of' support in Lancashire. Northumbrian Whigs agreed.[5]

It was not unreasonable for the Jacobites to expect support from Lancashire. England's strongest concentration of Catholics was to be found there. There were 469 estates in the county owned by Catholics, and in 1718 these were valued at a total of £27,031 11s 3d. Catholics were particularly numerous in the south and west of the county. Catholic gentry owned about a third of the land in the county and 1 in 10 of the population were Catholic: about 16,000–17,000. There had been strong Catholic support for James II in 1685–88 when Lord Molyneux, a leading Catholic peer, was made Lord Lieutenant. The discriminatory laws against Catholics had been briefly suspended in these years. The Jacobites promised to repeal all these laws and allow Catholics fully to participate in civil life, so there were powerful incentives for Catholics to support them.[6]

These penal laws dating from the late sixteenth century included the possibility of being fined for non-attendance at an Anglican church; in fact, Catholic churches were illegal, as was the holding of Mass. Catholics could not attend British universities. Furthermore, in 1661 there was the Corporation Act barring Catholics from posts in 'local government'; in 1673 the Test Act, barring them from the armed forces, court positions and Parliament; and in 1692 the imposition of double Land Tax hit the gentry's pockets. These laws were not always upheld, but the threat remained, depending on the zeal of the magistracy. For instance, in 1713 a clergyman had tried to have John Dalton and another seven Catholics in Lancashire indicted for recusancy, though in this instance the attempt was unsuccessful.[7]

Whigs were certainly concerned about the numbers of Catholics in Lancashire and the threat they might cause, in conjunction with a Jacobite army. Contemporary Whig sources reveal their fears of Catholics in this part of the country. Nicolson had written, in 1709:

> popery has advanced by very long strides of late years in this country and too many of our magistrates love to have it so. At the very time that the French were on our coasts and our people daily expected the news of their being landed, the

---

[5] *HMC*, Townshend, 174; Cowper, *Diary*, 188.
[6] Hibbert-Ware, 'Memorials', 244; R.G. Blackwell, 'Lancashire Catholics, Protestants and Jacobites during the 1715 Rebellion', *Recusant History*, 22/1, 1994, 42, 47.
[7] G. Holmes, *The Making of a Great Power, 1660–1722*, Longman, 1993, 455, 457; Tyldesley, *Diary*, 115.

wealthier of our papists, instead of being seized, were cringed to with all possible tenders of honour and respect.[8]

Similarly, the Rev. Samuel Peploe, Vicar of Preston, wrote to his bishop six years later:

> I beg leave to acquaint your lordship that there are three townships and part of another in this parish, which lie three, four and five miles from the church, and have no other convenient place of public worship; that by this unhappy situation they have still been exposed to temptations and popery, which is too prevalent in these parts of your lordship's diocese, and are thereby an easier prey to the priests of that communion, we having no less than six of these men in the one parish. From my first coming to this place I have wished for some hopeful remedy against this growing evil.[9]

Yet not all religious minorities, who were discriminated against (albeit to a lesser extent), were sympathetic towards Jacobitism. Dissent was relatively strong in Cumberland and Westmorland, with 5 per cent being Presbyterian and 3 to 4 per cent being Quakers.[10] Yet Dissent was strong in Lancashire, too, with about 18,000 in the county in 1718, though they lacked the monied and landed power of many of the county's Catholics.[11]

Religious differences were not the only issue at stake. Politically, the north-western counties were divided. The Lonsdales and Howards held influence over the six Parliamentary seats in Cumberland and in 1715 all were held by Whigs, who supported the Hanoverian succession. Westmorland was divided between two Whigs and two Tories.[12] There were seven constituencies in Lancashire. Except Lancaster, Liverpool and Preston, they were all held by Tories, Preston being divided. Of these nine, five Tory MPs have been identified as being Jacobite. Shuttleworth, who was an MP for Lancashire and 'is reputed one of the strongest Jacobites in England', and Henry Fleetwood, an MP for Preston, were both members of the Preston Jacobite Club. The other Lancashire MP, Bland, and Edmund Harvey, an MP for Newton, were both taken into custody in 1715

---

[8] *VCH Cumberland*, II, 1968, 104.
[9] *VCH Lancashire*, VII, 1912, 77n.
[10] Oates, *The Jacobite Invasion of North West England of 1745*, Lancaster: Centre for North Western Studies, 2006, 9–10.
[11] Eveline Cruickshanks, Stuart Handley and David Hayton, *House of Commons, 1690–1715*, II, Cambridge: Cambridge University Press, 2002, 319.
[12] Sedgwick, *History*, I, 221–3, 341–2.

on suspicion of Jacobitism. The latter was 'continously talking of designs to bring them back' and had been corresponding with the late French Ambassador for London and the Duke of Ormonde to solicit French aid to help restore the Stuarts.[13] Finally, three of the four Cheshire MPs were Tories and were thought to be sympathetic to the Jacobite cause.[14]

Some Northumberland Jacobites had estates in the adjoining county of Cumberland. Derwentwater, was one, for example: 'his Concerns in the Lead Mines in Alstone Moor are very considerable, where several hundreds of Men are employ'd under him, and get their Bread from him, whom, there is no doubt, he might have easily engaged'.[15]

Although there was no spontaneous Jacobite rising in the autumn in the North West until November, there was evidence in 1715 of Jacobite activity among men of all social orders. On 21 June, William Browne, a Manchester cordwainer, was overheard declaring, 'George is a usurper and we'll have him wafted over the main again'. John Ives, a chapman of the same, said, 'We can have no justice here'. Samuel Barker, a glovemaker attested, 'Now all things go well on our side and now we will be revenged on Mr Ainstough [minister of Cross Street chapel] for his sermon preached on the 31st January last'. Of course, as we have seen, Manchester was known for its Jacobitism, so perhaps this is not surprising, but Patrick Cairn, a bread baker from Liverpool, said, on 29 August, 'King George is no more fit to wear the Crown than my Dogg. And the only right king is King James' son, the Prince of Wales. And he shall wear it'. William Walmesley of Bolton, a linen draper, said, 'Down with the Rump and God bless King James'. William Johnson of Failsworth, a whistler said, 'if the Duke of Ormonde be impeached there is a league made for an army to be raised in a few days time of above 20000 against this King and government'.[16]

There was sometimes controversy in the toasting of healths, too. John Swarbreck, a yeoman of Westham, was in an ale house in Weetton and a group of Jacobites began to toast 'K. James ye 3rd's health and pulled off his hatt to drink it and was pledged by three of ye company'. Another man refused to join in, and so Swarbreck 'offered to pull off the informant's hat and presst him to drink the health'. The man left, but recalled that James's health was drunk to several times.[17]

It was not only in Lancashire that verbal signs of Jacobite support occurred, but also in Cheshire. On 4 October, it was noted that one William Robinson

---

[13] Sedgwick, *History*, I, 268–74.
[14] Sedgwick, *History*, I, 202–3.
[15] Patten, *History*, 47.
[16] TNA, PL1/28, 235, 238.
[17] TNA, PL1/27, 2.

was in the stocks for suspicion of disloyalty to George I. On 15 July he had said at Wrenbury, 'Either drive King George into his own Country or we'll have his head off'. Another Jacobite, had, at Eaton, exclaimed, 'By God, here's a health to James the third of England' and 'By God [I] wish all my heart I will ride my horse an hundred miles to do him'. At Hutton Magna, on 22 July, one John Dawson said, 'Here's a health to King James the third'. There are also cryptic references in late August to the Chester Recorder making out 'affidavits relating to what passed lately at Sir Richard Grosvenor's' and an order to 'discourage and suppress any disaffected proceedings'.[18] Two other Cheshire men who were suspected of Jacobitism were both clergy: the Rev. Thomas Wells, Vicar of Sandbach, and the Rev. Malton, Vicar of Congleton.[19] Perhaps the latter was suspected of encouraging the rioters at Congleton against the Dissenters. Another suspect clergyman was Mr Meakin of Mobberley, who apparently cried 'Down with ye Rump', and referred to the Whigs as 'Oliver's whelps, king killers and sequestrating rascalls'.[20]

There were no known instances of Jacobitism in Cumberland, though the assize records surviving for this period are patchy. However, in Westmorland, one Francis Willoughby was accused of 'seditious words against the King' in 1715.[21]

The only display of mass Jacobitism at this period occurred at Chester on 20 October, when the anniversary of the coronation was being celebrated. Jacobites were noted as taking the free drinks offered by the Whigs, but did not drink healths to the King or his principal generals, Argyle and Marlborough. Instead, one threw his pot of ale at the Whigs and others insulted them verbally. Houses which were lit up to mark the occasion had their windows broken. There was also a Jacobite mob at Partington, but in both cases the Jacobites were dispersed by resident soldiers without bloodshed, though on one occasion an alderman sided with the crowd.[22]

Elite Jacobitism was also in evidence, though of a more discreet nature. There was a meeting of Cheshire Jacobite gentry at Ashley Hall. Among those present were Henry and Peter Legh, John Warren, Robert Cholmondeley, Alexander Radcliffe, James Barry and Sir Richard Grosvenor. They debated whether they

---

[18] TNA, CHES24/152/3; SP44/118, 25.
[19] TNA, PL28/1, 235, 237.
[20] J.H.E. Bennett and J.C. Dewhurst, *Quarters Session Records with other Records of the Justices of the Peace for the County Palatine of Chester, 1559–1760*, RSLC, no. 94, 1940, 204–5.
[21] TNA, ASSI 41/1.
[22] *The Flying Post*, 3716, 27–9 October 1715.

should take part in the rebellion, but decided by the casting vote of their host, Thomas Assheton (1678–1759), that discretion was the better part of valour.[23]

It is also important to note that the regular forces in the north-western counties were few and far between. There were small garrisons at Carlisle and Chester, but these lacked the strength for any action apart from the strictly defensive. Formal opposition from these sources would, therefore, be limited.

Thus the Jacobites were not wrong to have expectations of sympathy in Lancashire, Cheshire and perhaps elsewhere. Let us not forget the rioting in Manchester earlier in the year, too. Whether this would translate into the active support which was needed for success would be another question. Although these counties did not see the Jacobite army in September and October, there was Jacobite activity there at this time, though this has traditionally been ignored.

Fears and Uncertainties

Few people in the North West of England had reliable and up-to-date news of events occurring elsewhere. Such was inevitable given the sources available to them, with no regional press. London newspapers gave news which was a few days old at best. They were unable to follow events happening at any distance away. Such is made clear by even a well-informed commentator such as Prescott.

It was not known for certain that there had been a rising in Scotland until late September. Prescott noted on 18 September, 'An Attempt on Edenborugh Castle defeated'. Two days later, he wrote, 'Wee are surpris'd today with the news of an insurrection in Scotland and that the Earl of Marr set up there the standard of K. James 8'. On 25 September, he wrote, 'The News magnifies the Commocion in Scotland'.[24] Yet knowledge of the progress of the Jacobites in Northumberland came quickly to those in the know. Nicolson recorded hearing news of the Jacobites there as early as 8 October.[25]

There was some discourse in Chester about the Jacobites, which annoyed Prescott. On 11 October, an Irish captain told him that 'If hee coud meet with the Pretender hee woud present his Head in a bag to the King & Parliament', and Prescott later abandoned 'this vain Furioso'. In the following week, Prescott and his wife talked with one Mrs Carter. According to Prescott, 'Her irreverent

---

[23] Bennett, 'Cheshire and the Fifteen', *Journal of the Cheshire and North Wales Archaeological and Historic Society,* New Series 21, 1915, 30.
[24] Prescott, 'Diary', II, 463–4.
[25] Nicolson, 'Diaries', V, 4.

and ingratefull mencion of the Royal Family [the exiled Stuarts], and peevish scandalous reflections on the Duke of Ormonde, provoke mee too much'.[26]

It was clearly an anxious and tense time, not made any better by the prevalence of rumour. Prescott recorded on 19 October, 'A rumor spreads today from a Letter from Ireland to Mr. Allen that Lord Marr is routed, taken and carry'd prisoner to London'. Yet the loyalists seem to have been in ascendancy in Chester. On 20 October, the anniversary of the king's coronation, the day was 'by one party kept with dull solemnity'. Furthermore, there was a demonstration by 'the yong Rakes of the Constitucion Club', who were presumably young loyalists who may have caused annoyance to local Tories, and they were bound over for future good behaviour by the mayor two days later.[27]

Loyalty

The other side of the coin was evidence of loyalty to the Hanoverian dynasty. One of the standard responses at times of emergency was that corporations and counties sent written messages of loyalty to the Crown, as they had done in 1714. Of course, it is possible to be cynical about these. Yet contemporaries thought they were important enough to pen them and that they should be printed in the press. In October, the following sent such addresses to the Crown: the corporations of Chester, Kendal, Clitheroe, Lancaster, Preston and Carlisle. Interestingly, Barrymore prepared the loyal address of Chester. The counties of Lancashire and Westmorland sent addresses, headed by the Lords Lieutenant.[28]

We do not know what most of these addresses declared. Typically, all that was stated in *The London Gazette*, where they were noted, were brief details:

> An humble Address of the Lord-Lieutenant, High-Sheriff, Grand-Jury, Deputy-Lieutenants, Gentlemen and Freeholders of the County Palatine of Lancashire; presented to His Majesty by the Right Honourable Earl of Derby.[29]

Yet the full text of one such address does survive. It was from the city of Chester and read thus:

---

[26] Prescott, 'Diary', II, 466–7.
[27] Prescott, 'Diary', II, 468.
[28] *The London Gazette*, 5262, 21–3 September – 5272, 26–30 October 1715.
[29] *The London Gazette*, 5263, 24–7 September 1715.

When the inveterate Enemy of our Religion & liberties in open violation of the most solemn Treaties is preparing to invade your Majesty's Dominions & to impose upon us a popish pretender to your Majesty's Crown, when many of your Majesty's deluded subjects insensible of the blessings of your Majesty's happy Reign have Given too much encouragement to this attempt by their late Riots & tumults in several parts of this Kingdom we think it high time for us your Majesty's most dutyfull & loyal subjects to prostrate ourselves at your Majesty's feet with the surest Assurance of an untainted affection & loyalty to your Majesty's person & government and that as we have hitherto preserved this City entirely free from the contagion of ill examples so we will upon all occasions to the last drop of our blood defend your Majesty's lawful & rightful title to the Crown of these Realms (to which we esteem our Religious & civil Rights as inseparably annexed) against the said pretender and all other your Majesty's enemies whatsoever.[30]

The Lieutenancy

More practical and physical was the work emanating from the lieutenancy, who were in charge of the militia. On 16 September, the Privy Council wrote to the lieutenants in the north of England. They acquainted them of the 'open and unaturall Rebellion … in that part of His Majesties Dominions in Scotland' and of the Jacobite attempt to restore James. In order to properly defend the kingdom they sent two commands: the first, 'to cause the Militia, both Horse and Foot, to be put in Such a posture as to be in readiness to meet upon the first order'. Second, they were to have the militia 'Seize, with the assistance of the Constable, the Persons and arms of all Papists, Nonjurors or other Persons that you have manner to suspect to be Disaffected'. All Lords Lieutenant were told to repair to their counties by a letter dated 19 September.[31]

As before, Carlisle was swift to act, given that he was in Yorkshire throughout the crisis. On 22 September, he wrote to the deputy lieutenants of both Cumberland and Westmorland. He commanded the deputies thus: 'I must recommend to your Care and Vigilance a Strickt and Due Execution of them'. Catholics who were arrested were to be sent to Carlisle castle, as 'the safest and properest place to send the persons you take into Custody to'.[32]

---

[30] Chester Record Office, AF/49g/50.
[31] Jarvis, *Jacobite Risings*, 149–50; TNA, SP44/118, 29.
[32] Jarvis, *Jacobite Risings*, 152–3.

After this, the senior deputy, Henry Lowther (1694–1751), Viscount Lonsdale, took matters into his youthful hands. He wrote to his fellow deputies on 25 September. He, too, saw that urgency was crucial, writing of the need for action against Catholics, 'I believe it will be adviseable to proceed as soon as possible upon the Order'. He also wished to have a meeting of deputies in early October, at Henry Hayton's house in Penrith. This occurred on 4 October. Fourteen men attended, including Nicolson and Sir Thomas Stanwix, Lieutenant Governor of Carlisle Castle. Some of those who had previously served in the militia were either dead or too old. They decided that each militia captain should send out instructions to the high constable of each ward in the counties, to order 'every Constable within the ward to Return and Summon three persons, between the Ages of Twenty and fifty, to appear before such Capataine at such time and place as he shall appoint for and respect of every one person so Deceased or Superannuated'. Each captain should then ensure that each constable should supply three men from his jurisdiction to serve in the militia. Constables were also to provide enough arms for these men. Each captain was to provide a report as to how many arms he had for his company by 17 October.[33]

Hugh Simpson, as clerk of the militia in Cumberland, was busy with paperwork in the next few days. Lonsdale told him to send copies of decisions made and letters written to Carlisle, so he could transmit these to the Privy Council. One item of information which he asked Simpson to distribute to the Earl of Carlisle was serious indeed. According to Lonsdale, 'I have received Certain Information of a Design to Invade this Countrey and Seize [the city of] Carlisle for the Pretender'. This required another meeting of deputies, Lonsdale concluded, and five days later another was held at Penrith, as before.[34]

Yet at the meeting (14 October), the decision was taken to fit out a troop of light horse militia. All those who had to provide a quota of horsemen were to send their contribution to Dalston Green, four and a half miles to the south-west of Carlisle, on 21 October. They were also to provide two weeks' pay for each man.[35] The horse militia of Westmorland and Lancashire in late October rode to Carlisle, in order to try to prevent the Jacobite march into England, and arrived on about 2 November.[36]

The militia was mostly made of companies of footmen. They were to be quartered in towns throughout the counties. Lonsdale's was to be at Appleby, two were to be stationed in Carlisle, and one each at Cockermouth, Penrith,

---

[33] Jarvis, *Jacobite Risings*, 153–5.
[34] Jarvis, *Jacobite Risings*, 157–8.
[35] Jarvis, *Jacobite Risings*, 159.
[36] Rae, *History*, 279.

Kirkby Lonsdale and Kendal. This deployment was to have occurred by the end of October. Each man was to have a musket and three pounds of ball. Simpson, as muster master as well as clerk of the peace, was to ensure that the men were paid.[37]

Carlisle approved of these measures and wrote to Lonsdale, to express his thanks: 'The Directions you have ... given in Relation to the Militia are very proper and what I intirely approve'. He wished to be kept informed of any new developments and promised that, in the event of 'any alarme or Apprehension of Danger', he would 'come immediately away'.[38]

Arming the militia, though, was a major concern. Carlisle pointed out what surely must have been obvious: 'The Men can be of no use unless fitly Armed ... take that particular into your Speedy and serious Consideration'.[39] This was, though, easier said than done. Lonsdale reported:

> The Militia throughout is ill armed, but I don't know how that can be remedied at present, for they can't be provided with better ones in this country and it will be a long time before new ones can be had from London. We have ordered them to throw away their pikes and get firelocks in their place, and also to put the arms they have into the best condition that is possible.[40]

Yet, according to Symson, 'Ours and Cumberland's militia both horse and foot are up ... and well armed and strictly disciplined every day'.[41]

Apart from measures taken concerning the militia, steps were also taken against Catholics. Carlisle noted on 25 October:

> You have perform'd what the Government expected from you in Securing all Roman Catholicks, Nonjurors [Anglicans who did not recognise monarchs following the overthrow of James II as being legitimate] and other Disafected People whom you had reason to Suspect would be Aiding to the Pretender upon this Occasion.[42]

Yet not all agreed with this, with Lonsdale writing, 'I was desired by some of these gentlemen to move the deputy lieutenants that they might have their liberty upon

---

[37] Jarvis, *Jacobite Risings*, 163.
[38] Jarvis, *Jacobite Risings*, 163.
[39] Jarvis, *Jacobite Risings*, 162; Historical Manuscripts Commission, *Manuscripts of the Earl of Carlisle*, London: HMSO, 18.
[40] HMC *Carlisle*, 18.
[41] Symson, *Letter Books*, 342.
[42] Jarvis, *Jacobite Risings*, 162.

their parole'. Lonsdale was adamant and replied, 'I told them that was what I could not possibly do: the Northumberland men, who were all their friends, were very near and that thought it not at all fit for me to meddle in at this time'.[43]

These instructions were obeyed. James Herbert, High Constable of Allerdale ward above Derwent, was active. He had 'been put to a great deal of trouble and Expence in rideing about to Summon Papists, &c., and Issuing forth Warrants pursuant to the Orders of the Court'. John Dean was similarly active in Cumberland Eskdale ward.[44] Militia officers were also reimbursed for similar activities. Thomas Wybergh was given £5 'for Seizing Papists with their Horses and arms' in Westmorland, and Mr Fletcher and two officers were given £6 'for Seizing Papists their Horses and arms' in Cumberland.[45]

Meanwhile, there were military preparations taking place in Cheshire. The county militia met at Chester on 28 October. Mr Ashurst, a deputy lieutenant, was in command of the infantry and Derby in charge of the horsemen.[46] However, not all the magistrates were eager to act against Catholics, and Townshend noted on 6 October that he was 'sorry to find that any of the gentlemen, should scruple the legality of securing disaffected persons by virtue of the late Order of Council'.[47] Whether this was a sign of Jacobite sympathies or the need to adhere strictly to the letter of the law whatever the circumstances is hard to discern. Perhaps most likely was the belief on the part of some JPs that their fellow gentry were harmless and so should not be molested.

Hoghton and his fellow deputy lieutenants were told by Derby (who, as with Carlisle, was largely absent during the crisis) to raise the Lancashire militia by a letter of 27 September. There was a meeting of the Lancashire lieutenancy on 29 October at Preston. Present were Derby, Hoghton and five others. They resolved that Hoghton, as colonel of the militia, should raise the militia of the hundreds of Amounderness and Lonsdale. They should be trained and meet at Preston on 3 November. The militia should be armed with bayonets and equipped with cartridge boxes, as well as muskets, and the cavalry 'with such arms and furniture as are wanting to make them compleat'. All Catholic gentry were ordered to be arrested, though it does not seem that this was very effective.[48] For instance,

---

[43] *HMC*, Carlisle, 17.
[44] Jarvis, *Jacobite Risings*, 179, 181.
[45] Jarvis, *Jacobite Risings*, 171, 170.
[46] Prescott, 'Diary', II, 469.
[47] TNA, SP44/118, 333.
[48] *A Calendar of the deeds and papers in the possession of Sir James de Hoghton, baronet of Hoghton Tower, Lancashire*, Record Society of Lancashire and Cheshire, 88, Chadwyck-Healey, 1936, 112.

Blundell was unmolested and, as shall be noted, numerous gentry were at liberty to join the Jacobites.

The parish constables were busy in their efforts to arm the militia, judging by the few constables' accounts which survive. The Downholland Constable spent six pence in 'repairing shooting buts'. The Formby constable did likewise. He also put muskets in order at the cost of 5s 4d, provided belts and cartridge boxes at 10s 4d, cleaned a halberd for two pence and put two swords and a pike in order for a shilling. He also advanced money to the men of the parish who served in the militia. The Tarleton constable paid 15 days' wages to three parishioners, Thomas Maudesley, Richard Starnge and Jeff Robinson, for service in the militia. This was on top of repairing and providing muskets and halberds.[49] At Halewood, the constable was even more enthusiastic, paying £10 14s 10d for muskets and swords and 7s 6d for cartridge boxes. Like his equivalent in Tarleton, he paid for 10 parishioners in the militia for a fortnight.[50]

The constables were active in other ways, too. The one for Downholland claimed a shilling for attending the High Constable in searching for horses and arms belonging to Catholics. His colleague claimed money for watching the Jacobites with soldiers and for making a search. The Halewood Constable made several searches and made a return to two magistrates of Catholics taking oaths, and arrested a 'young man on suspicion'. The Formby constable made two searches, almost certainly of Catholic property, and paid for a warrant to summon Catholics to swear oaths. The Tarleton constable did likewise, going to Ormskirk 'about ye papists'. Unusually, he had to find carts to convey army baggage.[51] Such activity is all the more noteworthy because the magistrates of the county included Tories installed in the previous reign.

The City of Carlisle

Concern was apparent in Carlisle, a key border fortress, as early as 21 September. The corporation noted that 'the present state of affairs in the north' required action on their part. They decided to have a count made of all able-bodied men in the city who were capable of bearing arms in case it needed defending. They also made orders that arms be distributed to these men if necessary. In the meantime, all weapons were to be lodged in the castle for safe keeping.

---

[49] Lancashire Record Office, PR29456/2/1; PR3360/4/1/1; PR3168/7/9.
[50] LRO, PR2724/15.
[51] LRO, PR2956/2/1, PR2724/15, PR3168/7/9, PR3360/4/1/1.

Anyone entering the city who was not a native was seen as a possible spy. All innkeepers were obliged to make a note of all such strangers and report them to the corporation. Failure to do so would result in the loss of their licences. Finally, additional bedding was to be provided inside the castle in case the garrison needed to be augmented at short notice.[52] Stanwix, however, seemed confident of the loyalty of the townspeople, writing on 14 October, 'As for this place, no people ever were more hearty or more honest, and the garrison very much improved'.[53]

Yet there was a perceived danger in some quarters. Lowther reported that Stanwix had 'received certain information of a design to seize Carlisle for the Pretender' in early October. Since the garrison of the castle was only 65 strong, any danger was not to be taken lightly. In addition, it is possible that the trained bands of the city assisted them.[54] Yet no more is heard of this threat. Indeed, later in the month, Stanwix was using his forces in a more aggressive role. He had begun corresponding with Lowland Whig gentry and they agreed to support one another. Furthermore, at the end of the month, he took the 60 militia horsemen who had recently arrived at Carlisle from Westmorland and Lancashire to Longtown, in order to garner intelligence of the Jacobites' whereabouts. In doing so, they arrested one Graham of Inchbrachy. Stanwix sent the information he gathered to Townshend, the latter thanking him on 25 October 'for your constant advices of the Rebells' motions in your parts', and later referring to intelligence sent on 1 November.[55]

The Church

Nicolson was the foremost cleric who was active in the North West of England at this time; Francis Gastrell (1664–1724), Bishop of Chester (and a Tory), was in London. Nicolson, on 15 October, issued a circular letter to his clergy:

> There being now a most unnatural and dangerous rebellion raised in the neighbourhood of this Diocese, by several papists and other wicked enemies to our happy Establishment in Church and State; I cannot but think it a necessary duty (on this pressing occasion) to exhort you, and the rest of my brethren, to

---

[52] CRO (C) CA2/3, 57r, 58v.
[53] *HMC*, Johnstone, 128.
[54] *HMC*, Carlisle, 16.
[55] *HMC*, Johnstone, 127–8; *The London Gazette*, 5378, 1–5 November 1715; TNA, SP44/118, 81, 102.

animate and encourage your respective parishioners, in the defence of their Religion, Laws and Liberties, against all such traiterous attempts towards the destruction of His Majesty's royal person, and the subversion of his most gracious government. Committing you and your flock to the protection of God and his good providence.[56]

Nicolson, as a deputy lieutenant, attended the meetings which Lonsdale arranged on 4, 14 and 26 October[57] His efforts did not go unnoticed, Townshend writing on 25 October to Stanwix thus: 'The zeal of my Lord Bishop of Carlisle has been particularly represented'.[58]

Unfortunately there are very few published sermons by the northern clergy during the Fifteen. One was made by the Rev. Christopher Sudell (1672–1735) of Holy Trinity Church, Chester, titled 'The People's and Soldiers' duty in this present time of war and rebellion'. He referred to the Jacobites as 'rebels against God and our excellent Constitution in Church and state' and declared that the defence of the government was 'the defence of everything that is sacred and dear to us'. Ironically, though, Sudell was tolerant towards individual Catholics.[59]

The first anniversary of George I's coronation fell on 20 October, and churches throughout these counties rang their bells to celebrate the event. In Lancashire, the parish of Downholland paid their ringers 8s 8d. Over Kellet's churchwardens were less generous – or poorer – and paid 3s 6d for the like.[60] At St Andrew's church, Penrith, the event was marked by bell-ringing, too. At Kirkby Lonsdale, 'Coronation ale' was given to the bell-ringers, costing the parish 8s. St Lawrence's, Appleby, gave their ringers the niggardly sum of one shilling on this occasion.[61] In Cheshire, 14 parishes are known to have rung their bells at this time, too, including those of Macclesfield and Stockport, but also smaller parishes of Goostrey and Farnsworth, and city parishes of St Martin's and St John's.[62]

Although all seemed quiet, matters changed as time went by. As late as 25 October, Carlisle could write, 'At present I perceive all is quiet'.[63] Yet only four

---

[56] William Nicolson, *Letters on various subjects, literary, political and economic, to and from William Nicolson*, London, 1809, 432.

[57] Jarvis, *Jacobite Risings*, 155, 159, 165.

[58] TNA, SP44/118, 81.

[59] P.G. Green, 'Charity, Morality and social control, clerical attitudes in the diocese of Chester, 1715–1795', *Lancashire and Cheshire Archaeological Society*, 141, 1992, 96.

[60] LRO, PR2956/2/1, 2566.

[61] CRO (C), PR110/75; CRO (K) WPR19, WPR28, 37.

[62] Oates, 'Responses', 89.

[63] Jarvis, *Jacobite Risings*, 162.

days later, Lonsdale had more accurate intelligence, which he communicated to Carlisle, letting him know that Lord Lumley of Northumberland had told him that he believed the Jacobites were moving 'as fast as they could for Lancashire'. Therefore, Lonsdale surmised, 'we shall have them with us very soon' unless the regulars pursuing the Jacobites could intercept them.[64] Likewise, the magistrates wrote from Preston on 29 October to Townshend, outlining their concerns that the Jacobites might arrive.[65]

Although there does not seem to have been much co-ordination or correspondence between different bodies throughout the North West, there was in the same county. Nicolson met Lonsdale on 4 October, and dined with Stanwix on 10 October and with Lonsdale on 14, 17 and 18 October. These dinners would undoubtedly have included discussion about the progress of the rebellion and of the steps needed to counter it.[66]

Conclusion

Despite the potential for support for the Jacobite cause in the North West in the autumn, open manifestations were understandably limited in the face of opposition from the agents of officialdom in the corporations, the counties and the parishes in order to demonstrate their loyalty to the status quo and also to take practical steps against anyone whose loyalty was thought to be suspect. Limited Jacobite activity did occur, either in public or in private, but was hardly a threat as it was not and could not be translated into action just yet. However, the activity of both sides was to be put into a higher gear as the Jacobite army decided to march through these counties and as yet the regular forces of the Crown were too few or distant to be effective.

---

[64] *HMC*, Carlisle, 18.
[65] TNA, SP44/118, 103.
[66] Nicolson, 'Diaries', V, 4–5.

Chapter 4
The Jacobite March South, November 1715

The Jacobite march through the north-western counties has been covered by those previously writing about the Fifteen; Baynes devotes a whole chapter to it.[1] However, there has been a tendency to downplay the independent behaviour in these counties of both those who opposed the Jacobites and those who supported them. Jacobite participation in the rising has been surveyed by Monod in his magisterial study of English Jacobitism.[2] The responses of those in authority throughout all the northern English counties have been studied by Oates.[3] This chapter surveys the Jacobite march southwards, detailing the activity of those loyal to the Jacobite cause and those to the Hanoverian cause, as well as detailing the activity of the regular troops who were opposing the Jacobites.

On 1 November the Jacobite army of about 1,400 men entered England at Longtown and marched to Brampton under Forster's command. There, as in subsequent towns which the Jacobites passed through, there were standard procedures to which they adhered. Firstly, they proclaimed James Stuart as James III. More practically, they collected the excise which lay in the hands of local tax collectors and was intended for George I's government. Apart from being a means to pay their men and also serving to underline that this was 'legitimate taxation' given to the true king's representatives, there was another benefit. It prevented looting, which might have led to local resistance against the Jacobites. Few people object to the loss of money which is no longer theirs. Patten claimed that 'the the Inhabitants cannot charge them with any Rudeness, Violence or Plunder in the least' and they 'behav'd very civilly' at Lowther Hall, though it was later claimed that they defaced statues and wrecked the gardens. Even Stout, who feared the worst, wrote 'but they were civil, and most paid for what they had'. Yet sometimes money was extorted from the citizenry, as in Kendal.[4] In all,

---
[1] Baynes, *Jacobite Rising*, 105–16.
[2] Monod, *Jacobitism*, 317–27.
[3] Oates, 'Responses'.
[4] Patten, *History*, 66–7; Stout, *Autobiography*, 270.

£379 5s 8¾d was taken from towns in the North West; if the Scots were being paid sixpence a day, this would pay them for about two weeks.[5]

This chapter will be divided by geography and also roughly chronologically, as the Jacobite army marched from Brampton to Preston. They arrived at Penrith on 2 November, leaving on the 3rd and arriving at Kendal on that day. They left Kendal on the 5th, reached Kirkby Lonsdale on the 6th and then marched to Lancaster.[6]

Before the Jacobite force were the resources of the civil state: the militia and posse. These were not deemed as sufficient to provide an adequate front line military defence, but as acting in support of regular troops. However, there were no field troops in these counties and so the prognosis for the Jacobites' enemies was not obviously good.

Cumberland and Westmorland

The only aim of the Jacobite army at this point was to gather support as they marched. Their progress was not entirely smooth, but it was not seriously hindered in the first 10 days and there was no known dissension among their leaders. On Wednesday, 2 November, on the heath to the north of Penrith, civilian forces mustered to oppose the Jacobite advance. There are considerable differences among both contemporaries and historians as to exactly who these men were, who led them and what their numbers were. Four well-known contemporary sources give their numbers as 8,000, 12,000, 14,000 and as high as 25,000.[7] Another source numbers them at 6,000–7,000.[8] Whilst we might expect Jacobite estimates to be inflated, in order to trumpet their triumph over mighty odds, Lonsdale numbered them at 13,000 and Dudley Ryder (1689–1756), a London law student, at 8,000, and both were strong Whigs.[9] These high numbers have been mostly accepted uncritically by historians, even the best of them.[10]

Cumberland's population was then approximately 60,000–65,000. This being so, the total adult male population was probably only about 16,000. It seems impossible that so many men could have been brought together in one place, even if only for a brief time. Some of the adult male population was serving

---

[5] Jarvis, *Collected Papers*, I, 187.
[6] Patten, *History*, 64–71.
[7] Ryder, *Diary*, 136; Rae, *History*, 279; Patten, *History*, 64; Clarke, 'Journal', 513.
[8] TNA, SP54/9/107.
[9] BL.Add.Mss, 63093, f60r; Ryder, *Diary*, 136.
[10] Szechi, *1715*, 117.

in the militia. We also need to recall that the county of Northumberland's posse numbered only 407 men.[11] Other doubts can be legitimately raised if we recall that the 'new' militia of Cumberland after 1757 numbered just 320 men and that the entire militia strength of the whole of Britain in the 1720s was 200,000.[12] We now must try to account for contemporaries referring unanimously to the force being in its thousands. It is possible that the men may have brought their families along, and spectators (including would-be looters) often congregated at the scene of conflict. These would considerably inflate numbers. The true figure will never be known, but it seems most likely that the posse numbered in its hundreds, not the thousands which are often accepted uncritically.

They were led by Humphrey Senhouse, the county sheriff. The posse was his remit. With him were Nicolson (and his daughter), Lonsdale and Sir William Dawes, Archbishop of York (1674–1724). Recent clergy involvement in civil strife was nothing new; the bishop of Winchester had lent his coach horses to bring artillery into action at Sedgemoor 30 years previously. However, according to Charles Owen (d. 1746), a Presbyterian minister of Warrington, Lonsdale was in charge.[13] Symson claims Lonsdale gave directions for the posse to be raised on 2 November, but Peter Clarke, a Penrith lawyer, states this was the sheriff's doing.[14] After all, the posse was under the command of the sheriff, not the Lord Lieutenant.

The main component of this force was the posse comitatus.[15] Yet Ryder noted that Owen thought they were 'militia and volunteers'.[16] Clarke hints that the militia of Cumberland, Westmorland and Northumberland (!) were present.[17] A number of clergymen accompanied them.[18] There was almost certainly a company of Cumberland militia with them, as one had been ordered to be stationed in Penrith.[19] Some apparently believed that the Jacobites had been defeated by Carpenter's men already, were merely the broken remains of the army, fleeing from the regulars, 'and that we should have nothing to do than to pick up some of their shattered fragments into which he would chop them: for such a service we were well enough prepared'.[20]

---

[11] HRO, D/EP F195.
[12] Jarvis, *Jacobite Risings*, 99.
[13] Patten, *History*, 64; Ryder, *Diary*, 136.
[14] Symson, *Letter Books*, 342; Clarke, 'Journal', 513.
[15] Patten, *History*, 64.
[16] Ryder, *Diary*, 136.
[17] Clarke, 'Journal', 513.
[18] *Original Weekly Journal*, 355, 19–26 November 1715.
[19] Jarvis, *Jacobite Risings*, 163.
[20] Ralph Thoresby, *Letters of Eminent Men addressed to Ralph Thoresby*, II, London: Colburn, 1832, 319.

They were probably poorly armed. According to Clarke, 'very few of them had any regular armes'.[21] A newspaper claimed they were armed with pitchforks, and a ballad states that two thirds had scythes, billhooks and pitchforks, with the remainder armed with rusty spears, swords and outdated muskets.[22] Yet they had had some instruction by half-pay officers – as Lonsdale wrote, 'by the assistance of some broken officers of General Elliott's regiment (who were extremely diligent) were put in a very tolerable order'.[23]

The force was completely useless. There are a number of accounts of the events leading up to their rout. According to Ryder, a scouting party saw the advance guard of the Jacobites begin to form up upon the moor, and then returned to their camp to give the news of the Jacobites. The Jacobite army advanced in several divisions; first were 400 horsemen, trumpeters blowing, then 300 Scots, then another 400 horsemen and finally another 300 Scots.[24] As Patten wrote, 'they broke up their Camp in the utmost confusion, shifting every one for themselves as well as they could, as is generally the Case of an arm'd, but undisciplin'd Multitude'.[25] A newspaper remarked, 'I never beheld such an instance of the cowardice of Rabbles'.[26]

A Lowlander wrote, 'they fled like sheep before us'.[27] Another possibility, voiced by Owen, was that resistance was never countenanced. Jacobite spies 'came unsuspected among the militia and heard what they said among themselves and then came where my Lord Lonsdale and others of the officers were consulting what to do and heard them determine not to fight'.[28] Clarke suggests that as soon as Senhouse, Lonsdale and Nicolson heard that the Jacobites were on their way, at about 11 in the morning, they fled.[29] Some men may have left because they wanted refreshment.[30]

There is also the suggestion that some of the men in the posse had Jacobite sympathies, for an anonymous Scots account claimed that when they ran, they called out 'down with the Rump', a well-known Jacobite cry of 1714–15. Another source claimed some of the men who surrendered said, 'God save King James

---

[21] Clarke, 'Journal', 513.
[22] *Original Weekly Journal*, 355, 19–26 November 1715.
[23] Thomas Sanderson, *The Life and Literary Remains of Thomas Sanderson*, ed. John Lowthian, Carlisle, 1829, 9. BL.Add.Mss. 63093, f60r.
[24] Ryder, *Diary*, 136.
[25] Patten, *History*, 64.
[26] *Original Weekly Journal*, 355, 19–26 November 1715.
[27] TNA, SP54/9/107.
[28] Ryder, *Diary*, 136.
[29] Clarke, 'Journal', 513.
[30] *Original Weekly Journal*, 355, 19–26 November 1715.

and prosper his merciful army'.[31] A Jacobite thought that 'by their expressions [they] did not seem to wish ill to our cause'.[32] Lonsdale was uncertain, writing:

> I don't know whether this rout proceeded from fear or Disaffection, what makes me imagine it was a thing designed is because most of the men came without any manner of arms and though the rebels knew their number to be so great they did not alter their march at all, which I fancy they would have done if they had not depended upon a great many friends who did not shew themselves.[33]

Clarke claims that if the posse and the militia had not fled, 'There is no doubt that had the men stood their ground the said earl [of Derwentwater] and his men (as it hath beene acknowledged by diverse of them) wood have retreated'.[34] This may seem unlikely, given that the men were poorly armed, led by amateurs and clearly low in morale. It was not their job to fight in battle – as Clarke stated, 'they were there, assembled at the place aforesaid for prevention of rebellion and riots'.[35] But on the other hand, as we have seen, the Jacobite army was hardly lusting for battle and had avoided action where it was probable they might have been successful, for instance over the outnumbered and exhausted regulars on the Borders, or over the militia of Dumfries a few days later. Perhaps a show of strength would have resulted in their avoiding battle, as before.

It is uncertain why morale was so low. Rae suggests that it was 'possibly with the false Accounts of their Numbers, industriously spread by their Friends in those Parts'.[36] Attempts were made to rally the men, Lonsdale writing that 'all the means that were possible were used by several of the gentlemen for keeping the men together but was all to no purposes'.[37]

Lonsdale remained with between 20 and 100 men including his servants. They remained until the Jacobite army came into sight, and then retired.[38] Taking the advice of the half-pay officers, the remaining men returned to Penrith 'to endeavour to defend that place'. They guarded the avenues to the town, but realising they were insufficient in number, withdrew.[39] Lonsdale's conduct was criticised by

---

[31] *A Letter*, 4–5; BC, Atholl Papers, 45/12/77.
[32] BC, Atholl Papers, 45/12/77.
[33] BL.Add.Mss 63093, f61v.
[34] Clarke, 'Journal', 513.
[35] Clarke, 'Journal', 513.
[36] Rae, *History*, 279–80.
[37] BL.Add.Mss. 63093, f61v.
[38] Rae, *History*, 280.
[39] BL.Add,Mss 63093, f61v.

some. However, as Patten noted, 'those who know how naked and unprepar'd that Multitude were of all warlike Arms and Stores, justly commend his wise conduct to retreat and prevent the effusion of so much Blood and innocent lives, which would have been of bad consequence, and no service to his master'. Lonsdale and his retainers rode south to Appleby Castle, where one Mr Carleton made difficulties in his lodging there. His conduct was further defended by the same chronicler: 'If Fear or Cowardice had possessed him, as one of Appleby hinted to the Rebel Lords and Forster, he might have, with a good Retinue well mounted, with ease gone over Stonemoor into Yorkshire'. Another wrote, 'my lord was doing the King and country the best service in his power'. Lonsdale had no option but to flee either to a castle in Westmorland or to a gentleman's house in Cumberland, where he remained for a week. Nicolson rode to Rose Castle. On 9 November, he was back at Carlisle, and associating with Stanwix.[40]

The Westmorland posse was to have mustered at Kendal on 3 November, and Symson and his son and servant were preparing to join it. However, as Lonsdale wrote, once they had heard of the rout of the Cumberland posse, this news 'so terrified the people, that those who were coming to the place appointed for the rendezvous turned back as soon as they heard the news and the rest would not stir from home'. He offered the following gloomy, but all too truthful, military analysis of the situation: 'The county is entirely without Defence and I am very much afraid these rebels won't be stopped till they meet with a Regular Force'.[41]

Townshend was sympathetic and wrote on 8 November:

> His Majesty is very sensible of your lordship's having done all that could be expected, and that it was not possible on a sudden and upon the first assembly of the people of the country, to raise a sufficient force to oppose them.[42]

Once the Jacobites arrived at Penrith, they were met with mixed responses. Some were averse to the invaders. Mr Johnson, Patten's brother-in-law and collector of the Salt Tax, escaped the Jacobites, who were sent to seize him. John Patterson, an attorney, hid weapons belonging both to himself and to Sir Christopher Musgrave of Edenhall. Yet other inhabitants had noticed his actions and told the Jacobites where the arms were, and this may have had official sanction. According to Patten:

---

[40] Patten, *History*, 64–6; Rae, *History*, 280; HMC 25, 12th report App. vii Le Fleming, 350; Nicolson, 'Diaries', V, 6.
[41] BL.Add.Mss. 63093, f61v.
[42] TNA, SP44/118, 116.

> The Chief People of this Town, with Mr [Andrew] Whelpsdale, one of His majesty's Justices ... by shewing all manner of civility ... agreed, when they heard of the Rebels' advance, wisely to consult their own interest their Enemies; Prudence-Necessity obliging them to act their Part, which force constrained them unwillingly to comply with.

In return, the Jacobites left the Presbyterian meeting house there alone, apparently on Forster's orders (some had wanted to destroy it, which would have been a disaster in propaganda terms). They also ate the dinner prepared for the Bishop and his men.[43]

There were other sympathisers en route. When the Jacobites arrived at Appleby on 3 November, some inhabitants told them the whereabouts of Mr Barnes, the local excise collector, and so his money was demanded once he was located and arrested.[44]

Some of the clergy in the towns which the Jacobites marched through acted ambivalently. According to Patten, he took the service in the church at Appleby himself

> if the Parson or Curate refused; but they were not very backward as to the thing itself, though they thought it their safest way modestly to excuse themselves, testifying however their satisfaction, in giving orders for the Bells to ring, and having all things made ready for the Service, nor did the Parson and his Curate scruple to grace the assembly with their Presence, or to join in the prayers for the Pretender, which encouraged the High Church party were entirely theirs, and would join in a little time.[45]

The clergyman at Penrith at this time was one James Lamb (d.1720).

The rout of the posse at Penrith was not immediately known in Westmorland. Symson wrote on the following day, full of enthusiasm and hopelessly ignorant of the true state of affairs, about the posse of Cumberland and of his own county:

> the like of this county of Westmorland rises this day to oppose the rebels, who we are informed are about 60 miles from us on the border of Scotland. We hope to join the Cumberland men this day or tomorrow and when so will be I hope many

---

[43] Patten, *History*, 66–7.
[44] Patten, *History*, 69–70.
[45] Patten, *History*, 69.

thousands well armed with courage, cheerfulness, and weapons that the enemy dare not stand against us.[46]

Although the posse were finished as a force on 2 November, not so the militia. On 9 November, the four companies of militia in Cumberland were ordered to appear, fully armed and supplied with muskets, powder and ball, at the Round Table, near Eamont Bridge, on 12 November.[47] We do not know what the next step was to be.

Yet if resistance to the Jacobites was limited, support for their cause was also minimal. When the army was at Appleby, Patten noted that 'there were none of any Account had yet joined them'.[48] Indeed, it would seem that only 29 men in the two counties joined them. Many of these waited until the last moment – just as the Jacobites did at Kirkby Lonsdale at the southern tip of Westmorland on 6 November. Some of these, perhaps most, were from Lancashire.[49] On the march from Appleby to Kendal, Francis Thurnburrow of Selfet Hall, near Kendal, joined; and on the following day his father sent a servant to attend him. At Kirkby Lonsdale, Esquire Carus and his two sons, Thomas and Christopher, three Catholic Jacobites from Hatton Hall, Lancashire, joined them. Others deserted; Mr Ainlsey and 16 or 17 men from Jedburgh left at this stage.[50]

There are a number of reasons for this. One was that these counties were fairly thinly populated and the numbers of Tories and Catholics there were limited. In 1696, Sir Daniel Fleming commented, about Westmorland, 'The papists are so few and inconsiderable'. Secondly, some had been taken into custody at Carlisle. For example, Henry Curwen of Workington Esq., 'a Gentleman of a plentiful Estate', Francis Howard of Corby Castle and John Warwick of Warwick Hall had all been secured. Thirdly, some were prevented from action by accident. According to Patten, 'it was reported that Mr Dacre of Abbeylanner-Coast [sic], a Papist, had promise to raise 40 Men; but he was taken with a fortunate Fever, which hindered him of his Design, and prevented him and his Family from Ruin.'[51]

Apart from the dismal performance of the posse, there were some other attempts at resistance, though on an inevitably mild scale. Patten had taken time away from his brothers in arms to drink with some of his friends in Penrith and was left behind by the army. Senhouse heard of this and 'spar'd no Diligence to have taken him, but came a little too late'. There were also a number of anti-

---

[46] Symson, *Letter Book*, 342–3.
[47] Jarvis, *Jacobite Risings*, 167.
[48] Patten, *History*, 67.
[49] Patten, *History*, 70–71; TNA, KB8/66.
[50] Clarke, 'Journal', 514, 516; Rae, *History*, p. 280.
[51] Patten, *History*, 67–8; *HMC*, Rydal, 341.

Jacobite spies at Appleby, including Thomas Wybergh, a militia captain, though perhaps not very efficient ones as they were all arrested and accompanied their captors to Preston, though one source states that Forster released at least one spy.[52] When the Jacobites read out their proclamation in Kendal, a Quaker in the crowd reacted by not putting his hat back on his head.[53] Kendal's mayor, Thomas Rowlandson, refused to tell the Jacobites where the militia's arms were and was arrested. Mrs Bellingham, Forster's godmother, would not allow him to see her, and when he went inside her house anyway, 'she met him on the stairs, gave him two or three boxes on the eare, and called him a rebel and a popish toole'.[54]

Not all of the clergy were ambivalent in their loyalties. Mr John Biggs of Kirkby Lonsdale fled on the army's approach on 6 November, so he would not have to acknowledge them by reading prayers at any church service they chose to hold.[55] The Rev. William Crosby (1664–1733) of Kendal prevailed upon the Jacobites in Kendal to have the mayor released.[56] Nicolson noted that, on 5 November, 'Mr Bolton [presumably John Bolton, Vicar of Workington, 1679–1724] preach'd on Luke 9, 5–6 against ye Spirit of Rebellion'.[57]

On 5 November, churches in these counties rang their bells despite the Jacobite presence there. The day celebrated Protestant England's God-given delivery from the Catholic menace in both 1605 and 1688. At Penrith, six shillings was given to the bell-ringers on this occasion.[58] Likewise at Kendal, four shillings was divided between the bell-ringers for ringing on this day and on Christmas Day. Heversham Parish also celebrated this red-letter day for Protestantism. At Kirkby Lonsdale the bell-ringers rang on this day, and were given ale to the value of 2s 3d – and on the next day the Jacobites arrived.[59] No wonder the vicar left the parish afterwards!

Finally, it must be noted that business was disrupted by the invasion. Although Symson makes no reference to the Jacobites in September and October and his business was uninterrupted in those months, it was a different story in November. As he admitted on 21 November, when the campaign was over, 'Indeed, we have been in such confusion of late by the Scotch and Northumberland rebels, who all went through this town, that we have minded no business else you might

[52] Patten, *History*, 68–9; TNA, SP54/9/107.
[53] Clarke, 'Journal', 515.
[54] Clarke, 'Journal', 515–16.
[55] Patten, *History*, 70.
[56] Clarke, 'Journal', 515–16.
[57] Nicolson, 'Diaries', 5.
[58] CRO (C), PR110/75.
[59] CRO (K), WPR18/W1; WPR43/W1; WPR19.

have heard a little sooner from me'. Symson often wrote several business letters each day. There are none between 3 and 12 November, when there is one on the latter day. Then there is another gap until 21 November.[60] Goods could not be despatched with safety, nor payments made, until peace returned. Symson wrote on 23 November, 'We were in great fear here of the Northumberland and Scotch rebels who came and lay one night in this town'.[61]

Threats were made to make civilians comply with Jacobite wishes. In Kendal, the bellman had to give notice to the town's tanners and innkeepers so that they would give the Jacobites the excise monies in their possession. According to Clarke, 'or else they that denyed should be plundered by Jack the highlander'. Others in the town were coerced. Clarke reported, 'They made the gunsmiths here work very hard all night and a Sunday morning likewise, for little or no pay'.[62]

The invasion disrupted civil life. But the Westmorland JPs still convened in early November. They ordered the High Constables of Kendal and Lonsdale wards to have the petty constables summon 'all the Papists, Non Jurors and all other persons disaffected to the king and government in their several constablewicks' to come to Kendal on 12 November in order to swear allegiance to the same.[63]

Lancashire and Cheshire

Much was expected of the Lancashire Jacobites. Although it is not known exactly what the assurances of support were that the Jacobites had about this, they were not entirely fictitious. Charles Widdrington, second brother of Lord Widdrington, had been sent southwards, perhaps on about 31 October, in order to discover what he could and 'to acquaint the Gentlemen of that County with their marching that Way'. He was a good choice because, as noted, Richard Towneley was a brother-in-law of his. Widdrington had good news for his colleagues, 'with News of their Cheerfulness and Intention to join them with all their Interest'. Furthermore, 'the Pretender was that Day proclaimed at Manchester, where the Town's-People had got Arms to furnish a Troop of Fifty Men at their sole Charge, besides other Voluntiers'.[64] Townshend shared

---

[60] Symson, *Letter Books*, 342–4.
[61] Symson, *Letter Books*, 345.
[62] Clarke, 'Journal', 515–16.
[63] CRO (K), WQ//O/2, 347.
[64] Patten, *History*, 56, 71; Dorothy Fitzherbert-Brockholes, 'A Narrative of the Fifteen', *LCHS*, II, 64, 1912, 250.

the Jacobites' predictions, commenting on 8 November on 'this march of the Rebels, into a county full of Papists and disaffected persons by whom they will probably be joyned'.[65]

Although some Lancastrians had some prior notice of the march of the Jacobite army towards them, 'little Credit was allowed' to such news until the Lancashire militia arrived in Lancaster on about 4 November.[66] Magistrates instructed the constabulary to secure horses worth over £5 belonging to Catholics. John Sparling, High Constable of Lonsdale, removed two from Albert Hodgson of Leighton Hall under the warrant of Edmund Cole, JP.[67]

There was some discussion as to whether the loyalist forces could have made a stand at Lancaster, where the 600-strong county militia had been gathered. Hoghton and fellow magistrates Charles Rigby and Colonel Francis Charteris suggested that the town's bridge over the River Lune should be destroyed so as to impede the Jacobite advance. Yet the townsmen were unhappy with this idea and put forward several reasons why it should not be done. According to Patten, these were that

> it would no wise hinder our Entrance into the place, seeing the River at Low water was passable by Foot or Horse, and that we could easily find Boats to pass into the Town; and that it would be a vast charge to rebuild the Bridge so strong and fine as before, so it would be a loss to no manner.

Hoghton then discovered gunpowder in the hands of local merchants. One of their number, one Samuel Sattherwaite, had thrown his down the well in the marketplace. However, they had insufficient time to be thorough, for they missed a number of arms held in the custom house. He then found that a ship, the *Robert*, in the docks, owned by William Heysham (1666–1716), an MP for Lancaster and a merchant, and Mr Lawson, a Lancaster Quaker (probably Robert Lawson the elder, 1652–1736), had six cannon mounted and also had other arms on board. He suggested the armament be removed from the ship and be used to defend the bridge. The owners demanded a bond of £10,000 because they feared their ship might be burnt if such an action were undertaken, as Hoghton was 'very obnoxious to the Rage of the Rebels for his Vigilance and Care'.[68]

---

[65] Leeds University Library, Special Collections, Townshend Papers, f.35v.
[66] Fitzherbert-Brockholes, 'Narrative', 250.
[67] TNA, KB8/66.
[68] Clarke, 'Journal', 518; Patten, *History*, 71–3.

Hoghton hoped to defend the town and sent an express to Colonel Stanhope, then at Preston with his regiment of dragoons, to come to their aid. He then summoned Robert Parkinson, the mayor, the aldermen and councillors together. Hoghton told them that they should persuade the two aforesaid merchants to deliver the cannon up to the King's service. Although they initially met with a refusal, he, Charteris and Rigby, all being JPs, could produce warrants ordering the seizure of the cannon, as well as other cargo on board the ship. Lawson finally gave in. But by this time it was too late. The mayor and his colleagues 'all agreed it was not advisable to make any opposition being so much inferior in Numbers to the Scots'. Instead they sent a letter to Townshend, imploring military support. Hoghton was told of the close proximity of the Jacobite army and realised the cannon would be of no use given that they had so few men; certainly not enough to properly defend the town. Lawson was told to sail down the river with his precious cargo, so it would not fall into Jacobite hands. He refused, so, when the Jacobites arrived, they helped themselves to the artillery.[69] However, it is possible that some steps were taken against the invaders; according to Clarke, the 'inhabitants of that towne had taken up the pavement of the bridge, and the side of the north arch'.[70]

Stanhope's dragoons did not march to the town's aid. Thus Hoghton and his men marched southwards. Apparently their march was made 'in a confused manner: happy was he that had the best feet! However, about two Hundred kept together'.[71] Meanwhile Hoghton wrote to Carpenter, informing him that the Jacobites were marching into Lancaster, and wrote again a few days later.[72] Another man who left the town was tax collector Joseph Bently, who 'scowerer'd off to the mountains and fells with above £400'.[73]

The Jacobite army arrived in Lancaster, unopposed, on 7 November. They took the six cannon, other weapons, claret, brandy and money, and left on 9 November. It is possible that they received an official welcome by the town's corporation. Owen later told Ryder, 'The mayor and aldermen, when the rebels came towards the town, met them in their robes and when they came in proclaimed the Pretender at the market in formality'.[74] Though Patten does not allude to this, the senior Jacobites certainly had dinner at the house of Robert

---

[69] Fitzherbert-Brockholes, 'Narrative', 250.
[70] Clarke, Journal', 517.
[71] Fitzherbert-Brockholes, 'Narrative', 250.
[72] Patten, *History*, 89.
[73] Jarvis, *Collected Papers*, I, 178.
[74] Ryder, *Diary*, 136.

Gibson, the Recorder.[75] Parkinson was probably related to the Parkinsons, who were friendly with the Jacobite Tyldesleys and so may have felt any kind of conflict with family friends to be anathema.[76] It is probable that the aldermen, fearful for their property and lives, and for those of their fellow townsmen, felt they had little choice but to obey as a necessary evil. Lancaster had, after all, been devastated during the Civil War and doubtless the folk memory of this lived on. Yet there is some hint that Parkinson was reluctant to do so, for in the evening six Highlanders 'by threats compeled Mr. Parkinson, the then mayore of this towne to goe along with them from house to house to search for armes'.[77]

Apparently Parkinson, Gibson and corporation officials were joined by a Jacobite quartermaster and visited households in Lancaster, demanding their arms. The vicar initially gave up a long fowling piece, but was asked for more and found other weapons. The widow Metcalfe was told, 'You had better deliver them quietly than have your house plundered'. All in all, over 20 'long guns', 60 swords and 'many' pistols were delivered to the invaders.[78]

It is also possible that Gibson was sympathetic to the Jacobite cause. One man recalled seeing Gibson and Thomas Westmore, an alderman, and Mrs Morley, an alderman's wife, looking from a window, 'having their hats off at the time of the proclaiming'.[79]

As in other towns that the Jacobites had marched through, threats were used to force the townsmen to comply with their demands, which suggests a degree of hostility on the townsmen's part. At Lancaster, when the Highlanders searched for weapons, 'At every house they demanded arms which if the owner did not deliver Jack the highlander was to plunder him'. Those arms they found were not paid for. However, no one was physically harmed, but the common soldiers did not pay for their accommodation or food.[80]

Yet some in the town were happy to see the Jacobite gentlemen. According to Clarke, 'This afternoone the gentlemen soldiers dressed and trimmed themselves up in their best cloathes for to drink a dish of teas with the laydys of this towne. The laydys also here appeared in their best riging, and had their tea tables richly furnished for to entertain their new suitors'.[81]

---

[75] Patten, *History*, 74; TNA, KB8/66.
[76] Tyldesley, *Diary*, 29, 78.
[77] Clarke, 'Journal', 518.
[78] TNA, KB8/66.
[79] TNA, KB8/66.
[80] Clarke', Journal', 518.
[81] Clarke, 'Journal', 519.

Certainly the clergy thought discretion the better part of valour. As usual, Patten read prayers in church, instead of the vicar, Dr James Fenton the Younger (1688–1767). As with the clergy at Appleby, his attitude was one of neutrality. Patten wrote that Fenton excused himself from taking the service, 'It seems not so averse to it any more than some of his Brethren; but he wanted to see how the scales would turn, before he could think of venturing so far'.[82]

There are other instances of Fenton's ambivalence. According to Clarke, 'This evening a discourse about religion hapned between the minister of this towne and two Romish priests'. Arms were taken from Fenton's house.[83] It is possible that Fenton was not wholly unsympathetic to the Jacobites. He was probably High Church; he certainly bore ill will towards the dissenters, Stout writing that he had local Quakers prosecuted for non-payment of tithes.[84]

Jacobite support, as was expected, was stronger in Lancashire than it had been elsewhere in England. In Lancaster 'our Number encreased considerably; and had we stay'd here, or kept a Garrison here, they would have continued so to do. For in that time a Great Number of Lancashire Gentlemen joined us, with their Servants and Friends'. These included Albert Hodgson of Leighton Hall, John Dalton of Thurnham Hall, John Tyldesley of the Lodge, Richard Butler of Rawcliffe and George Hilton of Cartmell. All these gentlemen were attended by their servants. A few townsmen joined, too, including Edmund Gartside, a barber, and a joiner. Lancaster Castle was emptied of its Jacobite prisoners, gaoled for their part in the riots in June and awaiting trial. These included Thomas Sydall.[85] Unlike in the case of Cumberland and Westmorland, prominent Catholics had not been arrested so were free to join the Jacobites if they chose, and many did. Yet the Merse officer wrote, 'Here several persons deserted us'.[86]

There were disappointments, too. The Scots expected that the High Church Tories would have joined in larger numbers. Few did. According to Patten:

> Indeed, that Party, who are never right Hearty for the Cause, 'till they are Mellow, as they call it, over a Bottle or two, begin now to shew us their blind side; and that it is their just Character, that they do not care for venturing their Carcasses any farther than the Tavern; there indeed, with their *High-Church*, and *Ormond*, they would make Men believe, who do not know them, that they would encounter

---

[82] Patten, *History*, 75.
[83] Clarke, 'Journal', 519–20.
[84] Stout, *Autobiography*, 170, 177.
[85] Patten, *History*, 78; Clarke, 'Journal', 517.
[86] *A Letter*, 5.

the greatest Opposition in the World; but after consulting their Pillows, and the Fume a little evaporated, it is to be observed of them, that they generally become mighty Tame, and are apt to look before they Leap, and with the snail, if you touch their Houses, they hide their Heads shrink back and pull in their Horns.[87]

Although the majority of the recruits were Catholic, even they did not join in the numbers anticipated – certainly the hope of 20,000 recruits was chimerical. As in Northumberland only a minority of Lancashire Catholic men of fighting age participated. Ryder wrote, 'The papists in Lancashire don't rise much to join them as was expected'.[88] It must be stated that participation in an armed uprising was a dangerous undertaking such that most, whatever their religious and political sympathies, lacking military experience or adequate arms would not feel it worth risking their lives in such a venture. Patten's condemnation, as an active Jacobite, is understandable, but to infer that the Tories were faint-hearted seems unduly harsh. Enlistments were in their hundreds, not thousands.

The additions to the Jacobite army were potentially important, even so, for it was feared that regular troops were marching towards them. It was also at this point that some form of medium-term plan emerged, apart from avoiding conflict and trying to gather support. They were to march to Preston, then to Warrington Bridge, then to Manchester, where additional recruits were promised. Finally, they would take the rich sea port of Liverpool. They left Lancaster on 9 November, and the advance guard of cavalry arrived at Preston in the evening; the infantry followed on 10 November. The two troops of Stanhope's dragoons stationed at Preston, on hearing of the Jacobite advance, retreated. Although this was militarily sensible, the dragoons being outnumbered, their departure led some Jacobites to believe that it was a sign that the regulars would not oppose them (Monmouth had had similar hopes in 1685, as did Charles Edward Stuart in 1745). Part of the county militia were here, too, and they also left, marching to Wigan.[89]

Whilst at Lancaster, Forster despatched the Rev. Buxton to deliver letters to potential gentry supporters in his own county, Derbyshire. The Rev. William Paul of Horton-on-the-Hill, Leicestershire, arrived with letters from Staffordshire to inform them (prematurely) that General Wills was at Preston. It was argued that the Jacobites should have stayed in Lancaster because it was a good defensive position, but they marched on, presumably to pick up more support in southern Lancashire.[90]

---

[87] Patten, *History*, 78.
[88] Ryder, *Diary*, 135.
[89] Patten, *History*, 79.
[90] Patten, *History*, 71.

On leaving Lancaster, the Jacobites found further recruits en route. Roger Muncaster, a Protestant attorney at law who lived in Garstang, joined them there. Several poor Catholics also enlisted at this point. Others gave hospitality to the Jacobite infantrymen on their march.[91] Derwentwater dined at Thurnham on 8 November.[92] There was a supper party at Stonyhurst, the seat of the Catholic Nicholas Sherburn (1658–1717), on 10 November, for 30 Jacobites. Although their host was infirm, he was sympathetic. As a Whig commentator observed in the following year, he 'has also been engag'd'. On the following day, the Jacobites left with seven or eight guns, a sack full of pistols, blunderbusses and four of his coach horses. They had also cast bullets there.[93]

There were other sympathisers. Thomas Townson, a Broughton husbandman, joined the Jacobites on 9 November, buoyed up by optimistic promises made by Derwentwater and Forster, who pledged that there was no force to oppose the army until they arrived in London. John Parker of Lancashire, on 9 November told the Jacobites of several places nearby where they could find horses, and they took horses from John Postlewaite of Lancaster, an innkeeper. He also told them about where the militia had hidden their arms and assisted in the search. Yet he later claimed that he had not actively helped and had only informed about one place where horses were held, but had not told about the location of the weapons. However, Parker was asked to drink James's health, and he replied, 'He would in puddle water and further saith yt he drinks a glass of ale ... to ye said health'. George Roskill claimed he had been forced to enlist by being threatened by Hillary Ashton of Overhill, a yeoman, with being locked in a barn, and if anyone sheltered him they would have their property plundered. Roskill claimed he 'would have gone to have served King George as a militia soldier'. William Taylor, constable of Preesal was threatened by John Wilkinson, a Jacobite miller and neighbour of his, with having his house burnt and plundered.[94]

It seems that Jacobite gentlemen summoned their tenants and servants to ride out with them to join the Jacobite army. On 9 November, John Clifton of Lytham Hall summoned all in the locality who wished to enlist, and one John Smith went to call on others who might accompany them. Ten did so, including three of Clifton's servants.[95]

Preston also offered support for the Jacobites. According to one source, on the arrival of the Jacobite army on 9–10 November, 'the disloyal [Jacobite]

---

[91] Clarke, 'Journal', 520.
[92] *The Flying Post*, 3772, 10–12 Nov. 1715.
[93] *Political State*, XII, 536–7; TNA, SP35/7, f.30r.
[94] TNA, KB8/66.
[95] TNA, KB8/66.

inhabitants received 'em with ringing of bells, illuminations, &c., and forc'd those who were averse to their Proceedings to do the like'.[96] Yet another source claimed that 'The Magistrates of the Town did not appear in the solemnity' when James was proclaimed.[97] They were also 'join'd by a Great many Gentlemen, with their Servants and attendants and some of very good figure in the County, but still all Papists'. These recruits included Richard Towneley and Richard Shuttleworth. Towneley brought with him a small retinue of followers, including his butler, postilion and coachman – one account says 18, another 60. Towneley's entrance was grand indeed if we are to believe a later Whig report:

> it is notorious to all the town of Preston that he marched in that Town at ye head of at least 60 men, swords drawn, flying colours for he had a standard, (viz) green damask, with like gold colour fringe round and his crest ye middle being a pelican, etc.

Towneley was also said to have threatened to shoot a man who did not show his respect by removing his hat when James Francis was proclaimed – so much for his alleged reluctance to join his fellows.[98] John Leyburn arrived there with two servants, armed with pistols and guns. So did Francis Legh, with six or seven armed men, with cockades in their hats, crying, 'Now for King James'. Their rendezvous in Preston was the Mitre Inn in the market place.[99] There were also recruiters elsewhere; Thomas Oliverson, once a servant of Mr Cholmey, had been to Chester to recruit incognito.[100]

There were other sympathisers, as there had been at Lancaster. According to Clarke, 'The laydys in this towne, Preston, are so very beautyfull and so richly atired that the gentlemen soldiers from Wednesday to Saturday minded nothing but courting and feasting'.[101] One Jacobite thought this delay was critical, writing, 'I'm perfectly persuaded that these delays were to give the enemie time

---

[96] TNA, KB8/66.
[97] John Estcourt and Edward Payne, *The English Catholics Non Jurors of 1715; being a summary of the register of their estates, with genealogical notes*, Farnborough: Gregg, 1969, 349–50; A. Nicholson, 'Lancashire and the Rebellion of 1715', *Lancashire and Cheshire Archaeological Society*, III, 1885, 82–3.
[98] *The Flying Post*, 3722, 10–12 November 1715
[99] Lyme Letters, 1660–1760, ed. Lady Newton, London: William Heinemann Ltd, 1936, 306.
[100] Prescott, 'Diary', II, 475.
[101] Clarke, 'Journal', 520.

(for had we got to Manchester we had done our business) ... they applyed only in feasting & revelling & playing the fool but not one farthing on Intelligence'.[102]

A different stance was taken by Peploe at Preston. According to an oft repeated story of the nineteenth century, when a Jacobite soldier heard Peploe pray in public for George I, he threatened him and was met with the following reply: 'Soldier, you do your duty and I will do mine'. Peploe was then left alone.[103] Yet his traditionally heroic role in the church is not backed up by contemporary sources. The only reference to his behaviour comes in a newspaper, which states that he had been threatened by the Jacobites prior to the arrival of their army. Thus he decided to flee towards the militia and regulars at Wigan. As noted, the Rev. Biggs also fled in advance of the Jacobite army. There was little else they could do.[104] Sensible though this action was, it was hardly heroic – Peploe was to flee from the Jacobite army in 1745, too.

Inhabitants of these Lancashire towns, especially those with property, were concerned at the approach of the Jacobite army. Stout noted that 'it was a time of tryall, and in fear that the Scots and Northern rebels would have plundered us'.[105] Likewise at Preston, on hearing similar news, 'Everybody was in great confusion. Most or all of ye Better Sort Removed themselves and effects'.[106]

Some actively resisted the Jacobites by whatever methods they could. At Lancaster, Christopher Hopkins, a stationer, and Ralph Fairbrother spied on the invaders. Hopkins made a list of their numbers, but he was seen and arrested. Fairbrother, however, escaped and went to find General Carpenter to give him what news he could.[107] More violently, it was said that after Towneley left with his followers to Preston, 'the mob there arose and gutted his house'.[108]

As with the two most northerly counties, the county militia had been summoned into being in Lancashire. Landowners were asked to contribute to their upkeep, however reluctantly. Blundell's disbursement book included the following entry: 'In November and December payed to the Militia ... £3 13s 9d'.[109]

The militia were certainly active in some quarters. Blundell recorded on 13 November, 'This Hous was twice sirched by some Foot as came from

---

[102] BC, Atholl Papers, 45/12/77.
[103] Baynes, *Jacobite Rising*, 111.
[104] *The Original Weekly Journal*, 355, 19–26 November 1715.
[105] Stout, 'Autobiography', 173.
[106] Brockholes, 'Narrative', 250.
[107] Clarke, 'Journal', 517, 518.
[108] BL.Add.Mss 37993, f30r.
[109] Blundell, 'Great Diurnall', 148n.

Leverpoole, I think the first party was about twenty six'.[110] Properties of other Catholic gentlemen in Lancashire, among them Towneley and Tyldesley, were also searched in early November. According to Towneley's housekeeper, the 20 militiamen who arrived at Towneley Hall were particularly aggressive; they 'would shoot him ... they fired a pistol into the Room where her master and mistress slept'. Some items were allegedly stolen from Tyldesley's house.[111]

Defensive preparations were being made at Lancashire's premier port. According to Blundell, on 5 November 'they began to fortify Leverpoole by kasting up great Banks for feer of my Lord Darwintwater'.[112] Here were a number of 'Merchants, Traders and other Loyal Inhabitants ... together with a Great Number of Country People'. They were helped by numerous sailors. They flooded a third of the approaches to the town, and in the remaining two thirds built earthworks, behind which were placed 70 cannon (presumably taken from ships in the harbour). Other ships were to put themselves at a distance from the shore, in order that the Jacobites would be able neither to enter the town nor to take the ships. The mayor also sent out spies to inform them of the Jacobite progress.[113] Six companies of volunteers were formed, one being led by William Crisp, brother of the high sheriff. One company consisted of young gentlemen and merchants' sons. Some 200 Dissenters also agreed to stand guard and their meeting house was turned into a storehouse for military supplies. Some of the Liverpool men ventured out of the town and arrested a number of Catholic gentlemen, including Lord Molyneux. They were accompanied by 'a vast mob of sailors and others', who threatened to destroy Molyneux's house if suspects believed to be within did not surrender.[114] As to this Catholic peer, 'he was concern'd in ye rebellion and put servants and horses to ye assistance of ye rebels at Preston', but there was no evidence to directly implicate him.[115]

They concluded, 'We are here well fortified, and are in a manner out of any apprehensions of the Rebels'. Those who had fled with their valuables returned 'for their greater Security'.[116] Yet, according to Defoe, all this would have been ineffectual had the Jacobites advanced resolutely towards the town. He later recorded, 'it would have fared but very ill with Leverpool, who could have made

---

[110] Blundell, 'Great Diurnall', 151.
[111] *Political State*, XII, 1716, 536–7, 541.
[112] Blundell, 'Great Diurnall', 151.
[113] Rae, *History*, 317.
[114] *The Flying Post*, 3731, 1–3 December 1715; Ryder, *Diary*, 175.
[115] BL. Stowe, 750, f158r.
[116] *St. James' Evening Post*, 72, 12–15 November 1715.

but little resistance against an armed and desperate body of men, such as they appeared to be, and by that time would have been'.[117]

Some fled before the Jacobite advance. On 13 November, Ryder met Owen at his brother's house in London. Ryder wrote of Owen, 'He is a brisk active man and is very much hated by the Tories in that country who do all they can to hurt him, his wife and brother, that are gone from Warrington for fear of the rebels'.[118]

However, though local efforts against the Jacobites were mixed, the regular forces were now advancing towards them. Having returned to Newcastle, Carpenter then marched towards Lancaster on hearing the Jacobites were there.[119] His dragoons left after he had rested them for two days. The infantry were left to guard the town because they would slow the march of the three mounted regiments. Carpenter reached Durham on 8 November.[120] At Barnard Castle he was met with a number of militia horse under Lord Lumley, Colonel Darcy, the Earl of Carlisle and Holderness, who told him that, with Wills at Manchester, the Jacobites would avoid him and march eastwards into Yorkshire via Clitheroe and Skipton. Therefore they should march that way. However, at Richmond, it was found that the Jacobites were marching towards Preston and so the route was adjusted accordingly.[121] On 10 November, they entered Ripon, having covered 38 miles in two days, and they received a warm welcome by the residents of that Yorkshire town.[122] On the following day they reached Garstang.[123]

Of more immediate danger to the Jacobites were the forces gathering under General Wills. In October, units of the regular army had been moving towards the North West of England, perhaps because the Jacobite danger in southern England was seen to be minimal. Three battalions of foot and one of horse had been shipped from Ireland to Chester. These included Pitt's horse and Preston's foot, the latter of which was initially stationed at Chester.[124] Munden's and Honeywood's dragoons were ordered, respectively, to Leeds and Halifax and to Nottingham on 19 October, and on the same day Stanhope's dragoons were told to march to Preston, which they reached at the end of the month. Two weeks later, Wynn's dragoons were ordered to march to Manchester and Wigan.[125]

---

[117] Daniel Defoe, *A Tour through the Whole Island of Great Britain*, ed. Pat Rogers, Penguin: Harmondsworth, 1971, 541.
[118] Ryder, *Diary*, 136.
[119] Rae, *History*, 318.
[120] Rae, *History*, 318.
[121] *Political State*, XI, 1716, 180.
[122] *The Daily Courant*, 4389, 17 November 1715; Prescott, 'Diary', II, 470.
[123] *St. James' Evening Post*, 72, 12–15 November 1715.
[124] *Political State*, X, 1715, 415.
[125] TNA, WO5/20, 98, 139, 140, 145.

Wills had been sent north to take command of the regiments in Lancashire, Cheshire and Shropshire on 28 October. His duty was to prevent the Jacobites taking Liverpool and reaching Manchester, by holding Warrington Bridge. On 5 November, he was told to 'immediately repair to Manchester and give orders ... to march upon the first orders'. He arrived at Manchester on 8 November. Here he received a letter from Carpenter to let him know that he was marching to intercept the Jacobites, and Wills replied, telling him that they were at Lancaster and they should attack them there. He also 'got to Manchester in time enough to prevent a pretended rising there'. Three days later, with Munden's, Wynn's, Honeywood's and Dormer's dragoons and Preston's foot having arrived at Manchester, Wills marched to Wigan, 'in a very hard frost', where he was joined by Pitt's horse and Stanhope's dragoons. Learning that the Jacobites were at Preston, he was determined to march there with his six regiments of cavalry and one infantry battalion on the following day. Newton's dragoons, who were on their way to join him from Worcester, were ordered to march to Manchester and stay there to deter any local rising. Sabine's and Fane's regiments were further away still.[126]

Although Forster knew of the whereabouts of Carpenter's force, it is uncertain whether he knew of Wills's presence. The Merse officer noted that they knew that two regiments were at Wigan with Wills on 10 November. He later wrote, 'Though we had an opportunity of cutting off the enemy, yet General Forster would not allow us, nor suffer us to march towards Manchester'. On the other hand, Patten stated that there was no such prior knowledge and Forster put his trust in Jacobites in southern Lancashire informing him of the approach of any enemy troops.[127]

Ironically, Marlborough, who was Captain General, on studying a map of England, said, 'You will find them there' or 'You will take them there'. The spot he pointed to was Preston.[128] Pulteney was convinced that the Jacobites' end was nigh, writing on 8 November:

> I believe it will not be necessary to send more forces that way in regard those under his command, with them he has will be sufficient to quell all the designs of the Rebels who I hope will have the mortification to fall between both your fires.[129]

---

[126] TNA, SP44/117, 309; *St. James' Evening Post*, 66, 29 October – 1 November, 1715; Rae, *History*, 317–18; BL.Add.Mss, 37993, f30r; TNA, WO4/17, 265.
[127] *A Letter*, 5; Patten, *History*, 80.
[128] Arnold, *Northern Lights*, 109.
[129] TNA, WO4/17, 265.

The government certainly saw Forster's army as a threat which had to be defeated. Townshend wrote on 8 November that it 'has occasioned some confusion here, and has had a bad effect upon the publick credit and it will be some time before Mr Wills who commands in those parts can have a sufficient Body together for reducing them, and can be joined by Carpenter'.[130]

There were also the irregular forces. Hoghton's militia were ordered by the deputy lieutenants to gather at Wigan and so join Wills, which they did.[131] The Mayor of Liverpool sent the regulars 'a great quantity of powder and ball, and other stores of war'.[132] Then there was part of the Yorkshire militia under Lumley, Darcy, Holderness and Carlisle, who were marching towards Lancashire with Carpenter. In Leeds, other Yorkshire volunteers and militia were preparing to ride westwards.[133]

Hoghton also requested further support. He was at Wigan with the regulars and wrote to the Rev. Woods of Chowbent on 11 November:

> The officers here design to march at break of day for Preston. They have desired me to raise what men I can to meet us at Preston to-morrow, so desire you to raise all the force you can, I mean lusty young fellows to draw up on Curedon Green to be there by ten o'clock to bring what arms they have fitt for service, and scythes putt in straight polls and such as have not, to bring spades and billhooks for pioneering with. Pray go immediately all amongst your neighbours and give this notice.[134]

The county community also assisted the regulars by the provision of transport from Wigan to Preston. John Pemberton supplied three carriages and six horses for £2 2s 6d on 11–12 November. Another seven carts were provided by four other contractors.[135]

In Cheshire, the militia had also been raised. Discussion had begun by 3 November, when it was known that there was a Jacobite army active in northern England. On 9 November, two troops of militia horsemen and seven companies of infantry were drawn up on Bridge Street in Chester. According to Prescott, 'The Militia seems unanimous and promise a saying, all of a Mind, which is

---

[130] Leeds University Library, Special Collections, 35v.
[131] *The Flying Post*, 3722, 10–12 November 1715.
[132] *The Flying Post*, 3722, 10–12 November 1715.
[133] *The Flying Post*, 3723, 12–15 November 1715; Leeds Central Library, Diary of John Lucas, 33.
[134] Hoghton, *Hoghton Tower*, 113.
[135] LRO, QSP1091/8.

interpreted, Not to be excersisd by half pay officers, nor to march but under command of their proper officers and many cry up For the Church'.[136] This would seem that the men did not want to be drilled by the half-pay officers sent to instruct them, that they would only obey the civilian militia officers, and that they were for the Anglican Church – perhaps in opposition to the Catholicism of the Jacobites.

On the following day, some of the militia, together with the city's recorder, were drawn up outside the city walls, 'in a military posture'. A proclamation was read out in the city to encourage more men to join the horse volunteers under Major Laurence. Finally, it was believed that on 11 November the militia were to depart the city, half going towards Warrington and half to Manchester.[137]

The militia marched out as planned. Colonel Samuel Daniel, with a troop of cavalry (50 men) and three companies (400 men), went to Manchester. The remainder, under Major Mainwaring of Caringham, marched to Warrington. Cholmondeley, however, did not accompany them. Yet the militia's departure resulted in 'the appearance and complaints of the soldiers wives and children a moving spectacle'.[138] On 12 November, Cholmondeley, with the half-pay officers and gentlemen volunteers, 50 men on horse and 600 foot soldiers in all, marched to Warrington.[139] Others stayed in Chester: Major Lawrence, Captain Harrison, half-pay officers and a company of gentlemen volunteers.[140]

There was also spiritual support for the troops. The bishops in London declared their loyalty to the King, but there were some exceptions. These included Francis Gastrell, Bishop of Chester.[141] Yet the Rev. Sudell of Chester, preached against the 'rebels against God and our excellent Constitution in Church and State'.[142]

There were other forms of loyalty shown in the North West in this period of intense danger. The fifth of November was celebrated throughout the parishes and cities. Prescott wrote:

> The day is usherd with Bells celebrated and carry'd on with the usual Solemnitys. That part of Delivery by King William is commemorated by the soldiers wearing

---

[136] Prescott, 'Diary', II, 471–2.
[137] Prescott, 'Diary', II, 472.
[138] Prescott, 'Diary', II, 472.
[139] Prescott, 'Diary', II, 473.
[140] Anon., *A Compleat History of the Late Rebellion*, London: W. Hinchcliffe, 1716, 71.
[141] *The Flying Post*, 3722, 10–12 November 1715.
[142] Green, 'Peploe', 96.

Orange ribbands, with particular respect. From Elixir last night, I confine myself today and read the History of it.[143]

Parishes in Lancashire rang their bells on 5 November. One such was Over Kellett, where seven shillings was spent on that activity. Formby's bells also rang. The bells of the parish church of Standish rang out, too.[144]

Also in Chester, on 4 November, Cholmondeley and the recorder, with 'zealous conduct and industry', called all adults to take the loyal oaths to the King and to subscribe to a loyal association. He was also thanked by Townshend for sending information to him about the Jacobites.[145]

In Cheshire, as in Cumberland, the JPs were told to put the laws against Catholics into action 'since there is open rebellion already begun in this country', as instructions sent by Cholmondely dated 1 November read. Peter Shakerley (c. 1650–1726), deputy lieutenant and leading JP for the division of Northwich, was unenthusiastic. There were only a few known Catholics within his jurisdiction and he deemed these to be

> poor little inoffensive Fellows ... I cannot think your lordship would give yourself or us the trouble of them since there is no information before us of any fact against them or indeed any of the rest. I personally know all the persons in the list save 1 or 2 and believe them to be peaceable and would live quietly and inoffensively under the government.

Generally, he believed that the county's Catholics, unlike others, were 'so quiet and behaved themselves so peaceably' and wondered 'whether your lordship's perseverance in the same mild and gentle methods will not more effectually preserve the peace of the county ... than rigid and severe methods'. In any case, it would be practically difficult to have the 14 Catholics summoned on the appointed day of 8 November, at Knutsford, before the deputy lieutenants.[146]

Yet there was some Jacobitism noted even here. On 2 November, a number of men gathered at an inn in Macclesfield. One John Harrison of the same, a thread dyer, declared, 'Here's King James' health'. With him were Joshua Rowbotham, a whitesmith of Nether Knutsford, and William Pimlott, a groom. They toasted

---

[143] Prescott, 'Diary', II, 471.
[144] LRO, PR2566; 3360/4/1/1; PR183.
[145] TNA, SP44/118, 117.
[146] CRO, DSS1/3/88/6.

James again and also said, 'Down with the Rump', and cried hurrah for the Jacobite cause.[147]

Civilians were very anxious throughout these two weeks. Stout wrote, 'this was a time of much trouble and danger, on account of the Rebellion, in which we were in feare of being plundered or worse'.[148]

Prescott notes that he was not aware of the rising in Northumberland until 2 November – almost four weeks after it had begun – and we can probably assume that most of Chester was in such ignorance, too. Yet for the next 12 days, the subject of the progress of the Jacobite army was seldom absent. On 3 November, there is indeed alarm in his following words:

> Wee are startld with 2 Expresses from Penrith in 2 hours, telling the Rebells are advanc'd on this side Penrith, hastning the march of the Squadron in Wigan, and proceeding with all dispatch to the other places, the squadron (about 120 Horse) march toward Preston.[149]

Often news was imprecise, Prescott writing on 6 November, after 'a disturb'd sleep', that 'the Letters bring little of News, the Rumors very much, but incertainly, from Lancashire'. Likewise, on the following day, 'The Town is full of Rumor and Invencion about the Motions in Lancashire'. On the 8th they were no better: 'The News from London magnifies the Insurrection in Scotland. Some Letters from Lancashire remove the rebels to a great distance, others bring them betwixt Lancaster and Preston'.[150]

More reliable was news of the Jacobite march through Lancashire in the following days. The scene was set for a major clash of arms, the first in the whole campaign in Britain, as the regular troops, eager for battle, were marching towards the Jacobites at Preston. Whether the latter were willing or not, conflict seemed inevitable.

Neither side could realistically feel confident as to the outcome of battle. The Jacobites had been severely disappointed by the lack of active support that had been promised by Lancashire Jacobites. Confidence would also have been dented by the desertion of so many Scots on the eve of the march into England. Those recruits who had come in were variously armed, largely untrained and led by amateurs. Dissension between the leadership may have occurred, as had happened in the days between the amalgamation of forces at Kelso and their

---

[147] TNA, CHES/24/152/4.
[148] Stout, *Autobiography*, 176.
[149] Prescott, 'Diary', II, 470–71.
[150] Prescott, 'Diary', II, 471–2.

arrival into Cumberland, and though this may have been less remarked upon on the march south, it was still latent.

Similarly, the government's supporters had no obvious reason to cheer. Their forces had been unable to offer any effective resistance to the advancing Jacobites. The posse had fled at Penrith; the militia and dragoons at Lancaster withdrew less precipitously, but withdraw they did. Retreat is poor for morale. Although a force had been finally drawn together under Wills, it had not made contact with Carpenter's forces from Newcastle. Elsewhere, their colleagues in Scotland were heavily outnumbered by the Jacobites. There might be potential Jacobite supporters in England and elsewhere, whose future conduct would be based on the result of a battle in England. The stakes for all involved had now risen considerably as that battle drew close. It is possible that the Jacobite army in Lancashire was viewed by those in government as a more significant threat than the far larger Jacobite forces in Scotland because of its closer proximity to them. England was their heartland. Scotland could be lost and retaken (as in 1650); once England was lost that was the end, as Charles I learnt in the previous century.

The result of the forthcoming battle, the first of the whole campaign, would be decisive in shaping the future of the whole struggle. Unlike previous potential clashes, this one could not be avoided. For both sides the outcome was of supreme importance and not only for the immediate participants at the sharp end.

Chapter 5

The Opposing Sides

With conflict imminent, it is necessary to survey both sides in the struggle. Whereas there has been military analysis of the Forty Five in recent years by Stuart Reid and Christopher Duffy,[1] and while the Fifteen is long on narrative of the campaign and its aftermath, there has been little systematic analysis of the forces involved on either side, of their commanders and capabilities. On the Jacobite side, Gooch has provided a study of the Northumbrian gentry and their followers.[2] Military analysis of the regulars and militia in the Fifteen was published by Oates in more recent years.[3] The campaign in England has also been subjected to the same historian's analysis.[4] Of the commanders, Thomas Forster has come in for considerable abuse. According to the Taylers, he was 'an even more unfortunate choice than the Earl of Mar – no soldier, and had not even the merit of personal bravery'.[5] Baynes wrote that Forster had few qualifications for the position. He had no military experience at all and was not especially admired'.[6] Finally, Arnold wrote, 'Tom Forster had no qualifications for leadership. He had no military experience, and his martial failings will become all too apparent'.[7] More recently, a more kindly assessment comes from Gooch, arguing that he was let down by allies and faulty communications and so should be exonerated.[8] Here follows a description of both sides and an analysis of their military capacities.

One point stands out above all. As far as the North West was concerned, this was primarily a rebellion of the rural Lancashire Catholics and of the gentry

---

[1] S. Reid, *Like Hungry Wolves*, London: Windrowe and Greene, 1994; *1745: A Military History of the Last Jacobite Rising*, Spellmount: Staplehurst, 1995; C. Duffy, *'45*, London: Cassell, 2003.
[2] Gooch, *Desperate Faction*, 51–68.
[3] Oates, *The Jacobite Campaigns* 2011.
[4] Oates, 'The Armies operating in Northern England', *Journal of the Society for Army Historical Research*, 362, 2012.
[5] Taylers, *Story of the Rising*, 80.
[6] Baynes, *Jacobite Rising*, 86.
[7] Arnold, *Northern Lights*, 92.
[8] Gooch, *Desperate Faction*, 84–5.

(in contrast to the rebellions of 1685 and 1745, in both of which the gentry were conspicuous by their absence, but even in 1715 only a minority of Catholic adult men took part). To an extent, we should not be surprised. Lancashire was the most populated of the three north-western counties which the Jacobite army marched through, and it was the most Catholic of them. Cumberland and Westmorland were more thinly populated and contained far fewer Catholics, and the Jacobites never reached Cheshire. Of the 429 known active Jacobites in the North West, 396 were from Lancashire – just over 90 per cent of the total.[9]

Those who took a rather more active part were from a variety of social backgrounds, as well as being more geographically diverse. Of the north-western Jacobites that we know of, 133 were husbandmen, farmers and yeomen (32%); 109 were gentlemen and esquires (26%). These were men with a stake in the landed society of the time. With them were 48 servants (11%), 34 weavers (8%) and 18 labourers (4%). Finally, there were 80 men from a total of 29 other callings (20%). This was not a typical cross section of society, though it did show that Jacobitism had its followers in all ranks. As noted, gentlemen and esquires were represented out of all proportion to their percentage of the population. They were also overwhelmingly Catholic – of those of whom we know the religious affiliations, 200 (74%) were Catholic and 72 (26%) Protestant. In total, there were 396 Lancastrians, 23 from Cumberland, 6 from Westmorland and 4 from Cheshire. A list of these men appears in Appendix 2.[10]

They came from all over the counties of the North West, but there were a few concentrations. Preston supplied 48 recruits and the adjoining Walton 36. Twenty-five men came from Burnley, doubtless influenced by Richard Towneley of Towneley Hall, Burnley. Myerscough supplied 18 men, Singleton 12, Claughton 11 and Lancaster 10. Wetheral in Cumberland provided 10 men, the largest single number for a parish outside Lancashire. Many parishes in Lancashire supplied one or two men to the army, including parishes that were over five miles from the army's march. However, the vast bulk of the recruits came from places which the army marched through or from those adjacent.[11]

An analysis of parish registers clearly identifies 24 out of 429 Jacobites where parish of baptism equates with parish as noted in the prisoner lists (about 6%), so the validity of the following may be questionable. The oldest active Jacobite was 57 in 1715; four had been born in the 1660s, three in the 1670s, five in the 1680s but 11 in the following decade, the youngest three being teenagers. At least five

---

[9] TNA, KB8/66.
[10] TNA, KB8/66.
[11] TNA, KB8/66.

were married and at least two of these had children (Thomas Sydall had at least five children, for instance). Jacobite recruits were thus from a diverse range of ages and included both married men and bachelors, but with a preponderance of the latter.[12]

The true numerical strength of active English Jacobitism cannot be known for certain. The number of English prisoners taken after the battle of Preston numbered 744, but many, possibly several hundred, escaped prior to the surrender. Therefore, an absolute minimum must be about a thousand, but quite possibly more.

A study of the Jacobites from the three north eastern counties of England reveals that of the 84 nobility and gentry among them, 39, or just under half, were Catholic. There were at least 236 Northumbrians, 24 from Durham and a dozen from Yorkshire. The Midlands and southern English counties contributed a mere handful of recruits, suggesting that geographical proximity to the Jacobite army was a major factor in recruitment.[13]

As regards motivation, the Jacobitism of some derived in part from their family history. Men whose ancestors had fought and died for Charles I and supported his son were often sympathetic towards Jacobitism. Among these were Lord Molyneux and Sir Thomas Tyldesley, who led regiments for the king in 1642. The latter was killed at Worcester in 1651. A study of 42 Jacobite gentlemen out in the Fifteen revealed that the families of 28 of them had been active in supporting the King in the 1640s and 10 had been passive supporters. Only four had sided with Parliament.[14]

One of the leading Lancashire Jacobites was Richard Towneley of Towneley Hall, near Burnley, a Catholic gentleman. In 1713 he had married Mary, daughter of William, fourth Baron Widdrington, a leading Northumberland Catholic peer, who was also a leading light in the rebellion. Towneley was able to lead a contingent of men to join the Jacobite army at Preston, with estimated numbers ranging from 18 to 60. These included his servants – his butler, his postilion and his coachman – but not his priest. His great-grandfather had died fighting for the King at Marston Moor in 1644. He was also a member of the mock corporation of Walton-le-Dale, being appointed mayor in 1713.[15]

Another Lancastrian Jacobite gentleman was Ralph Standish, Esq. The Standishes were an ancient family, dating back to the thirteenth century. Ralph's

[12] International Genealogical Index.
[13] Gooch, *Desperate Faction*, 60–61; TNA, KB8/66.
[14] P.J. Gooderson, *History of Lancashire*, 1980, 85, 90; Blackwood, 'Lancashire Catholics', 51–4.
[15] *Burke's Landed Gentry*, 1855, 1217–18; J.P. Earwaker, ed., 'The Mock corporation of Rochdale', *Lancashire and Cheshire Archaeological Society*, New Series 4, 1884, 100; Nicholson, 'Lancashire', 82–3.

grandfather and namesake had been a cavalry colonel with Charles I. He himself had married Philippa Howard, daughter of the Catholic Duke of Norfolk.[16]

Other Lancastrian Jacobites had similar pedigrees. The grandfather of Sir Francis Anderton (d. 1760) of Lostock Hall fought for Charles I. So did an ancestor of Gabriel and Cuthbert Hesketh, though one also fought for Parliament.[17] These were men of substance in the county. Ralph Standish was 'a Gentleman of very good Repute; having a plentiful Fortune'. John Dalton was 'of a good Estate'. Anderton's lands were worth £2,000 per annum.[18]

We know rather more about George Hilton (1673–1725), a Catholic from Westmorland, than most for he kept a diary for part of his life (frustratingly not for the period 1714–16). Although he was married, he was separated from his wife for most of his married life. He was also impoverished, having to sell in 1696 much of the land he had inherited on his father's death. He was a violent young man, knocking out a man's eye at the Assizes at Appleby in 1701, and fond of drinking, so much so that many entries record that at the end of the evening he was 'fuddled'. The diary makes no note of his political and religious feelings, but without children and with little property or money, he was probably an ideal candidate to take part in so risky an undertaking as an armed rebellion.[19]

In Lancashire, it was common for more than one male member of the family to ride out to join the Jacobite army. These included William and John Brockholes, Catholic gentlemen of Claughton. Richard and Charles Chorley, father and son, of Chorley were another example. Four members of the Hesketh family – Cuthbert, Gabriel, Thomas and William – participated. This was also the case with men lower down the social scale, especially in Lancashire. To take a few examples, James, John and Peter Wyke, all husbandmen from Walton, and all Catholics, joined. So did Evan, Roger and Thomas Hodgson, three Catholic husbandmen from the same village. Four members of the Cowp family, all weavers from Walton, also enlisted, though only two were definitely Catholic. Of the far fewer Jacobites from Cumberland, Westmorland and Cheshire, in only one case did more than one member of the family take an active part in the rebellion – John and William Willson of Wetheral.[20]

According to a government source, even more men would have joined the Jacobites had they marched south from Preston: 'the rebels in two or three days

---

[16] *Burke's Landed Gentry*, 1131.
[17] *VCH Lancashire*, V, 297, VIII, 407.
[18] Patten, *History*, 114, 115.
[19] George Hilton, *The Rake's Diary: The Journal of George Hilton*, ed. Anne Hillman, Kendal: Curwen Archives Trust, 1994.
[20] TNA, KB8/66.

would certainly have been joined by as many thousands well armed and well mounted'.[21] A Jacobite source concurs with this.[22] Whether this would have been the case, is, of course, an unanswerable question, but it is difficult to resist the conclusion that further support from Manchester would not have been forthcoming; as it was, only five men from Manchester were involved.

It is also worth adding that there were some startling omissions from the list of known Jacobite supporters. There was only one Catholic clergyman (one Littleton), and no one from the Anglican Church from the North West. Perhaps Catholic clergymen were not encouraged to participate because of the propaganda value in not being seen as a Catholic army. As to the latter, it is possible that the presence of so many Catholics among Jacobite ranks dissuaded them from active participation.

Their motives were mixed, but religion was probably uppermost for both Catholic and Protestant Jacobites. Old grievances may have rankled. John Leybourne, Esquire, had been executed for his faith in 1583. According to Patten, Roger Muncaster, a Protestant Jacobite, joined because of the 'blazed Rumour of the Church being in danger', and it was added that he 'had been corrupted by conversation with papists and others not affected to the government'.[23] Only Muncaster made a recorded dying speech, as far as is known, and that was to apologise for his actions. A Whig report claimed that other prisoners who were about to be executed 'all being papists, dyed obstinately'. This would indicate that they affirmed their Jacobite beliefs at the scaffold, probably stating that James was the rightful king.[24] Family history was also important. As noted, many of the families who were represented in the rebellion had also been involved in the Lancashire Plot of 1694, such as Tyldesley, Dalton, Legh and Towneley. Chorley had been arrested for his support of James II after 1688. The remembrance of martyred Lancashire Catholics during the persecutions of the past as well as the Civil Wars may also have rankled with some.

Were some men reluctant Jacobites – reluctant, that is, to enter into arms? John Dalton, a Catholic squire, had a party of the Jacobite army at his house on 8 November, and later claimed he was then obliged to accompany them, declaring, 'The Business is now done, we have nothing to do but to march to Preston'. Earlier, he had been warned by an Anglican clergyman not to take up arms, and replied that 'he had neither intention nor inclination to do it; that he lived very happily and would not endanger himself'. The same clergyman said that Dalton

---

[21] BL. Stowe 750, f157r.
[22] Patten, *History*, 94.
[23] *Faithful Register of the Late Rebellion*, London: T. Warner, 1718, 28.
[24] TNA, PL28/1/37, 234; BL.Stowe, 750, f.157r.

was a man 'whom he never heard to express himself against the government', that 'his character [is] of a very peaceable Roman Catholic' and that once he 'heard him drink King George's health'. Similar remarks were told of others: Sir George Warburton said of Edward Tyldesley, 'they never heard him speak with Disrespect of the government ... a facetious, inoffensive man'. Finally, Towneley claimed that he only joined the Jacobites because 'he left his house for fear of being secur'd by the militia of the county, who were then gathering together to secure papists and persons reputed to be disaffected to the government'.[25] Of course, these may well be excuses in order to avoid the gallows, and given these men's pedigrees, this seems likely. Another reluctant Jacobite was a thief who joined in Cumberland only to escape the constables.[26]

Another was Thomas Carus, whose father allegedly forced him into the rebellion. Apparently, Carus senior 'being zealously affected towards them [the Jacobites] made preperations to meet them ... both urged and constrained this your petitioner ... to goe along with them ... threatened to turn his wife and tender infants out of home and lett them starve unless he would goe along with them'.[27] Edward Shafto later wrote of his son, John that 'with inexpressible grief he made his best endeavours to dissuade his son from such an enterprise but to no purpose, though he followed him through all the towns the rebels marched'.[28]

An allegedly more militant Jacobite was Richard Shuttleworth, who, according to news reported by the Whiggish Lady Cowper, 'was famous for saying he hoped in a little time to see Preston Streets running as fast with heretic Blood as they do with Water when it has rained twelve Hours'.[29]

There were Jacobites who did not enlist in the Jacobite army, but who showed their sympathies in other ways. Principally, these were the members of the mob which attacked Dissenting chapels in the summer of 1715. They are thought to have numbered about 500 to 600. There are five surviving lists of men charged with these riots, and the lists are mostly dissimilar; they give 54 names in all. The rioters were wholly plebeian, as we would expect. They include eight husbandmen, five weavers, four labourers, three fustian cutters and men from another 18 occupations.[30] All were from Manchester, except four from

---

[25] *Political State*, XII, 580, 583, 542, 536–7.
[26] Clarke, 'Journal', 514.
[27] TNA, SP35/7, f30r.
[28] *Calendar of Treasury Books*, XXI, Part III, 1717, London: HMSO, 1957, 720.
[29] Cowper, *Diary*, 84–5.
[30] LRO, GJ1/2//10, 522–3; TNA, PL28/1, 234–8.

Salford. Although we know the names of less than 10 per cent of the rioters, this is probably a fair cross sample of those plebeian Jacobites from Manchester.[31]

We know far less about these rank and file Jacobites. Thomas Sydall is perhaps the only significant Lancastrian Jacobite who was not a gentleman. As a middle-aged Manchester blacksmith, he was prominent in the rioting there against the Dissenters. Thomas Bootle, in 1716, referred to his evident notoriety: 'Sidall who was called Colonel of the Mob at Manchester and being a notorious offendr & of great esteem there amongst the disaffected'. Apparently, 'when he was in his pomp, pretended to dispense pardons and protections upon his honour'.[32] Another significant plebeian was James Blundell, a tanner, who was also a churchwarden of the parish of Standish. Apparently, he 'came with horse and arms to the Rebels, and was to have been one of the militia, who were then to be raised and was said to have been approached by the vicar'.[33]

Jacobitism was a many-layered phenomenon. Apart from those taking direct action, there were others who were less militant. It was also celebrated in private, too. A number of Jacobite clubs had been founded in Lancashire and Cheshire after 1688. They numbered seven in all. Four seem to have been drinking clubs; these were the Cheshire Gentlemen (founded 1689), the Crosby Bowling Club (founded 1708) and the short-lived Mar Club (1715), and there were meetings at Conder Green from 1689–1715. They met at gentlemen's seats or at country inns.[34]

There were also more formal clubs, which had constitutions, proceedings, officers and membership lists. These were often termed 'mock corporations' because, to an extent, they mirrored the corporations which actually governed towns and cities. These were the Ardwick Corporation (founded 1714), the Walton-le-Dale Corporation (founded 1701) and the Rochdale Corporation (founded 1712). The Walton Corporation met at the Unicorn public house once a year. They appointed members to different offices, such as mayor, recorder, sheriff and chaplain.[35]

One of the main purposes of these groups was so that like minded-men, mostly Catholics and/or those with Jacobite sympathies, could meet to eat, drink and discuss topics of mutual interest. Politics and religion would inevitably be on the agenda. But some did more than just talk. As said, the active Richard Towneley was a leading member of the Walton Corporation. Perhaps it is significant that none are known to have existed in Cumberland and Westmorland.

---

[31] LRO, GJ1/2//10, 522–3; TNA, PL28/1, 234–8.
[32] BL, Stowe, 750, f157r; *Flying Post*, 3728, 19–21 Feb. 1716.
[33] Prescott, 'Diary, II', 492; *Faithful Register*, 33.
[34] Lole, 'Jacobite Clubs'.
[35] Earwaker, 'Mock Corporation', 100.

There were also other sympathisers. For example, when Sydall and other rioters were put in the stocks in Lancaster in August 1715, 'no person was allowed to fling anything at them'.[36] Others included William, fourth Viscount Molyneux of Maryburgh (1656–1717), and the elderly Nicholas Shirburn. Apparently, the former 'has a Deposition made against him by his gardener that shews his Lordship to have been as directly concerned in the late Rebellion as any man who was executed for it'. Dudley Ryder added that he was 'known to associate with the rebels'.[37] Yet Molyneux was elderly and not in good health, as Blundell recorded on 14 January 1715, 'ill of the Gout' and so unavailable to see visitors. Clearly he was in no position to aid the Jacobites directly.[38] Yet he was later accused of trying to persuade his servants and others to join them.[39]

Several MPs from the North West had Jacobite sympathies, too. Charles Cholmondeley (1685–1756) of Chester had been present at a meeting where James's health had been drunk (see below). Others were members of Jacobite clubs, such as Henry Fleetwood (1667–1746), an MP for Preston, and Barrymore. Bunbury was thought to have been involved in distributing Jacobite pamphlets. He, too, had been recently dismissed from a position of authority – from the Irish Customs.[40]

The Jacobite meeting alluded to above took place on 24 August 1715 at a country house, Rocksavage in Cheshire, and was described by Prescott thus:

> My Lord Barrymore appears great in Servants attending. Hee treats with a fine Ayr and full generosity. In the middle of dinner Mr Chomley, his brothers Seymor and Banks come [Bunbury was also present]. That over ... Toasts are first promoted, the Circle takes about 14, the wine and ... old Beer perform a perpetual motion, till six, when a Health to our absent Friends, and that they may return with Honor, prosperity and Glory concludes and Crowns the Entertainment.

The absent friends who hopefully would return are presumed to include James Francis Stuart, with Bolingbroke and Ormonde.[41]

Some Anglican clergymen were thought to have had Jacobite sympathies. One was Francis Gastrell. Among his friends and supporters were the Tory Robert Harley, who was imprisoned in the Tower for treason in 1715 (but

---

[36] Clarke, 'Journal', 518.
[37] Ryder, *Diary*, 175.
[38] Blundell, 'Great Diurnall', 122.
[39] Henry Hoghton, 'The Jacobite Rebellions' in 'De Hoghton Deeds', 276.
[40] Sedgwick, *Commons*, I, 202–4, 440, II, 39.
[41] Prescott, 'Diary', II, 459.

was not convicted), and who had been instrumental in Gastrell's promotion to the bishopric of Chester in 1714. Francis Atterbury and George Smallridge, Bishops of Rochester and Bristol respectively, were other friends of Gastrell's, and were Jacobite inclined.[42]

Although there were many in the North West who were sympathetic towards the Jacobite cause, especially among Lancashire Catholics, as with any political movement, only a minority were active. Yet a minority, if determined enough, and if its opposition is enfeebled, can achieve much (as proved in 1688 by James II's opponents). We now turn to their opponents.

The Whigs

George I has often been portrayed as an unappealing and uncharismatic figure, remote from the majority of the nation and unable to speak much English. Yet some of this image is the result of Jacobite propaganda. At any rate, he was an experienced soldier and diplomat and did not lack for supporters. Crucially, he was Protestant. There were the Dissenters who supported him on religious grounds. Secondly, and again on religious grounds, most Protestant Englishmen were anti-Catholic and a return of the Stuarts almost certainly meant the promotion of Catholicism, which had happened during James II's reign. George I was important for what he was not as well as for what he was. Then there were secular reasons. The Whigs had been handsomely rewarded with offices and places of profit, and they certainly wanted to maintain these against any Jacobite threat. Those who supported George wanted to maintain, and perhaps further, their position in the new status quo. They included noblemen, gentry and clergy.

Principal among the Whigs in the counties were the Lords Lieutenant. The third Earl of Carlisle was the eldest of these. He succeeded to the title in 1692 on his father's death and was given the appointment of Governor of Carlisle Castle. In 1694, on the first Viscount of Lonsdale's death, he was made Lord Lieutenant of Cumberland and Westmorland. In the following decade, further honours followed – Deputy Earl Marshal of England in 1700, member of the Privy Council, 1701 and First Lord of the Treasury in the same year. Although he lost these posts in 1712, he was reinstated in 1714 and in 1715, as First Lord of the Treasury (until October) and then Constable of the Tower.[43]

---

[42] *ODNB*, 31, 620–32.
[43] Jarvis, *Jacobite Risings*, 91.

Viscount Lonsdale was another key supporter of the Hanoverian state in the North West. Symson wrote of him thus: 'The worthy Lord Lonsdale, who is now in this county is warm in the defence of King George And this country against Popish tyranny and slavery and may truly be styled the northern Hero'.[44] Patten wrote likewise: 'The Lord Lonsdale whose Predecessors have been famous for their loyalty as well as Antiquity, had still considerable Interest in that County. This Nobleman, tho' young, has still very valuable and endearing Accomplishments, and no small share of Courage'.[45]

Lonsdale was Henry Lowther (1694–1751), and had become third Viscount on his brother's death in 1713. Their father had played his part in promoting William's interests in the North West in 1688. Although he was only a deputy lieutenant in 1715, he was the most senior among their number, being the only peer therein.[46]

Another Lord Lieutenant was Hugh Cholmondeley (c. 1662–1725), first Earl of Cholmondeley. He had been a critic of James II and supported William III. Created Lord Lieutenant of Cheshire in 1704, though dismissed in the Tory purge in 1713, he was reinstated on George I's accession. He was also made an official of the Royal Household at this time.[47]

Then there was Edward Stanley (1664–1732), tenth Earl of Derby. Although his family had supported Charles I in the Civil War, and the seventh Earl had been executed for his royalism, the tenth Earl was a staunch Whig, and had been an officer in one of the regular units which had been stationed in Holland in the 1680s. He came over with William's fleet in 1688 and subsequently saw service in Ireland and in Flanders in the following decade. In the 1700s, he was promoted to brigadier, but soon afterwards inherited the title and estates and became Lord Lieutenant of Lancashire. He had been dismissed in the Tory purge in 1710, but was reinstated after George I's accession in 1714.[48]

Two of Lancashire's deputy Lords Lieutenant and JPs were also prominent in the Whig cause. Sir Henry Hoghton, a Whig MP for Preston, with the family seat at Hoghton Tower and a town house in Preston, was one. He came from a wealthy family of Dissenting merchants. Although the Hoghtons were an ancient family, dating back to the fourteenth century, and had opposed the Reformation of the sixteenth, matters changed with the succession of Richard as third baronet in 1647. He was a Puritan, and since then the family home had

---

[44] Smith, *Letter Books*, 342.
[45] Patten, *History*, 64.
[46] Jarvis, *Jacobite Risings*, 92.
[47] *ODNB*, 11, 508.
[48] *ODNB*, 52, 225.

become a haven for Presbyterians. It was registered as a Dissenting meeting-place after 1688 and had a growing congregation. Hoghton himself supported the building of Presbyterian chapels in Preston and Walton-le-Dale. The Hoghtons also owned the advowson to Preston and always nominated Low Church clergy who would be sympathetic to their religious and political views.[49]

The other was Francis Charteris, (1665–1732), a Scottish soldier, who had bought Hornby Castle, near Lancaster. He had an unsavoury reputation as a card cheat and had been found guilty of financial irregularities when serving in the army.[50]

Another leading Whig was Sir Thomas Stanwix (1670–1725). He was the Lieutenant Governor of Carlisle Castle and had been one of the MPs for the city since the reign of Queen Anne. As a loyal Whig, he was appointed as Governor of Chelsea Hospital after George's accession. In the following year he was given a commission to raise a regiment of infantry.[51]

The men who were officers in the Cumberland and Westmorland militia were all men of property and rank in these counties. Most held, or were to hold, important civil offices, such as those of deputy lieutenant, MP, or sheriff. One such was Edward Wilson (1680–1754) of Dallam Tower, Westmorland, who was captain of the Kirkby Lonsdale company. He was later to serve as an MP and county sheriff. Thomas Lamplugh (1656–1734), captain of the Penrith Company, had been MP for Cockermouth.[52]

There were also clergy who were enthusiastic in their defence of King George. The leading cleric in the North West was Nicolson. Patten described him thus: 'not only a compleat scholar in all manner of learning, but likewise a Man of Courage and brave soul'.[53] Nicolson had been born in Orton, the son of the rector there, in 1655. He became Archdeacon of Carlisle in 1692, having promoted William III's cause on 1689. In 1702, he became Bishop, because he had the support of Sir Christopher Musgrave of Edenhall, a Whig. Two years later he refused to induct the Jacobite Atterbury to the diocesan deanery. On George I's accession, Nicolson was rewarded with the post of Lord High Almoner.[54]

Another Whig clergyman was Peploe. He was nominated for this post by Sir Charles Hoghton (father of Sir Henry), a leading county Whig, because of

---

[49] Eveline Cruickshanks, Stuart Handley and David Hayton, *The Commons, 1690–1715*, IV, Cambridge University Press, 2002, 377–8.
[50] *ODNB*, 11, 209–11.
[51] Sedgwick, *Commons*, II, 440–41.
[52] Jarvis, *Jacobite Risings*, 156n.
[53] Patten, *History*, 65.
[54] Jarvis, *Jacobite Risings*, 39–40.

his similar politics. Peploe had two schools built in Preston in the first decade of the eighteenth century, but was overbearing and uncompromising in his beliefs and so antagonised many in Preston, especially those who were High Church or Catholics.[55]

Dissenting clergymen opposed the Jacobites, too, unsurprisingly given the attacks on Dissenting chapels in 1715. Foremost among these was James Wood (1672–1759), a Dissenting minister of Atherton. His father had also been a minister. John Walker of Horwich and John Turner of Preston were two other Dissenting ministers who rallied to the Hanoverian cause. All were from Lancashire, a county renowned for its Jacobite sympathisers. Doubtless they felt very vulnerable and so gravitated towards the new status quo – at least in part because of their fear of Jacobitism.[56]

Other less exalted folk were anti-Jacobite, too. Symson described himself thus to Peter DeSitter, a London merchant, on 3 November: 'I am, with my second son and a servant well armed, just going to mount with my neighbours in defence of His Majesty King George and the Protestant religion'. Other mercantile support came from those in Liverpool, as we have seen; merchants and office holders, who probably feared a change for the worse if the status quo was altered.[57]

It is unfortunate that we do not know the make-up of the rank and file of their supporters, as we do for the Jacobites. Many were probably co-religionists, especially with the Dissenters, or dependants, such as tenants or junior clergy.

These men represented the new Whig establishment, but many of them were from old and established gentry and noble families, just as many of their Jacobite opponents, were, too. They could mobilise the official forces of the counties, such as the militia, the posse and the Anglican clergy. If these forces did not support the new government, then the latter was indeed in dire straits, as it had been in 1688 in the wake of the invasion of William of Orange.

It is also worth mentioning that most people in the counties were neutral. They had no strong views either way, at least to the point of committing themselves to action, but did not want to see a return to a prolonged civil war and military rule. Nicholas Blundell was certainly one man who wanted to live peacefully with his neighbours. Yet even he could not avoid being swept up by events.

---

[55] *ODNB*, 43, 630–32.
[56] *ODNB*, 60, 108–9.
[57] Smith, *Letter Books*, 343.

Military Force: An Evaluation

These, then, were the men who made up the opposing sides in the North West of England. Yet the issue would be resolved by military force, and so the military aspects of the campaign must be now discussed. We will now consider the leadership, training, weaponry and morale of both sides. A successful rebellion requires the creation of an army, which needs leaders, men, money, arms and supplies. It needs experienced men to lead and train the recruits and enough time to organise and create an effective force. This put the Jacobites at an immediate disadvantage as they had to create these from scratch.

Leadership was critical. As has been said, it has been traditional for historians to decry the Jacobite leadership, which mostly rested with Thomas Forster. More recently, there have been efforts to rehabilitate his reputation.

Yet, as is usually cited, for his role as commander Forster had no military experience whatsoever. He was a landed gentleman and a politician, being one of the two MPs for Northumberland from 1708–15, sitting as a Tory; in three elections out of four he had taken the seat without a contest and had emerged victorious in the other. He was also a JP for the county and had survived the recent purge of the Bench. His aunt had married the elderly Bishop of Durham, Nathaniel Crewe, who had been a supporter of James II. Perhaps most importantly, he was an Anglican.

Patten wrote of Forster:

> I cannot but justify him against the many Aspersions he lies under ... I mean, as a Coward. It must be owned that he was no Soldier; nor was the Command given to him a such, but as he was the only Protestant who could give credit to their Undertaking, being of Note in Northumberland, of an ancient Family, and having been for Several years been Member of parliament for the County, and therefore very Popular: For if the Command had been given to either of the two Lords, their Characters as Papists, would have discouraged many of the People.[58]

Lady Cowper noted:

> 'I conjecture that it was for the sake of his Uncle [Nathaniel Crewe, bishop of Durham] and Aunt that he was made General, and not at all from the Fitness of the Thing, for he had never seen an Army in his Life'.[59]

---

[58] Patten, *History*, 97.
[59] Cowper, *Diary*, 57.

Forster was criticised by friend and foe alike. Clerk of Penicuik, a leading Scottish Whig, wrote that he was 'an idle, drunken, senseless man, not good enough to head a company of militia'.[60] A Scottish Jacobite stated, 'I humbly conceive all our Misfortune is not entirely owing to him [Forster]'.[61] Rae referred to him as the 'cowardly general'.[62] Even Derwentwater was not wholly enthusiastic, declaring, 'What could we do better? The Catholics were not to appear at the head of the business; High Church was to do it. And who could we in Northumberland pick out to please High Church better, than Mr Forster, Knight of the shire, who represented them all?'[63]

Indeed, it is hard to think who else could have been the Jacobite leader. There were no Protestant nobility involved in the rising, so he was the most socially senior figure who was also an Anglican. An Anglican was needed in order to attract other Anglican supporters; Catholic support was taken for granted, but was insufficient in itself (Catholics making up a minority of the population even in Northumberland and Lancashire), and in any case a Catholic leader would be an excellent propaganda weapon for their enemies. That Forster had no military experience was not as damning as it might seem; figurehead leaders were not uncommon in this period and were not necessarily a handicap. Louis XV led the French armies in 1745, and his military experience was no greater than Forster's; as did Charles Edward Stuart in the same year (it was only when the latter sought to exercise real command in battle that matters went awry). However, he does not seem to have encouraged the men by personal example or by rousing speeches (Mar gave one on the day of Sheriffmuir). In any case, military experience in a leader was no guarantee of success; Monmouth had successfully led troops into battle but his rebellion in 1685 ended in disaster.

The key was that a leader must have sound advice from experienced soldiers who knew their business. For military wisdom, Forster relied on Colonel Henry Oxburgh. Although he had lived as a civilian in Lancashire for the previous 15 years, he had served as an officer in the French army in 1695–1700.[64] Yet Oxburgh, as Patten comments:

> was formerly a Soldier, and had obtained a great Reputation; tho' it is manifest in our Case, that he either wanted Conduct or Courage, or perhaps both. He was

---

[60] John Clerk, 'Memoirs of Sir John Clerk of Penicuik', *Scottish Historical Society*, 13, 1892, 91.
[61] *Political State*, XI (1716), 166.
[62] Rae, *History*, 239.
[63] Hibbert-Ware, 'Memorials', 50.
[64] *ODNB*, 42, 278.

better at his Beads and prayers, than at his Business as a Soldier and we all thought him fitter for a Priest than a Field-Officer.[65]

Forster also took advice from Widdrington. Patten is equally disparaging about him, writing, 'Lord Widdrington had too great prevalency over Mr Forster's easy Temper; and this Lord we thought understood so little of the Matter, that he was as unfit for a General as the other [having no military experience whatsoever]'.[66]

An anonymous Lowlander was vitriolic in his condemnation of the Jacobite leadership, writing after the defeat at Preston:

> But our generals and Lords were all alike, either fools, knaves and cowards, or all three (except the Earls of Winton and Derwentwater and Lord Nairn, who were all very tight and firm), for they changed their minds, & kept no resolution, but those which were ridiculous to any person, and ended in our ruin.[67]

There were some mid-ranking officers who had seen military service. Foremost among these was Mackintosh of Borlum. He had served as a captain in Gage's regiment in the Spanish Netherlands in 1681. He had then served under James II in the 1690s and under Louis XIV in the next decade, allegedly ending his service there as a colonel, having 'the Character of Brave and Bold: He has given Signal Instances thereof beyond Seas'.[68] Yet the Jacobite leader in Scotland, the Earl of Mar, did not see fit to appoint him to command the army. He preferred titled men, such as Kenmure, as was natural for a nobleman in a society with the nobility at the apex.

William Gordon, sixth Viscount Kenmure (d. 1716), was given command while the force was in Scotland, and he lacked such knowledge. According to Patten, 'He was a grave full-aged Gentleman of a very ancient Family, and he himself of extraordinary Knowledge and experience in Politics and Political Business, tho' utterly a stranger to all Military affairs; of a singular good Temper, and too Calm and Mild to be qualified for such a post'.[69]

The junior officers in the Jacobite army who led the troops and regiments were young gentlemen, though most lacked any military experience either. For example, the Hon. James Home, captain of a troop of Lowland horse,

---

[65] Patten, *History*, 97.
[66] Patten, *History*, 97.
[67] TNA, SP54/9, 107.
[68] *ODNB*, 35, 686–7; Patten, *History*, 98.
[69] Patten, *History*, 39.

was described thus: 'of a very good Temper, but not very capable of having the command of a Troop, as well on Account of his Age as well as other Incapacities'.[70]

However, several of them were half-pay officers, that is to say, they had seen service as junior officers in the regular army in the recent war, but with its end were no longer on active duty, and others had fought in that war. Some were appointed as captains of troops and companies in the Jacobite army. They would help lead the men on the march and in battle and could help with drill and training, though there was little enough time for such vital tasks.[71]

They included Lord Charles Murray (1691–1720), who had been a cornet in Ross's dragoons in Flanders during 1712–13.[72] Another was Philip Lockhart (c. 1689–1715), who had fought in Kerr's regiment in the War of the Spanish Succession, and John Nairn had been in the same regiment as a captain since 1706 and was previously an ensign in McCartney's from 1704. He was described as a man of 'extreme courage and conduct at the battle of Almanza'. Simon Fraser was in the same regiment as a lieutenant from 1710 to 1713. John Shafto had been a captain in Frank's regiment.[73] Captain James Dalziel had served in Lord Orkney's regiment as an ensign. John Erskine had been an ensign in Preston's.[74] Another captain was Thomas Errington, 'formerly an Officer in the French service, where he had got the Reputation of a good Soldier'.[75] John Hunter had been a quartermaster in Ross's dragoons since 1702.[76] Robert Douglas had been an ensign in Maitland's horse since 1702.[77] Richard Stoke had served in the Scots Greys.[78] In the Jacobite army, Murray had the charge of a regiment of Highland infantry, Lockhart commanded a troop of Lowland horse; Hunter and Errington led troops of English cavalry.[79]

A more senior officer serving with the Jacobites was a man called Colonel Brereton. There are several men of this surname in the army lists, none of whom was a colonel, so he was probably promoted by the Jacobites. He was probably William Brereton, who had been a captain of a Grenadier Company in 1708

---

[70] Patten, *History*, 39.
[71] Patten, *History*, 38–50.
[72] *ODNB*, 39, 874; TNA, WO71/122.
[73] Patten, *History*, 41; *ODNB*, 34, 250–51; TNA, WO71/122; Dalton, *List of Half Pay Officers*, London, Private Circulation, 1900, 19. Dalton, *English Army Lists*, VI, London: Eyre and Spottiswoode, 1904, 171, V, 224–5; TNA, SP54/10/75.
[74] TNA, WO71/122; Dalton, *Army Lists*, V, 48.
[75] Patten, *History*, 48.
[76] Dalton, *Army Lists*, V, 233.
[77] Dalton, *Army Lists*, V, 222.
[78] Patten, *History*, 114.
[79] Patten, *History*, 44, 41, 49, 48.

and then major in Jones's horse in the War of the Spanish Succession, but who had been put on half pay when the regiment was disbanded.[80] It is not known if he was given any command.

The main difficulty for the Jacobites was that no one had any experience of military leadership at a senior level. None had that sense of strategic thinking that was necessary in order to plan a campaign and to set long-term goals. Instead, decisions were only made when they had to be made by force of circumstance, often responding to the actions of others. There was little aggression or initiative. Most decisions were compromises between different factions within the army. As one disgruntled Jacobite wrote, 'our Generalls courage was so great that they never durst look any body in the face and altered their resolutions every half hower'. He added, 'our Generalls & lords were all of a piece, either Rogues or Cowards save two Darwentwater & Wintoun'.[81]

The Jacobite army was not a peasant force of insurgents but for the most part organised on conventional military lines, with regiments, troops and companies. It was also, at least from 1 November, properly paid. Money for pay came from the English tax collectors at the towns through which the army passed, so there was no need for looting. The army also had a number of men assigned as quartermasters, such as Richard Stoke and William Tunstall, the latter being Paymaster General.[82]

The bulk of the Jacobite army under Forster were Scots infantrymen. On 1 November, the Jacobite infantry consisted of six infantry units and one of gentlemen volunteers of Scots from Mar's army. By the time of the army's arrival in Cumberland, after the desertions, they may have numbered about 1,000 men. About half of these were Highlanders and the other half Lowlanders.

Much of the Jacobite army, as has been seen, was organised into regiments of infantry and troops of cavalry. The Highlanders and Lowlanders under Mackintosh's command, 'who are extremely good Marksmen', would have been armed with muskets and many had broadswords and so were able to engage their enemies in a fire fight and also to attack them by charging. Contrary to popular received opinion, the Jacobite Scots were in many ways a conventional force. They were certainly organised as such; Panmure's Battalion, part of Mar's forces, was divided into companies, each with 3 officers, 2 sergeants, 2 corporals, a drummer and a piper and between 29 and 44 privates.[83] They certainly

[80] Dalton, *Half Pay Lists*, 24 and *Army Lists*, VI, 254.
[81] BC, Atholl Papers, 45/12/77.
[82] Patten, *History*, 112, 114.
[83] National Archives of Scotland, GD45/1/201.

looked more convincingly military. All apart from Strathmore's regiment wore Highland garb. They had drummers and pipers and carried standards.[84]

Mackintosh's battalion consisted of 13 companies of about 50 men each prior to the desertions at Langholm. There was a colonel, a lieutenant colonel, a major and 10 captains; 15 lieutenants, two of whom were ADCs; an adjutant, a paymaster, a quartermaster and another ADC. Only part of Strathmore's Battalion crossed the Firth, but there were about four companies; four captains and four lieutenants, five ensigns and a quartermaster. Only part of Lord Drummond's regiment arrived; three captains, a lieutenant and three other officers. There were three companies of Mar's battalion; a major, three captains and three lieutenants. Lord Nairn's regiment was commanded by himself as colonel and included five companies, and Lord Charles Murray's regiment was similarly composed.[85] There were also 30 doctors and apothecaries in the army at Preston, a far higher proportion than in 1745,[86] and an absence of camp followers, again in contrast to 1745.

Jacobite tactics were to loose off a volley of musketry at long range and then to charge, broadswords in hand, to engage the enemy at close quarters, which often made them flee in terror at such an unorthodox tactic. This proved most effective at Killiekrankie in 1689 and was similarly so at Prestonpans in 1745, but was less effective at Sheriffmuir in 1715 and Falkirk in 1746, and ended in disaster at Culloden in 1746. Although many were musket armed, ammunition was often limited; in 1745 this averaged about 12 balls per man.[87] Given that firing two shots per minute was possible, this meant that a fire fight could not be sustained.

James Maxwell, a Jacobite officer in 1745, made the following comparison between the Jacobite and Regular modes of combat:

> A Highlander with a broad sword and target, has a great advantage over a soldier with a screw bayonet, when his fire is spent, so that the advantage regular troops have over Highlanders, consists in their fire and discipline, and if these don't prevail, a body of Highlanders, completely armed and in good spirits, will get the better of an equal number of regular troops.[88]

---

[84] Patten, *History*, 30, 42.
[85] Patten, *History*, 120–22.
[86] TNA, KB8/66.
[87] Barthorp, *Jacobite Rebellions*, 18–21.
[88] J. Maxwell, *Narrative of Prince Charles' Expedition to Scotland*, Edinburgh: T. Constable, 1841, 26.

The lack of ammunition on the Highlanders' part was noted by Sibbitt on 14 October: they 'arrived with musket, sword and target according to the Highland manner ... they have neither ammunition nor provisions but what each man carries for himself'.[89] This would seem to suggest that a prolonged fire fight, as had occurred with such fatal results at Dunkeld in 1689, was untenable

Then there were the cavalry. There were five troops of Lowland horsemen and five of English horsemen, plus two groupings of gentlemen volunteers who were not attached to any unit. These cavalry numbered about 400–500. The role of the horsemen would have been to act as the army's vanguard on the march and to scout ahead for the enemy. It is to be doubted, though, whether they would ever have been capable of mounting a charge against any formed unit of the enemy. As to the several hundred English recruits who were on foot, their role would seem to have been minimal in any battle – untrained and under-armed, it seems that both firing volleys and fighting hand to hand might have proved difficult.

Jacobite cavalry and artillery were traditionally their weakness, unless they had allies from among the regular forces of Europe, which was not to be the case in 1715. As we have seen, there were five troops of Lowland cavalry and five of English cavalry, though perhaps the use of the term 'cavalry' is being generous. It is true that the Lowland cavalry were able to undertake reconnaissance work and had done so among the Borders, and this was one of the key duties of the mounted arm in this era. Yet they were unable to act as cavalry in battle by engaging the enemy cavalry or attacking infantry. To be fair, there was no opportunity for either in the campaign, but there seems little doubt that their performance would have been limited.

Of the Lowland horsemen, Patten writes that they 'were well Mann'd, and indifferently Armed; but many of the Horses small, and in mean condition'. The English were in a worse condition, being 'not altogether so regulated nor so well armed as the Scots'.[90] The Master of Sinclair was also scathing, writing, of the English, 'their number was not five hundred when he left them, and of those few or none well arm'd, all the greatest part altogether without armes; that their horses were light hunting horses, and hunting saddles and snaffles made up their accoutrements; that there was scarce a cutting sword among them all', though he thought the Lowland horsemen 'much better horsed

---

[89] TNA, SP54/9/47.
[90] Master of Sinclair, *Memoirs of the Insurrection in Scotland in 1715*, ed. Walter Scott, Edinburgh: Abbotsford Club, 1845, 191.

for the purpose, because they had strong ruff horses, and were all very well armed ... in comparison with the English'.[91]

A Lowlander noted of the English, 'he most will proper to blame that not above 8 or 10 of a Troop of the English were better armed with a whip and small sword, many of their horses were but indifferent, and their men raw and untrained'.[92]

Yet some of the English recruits were not so ill prepared. An anonymous Scots source claimed that the 200 English Catholics who joined at Preston were 'well arm'd', but 'the rest had no better armes than a whip or a broken sword'. Some had 'guns, some with pistols'.[93] Mackintosh said of his allies that they were 'a parcel of north country jockeys and fox hunters ... This will never do'.[94] Another Scottish criticism of the English contingent was that 'The Scots seemed afraid, when they should come to action, of the English running away from them on their fleet horses'; though some gentry had mounted their servants on coach horses.[95] In most towns which the Jacobites passed through, frantic searches were made for weapons – clear evidence that the army had a shortage of them.[96]

Furthermore, most of the English rank and file had no experience of using weapons in battle – the gentry would have used guns while shooting and been skilled horse riders because of the hunt. Because the army was on the move almost all the time, it was impossible to train any of the men. Even with time, the scarcity of trained officers and weapons would have meant that such training could only have been rudimentary.

There were no English infantry regiments, as there were with the Scots. Some Englishmen, especially those who joined in Lancashire, were not even assigned a unit. According to the lists of prisoners, only 10 were in any company (less than 5%), though most of the Cumbrians had been allotted to companies. The military usefulness of such unformed men, even if armed, would have been almost nil.

Finally, it is worth mentioning that this little army did possess artillery. Two cannon seized at Kelso (originally taken from Hume Castle) had been abandoned, but six more were acquired at Lancaster. These were fired at Preston. Patten noted:

---

[91] BC, Atholl Papers, 45/12/77.
[92] BC Atholl Papers, 45/12/77.
[93] TNA, SP54/9/107.
[94] John Oldmixion, *History of England during the reigns of the royal house of Stuart*, London: J. Pemberton, 1730, 616.
[95] Sinclair, *Memoirs*, 191.
[96] Clarke, 'Journal', 515–18.

the Rebels, though they had Six Pieces of Cannon, did not much use them, except at first only; in short, they knew not how, having no Engineers amongst them; and a Seaman who pretended Judgement, and upon his own Offer took the Management of the Cannon ... acted so madly, whether it was he had too little Judgement, or too much Ale.[97]

It is difficult to know how the Jacobite army would have fought a conventional battle. Its cutting edge was the Scottish troops under Mackintosh, but the force was very small. Lacking adequate leaders, and many with inadequate arms and ammunition, the military ability of the Jacobite army did not appear to be high. Perhaps it should be seen as more of a political gesture, in order to win over the doubtful and succeed without a fight. This was to prove wishful thinking, however.

The Jacobites did not wear uniforms and many of the English and Lowlanders would have looked little different from conventional civilians. The English Jacobites wore red and white cockades in their hats and the Scots had blue and white cockades (the Jacobites' colour was white).[98]

The Jacobites' regular military opponents were led by Major General Sir Charles Wills (1666–1741) and Lieutenant General George Carpenter (1657–1732). Both these men were experienced soldiers, having entered the army in their mid teens. They had both served in Ireland and Flanders during the War of the League of Augsburg and in the War of the Spanish Succession. Carpenter joined the Foot Guards as a private in 1672, becoming quartermaster in Peterborough's horse in the following decade. He was Lieutenant Colonel of the Royal Regiment of Dragoons in 1703, a brigadier in 1705, major general in 1708 and lieutenant general in 1711, having served in Flanders and Spain, and had received wounds in battle.[99]

Wills was an infantryman, receiving a commission as ensign in Erle's horse in 1682, becoming a captain in 1691 and then a major in Sanderson's horse in 1694. He was a lieutenant colonel by the end of the War of the League of Augsburg (1697). In 1701 he was a lieutenant colonel in Caulfield's horse, a brigadier in 1707, and major general in 1709. However, although he lobbied the commander in chief, Marlborough, for the rank of lieutenant general, he was unsuccessful; this still rankled in the following years and he was probably jealous of Carpenter's rise. He had served in Ireland, the West Indies and Spain,

---

[97] Patten, *History*, 90.
[98] LRO, DDX2244/1.
[99] *ODNB*, 10, 225.

was a brave soldier and had suffered wounds. He was enthusiastic for battle and for victory in order to gain promotion.[100]

Admittedly, neither was brilliant, nor had they had independent commands previously. But both possessed a dogged persistence which was to hold them in good stead during the brief campaign of the Fifteen. And, unlike the Jacobite high command, they had a clear objective – to bring the Jacobite army to battle and to defeat it. Although the achieving of that aim was not necessarily easy, at least their goal itself was straightforward.

Wills's three brigadiers were also experienced officers. James Dormer (1679–1741) had been a lieutenant and captain in the First Foot Guards in 1702, serving at Blenheim and Ramillies. He was colonel of Mohun's horse in 1708 and a brigadier in 1711. In 1715 he raised a regiment of dragoons.[101] Richard Munden (1680–1725), as with Dormer, was a captain in the Foot Guards in 1702, a lieutenant colonel with Lovelace's horse in 1706, a colonel in 1708 and a brigadier in 1712. He had seen service at Blenheim and Ramillies and in Spain. Again, as with Dormer, he raised a regiment of dragoons in 1715.[102] Philip Honeywood (c. 1680–1752), the third brigadier, also raised a new regiment; he had 21 years' military experience prior to the Battle of Preston and had been a brigadier since 1710.[103] It is perhaps worth noting that Wills, Carpenter, Munden and James Stanhope all spent time in captivity at Brihnega in 1710.

Yet of Wills's command, only two units were veteran (Preston's foot and Pitt's horse); the other five had only been raised in July 1715. Carpenter had one veteran regiment (Cobham's dragoons) and three of newly raised men (the better units mostly were sent northwards to join Argyle to face the principal Jacobite threat). Ten members of Preston's foot who saw service at the battle had a total of 154 years' service between them and had an average age at the battle of 42½ years. Two of Pitt's horse had 36 years' experience between them and were aged 49 and 52. Yet not all the men from the veteran units were veterans. Preston's had undergone a recruiting drive only weeks before the battle. John Jones and Francis Suthran, privates in Preston's, had joined as recently as 19 October at Chester.[104]

Some of the junior officers were also experienced soldiers. Those we know of are those who served in Preston's Foot, a veteran battalion of infantry, raised in 1688, which had fought in all the battles of the War of the Spanish Succession.

---

[100] *ODNB*, 59, 430–31.
[101] *ODNB*, 16, 575.
[102] Cruickshanks, Handley and Hayton, *Commons*, IV, 954.
[103] Dalton, *Army Lists*, I, 115.
[104] TNA, WO71/122, 116/1.

Lord George Forrester was lieutenant colonel. He had joined the army in 1707 as a cornet in the Royal North British Dragoons, served at Oudenarde and Malplaquet, and led the battalion from 1709. His second in command was more experienced. This was Major James Lawson, ensign in 1691, lieutenant in 1694, captain by 1704 and major in 1711. He had served at Schellenberg and Blenheim in 1704 and at Malplaquet in 1709. Of the captains, two had military careers dating from 1704, one from 1706 (Robert Ferguson who was at Blenheim), and the remaining four had commissions dating from 1711. The lieutenants had commissions dating from 1704 (one), 1706 (three), 1707 (one), 1709 (two), 1710 (one), 1711 (two) and 1713 (one). The ensigns had seen a little less service; at the time of battle, one had seen 11 years' service, three 7 years, one had 6 years, one had 5 years and four had 1 year each. Charles Colville, an ensign, had been at Malplaquet. Alexander Arthur, the surgeon, had been with the army since 1696; the chaplain, Samuel Holliday, since 1708; and the adjutant, John Gilchrist, since 1715.[105]

We do not know how experienced all the officers in the other units were. An examination of the army lists of officers for the reign of George I shows that some were certainly inexperienced. Of the seven newly raised regiments under Carpenter and Wills, of 35 captains, only 8 had previous military experience; and none of the lieutenants, ensigns and cornets did. One of these newly commissioned men was Henry Pelham (1694–1754), a country gentleman, who, fresh from university, bought a commission as captain in Dormer's dragoons on 22 July 1715. He later became George II's leading minister from 1743 to his death.[106] Yet others were veterans. James Gardiner (1685–1745) had been a cadet in a Scots unit serving with the Dutch in Flanders and rose to ensign by 1702. He transferred to Borthwick's regiment in the War of the Spanish Succession and was wounded at Ramillies. In 1714 he was a lieutenant in Kerr's dragoons and in 1715 became a captain in Stanhope's newly formed dragoon regiment.[107]

However, all the lieutenant colonels and majors of these regiments had prior military experience garnered from the War of the Spanish Succession, and some from the War of the League of Augsburg, too.[108]

Yet if the leadership of the regular army was at least up to standard, could the same be said of the rank and file? Following the great demobilisation of 1713, the veteran regiments mostly ceased to exist. As noted, new regiments

---
[105] Dalton, *George I's Army*, I, London: Eyre and Spottiswoode, 1930, 351–2.
[106] Dalton, *George I's Army*, I, 106, 113, 115, 117, 118, 120, 123, 124.
[107] *ODNB*, 21, 421.
[108] Dalton, *Army Lists*, I, 106, 113, 115, 117, 118, 120, 123, 124.

were raised in July 1715. Most of those under the command of Carpenter and Wills were the newly raised regiments, including Churchill's and Molesworth's dragoons and Hotham's horse (Carpenter), and those of Munden's dragoons, Dormer's dragoons, Honeywood's dragoons, Stanhope's dragoons, Newton's dragoons and Wynn's dragoons (Wills). The only veteran units were Cobham's Dragoons (Carpenter), Sabine's, Fane's and Preston's regiments of infantry, and Pitt's horse. (Wills).

These units had been raised as part of a government order of July 1715 to raise 13 new regiments of dragoons to total 2,574 men, and eight battalions of foot to total 3,440 men. The dragoon regiments were to comprise six troops each. Each troop would have three officers (captain, lieutenant and cornet), a sergeant, two corporals, a drummer, a hautbois and 28 troopers. The infantry should be made up of 10 companies per battalion, each to possess, apart from three officers (as with the dragoons, but with an ensign instead of a cornet), two sergeants, two corporals, a drummer and 38 privates. A bounty of 40 shillings was payable to each recruit. Lists of men selected as officers were sent to the Secretary at War immediately the colonel had selected them.[109]

On 4 August, Munden wrote to Pulteney to tell him that his dragoon regiment 'was near Compleat, Arm'd & mounted'. He asked about his powers to hold courts martial in case of desertion. On 22 August, gunpowder was issued to the new regiments.[110]

Some of the men in these units had probably never previously fired a shot in anger. Yet others were veterans of the recent war who re-enlisted, especially if they had not yet found gainful employment following demobilisation, judging by the men from these units who were later awarded disability pensions. Among the five cavalrymen that we know of, there was between four months' and 15 years' experience, and they were aged on average 28 years.[111] Even so, they might not have coalesced in their new units, and so morale might not have been as high as it would have been in a more veteran unit where the men knew each other.

At least they were all well armed, with flintlock muskets and bayonets for the infantry, and basket-hilted swords and carbines for the dragoons. They would have had some training, too. Neither general possessed any artillery, though, but in the mobile campaign that this was, these would have only slowed down their forces. Yet they might have been useful for battering the Jacobite army at Preston.

---

[109] TNA, WO4/17, 148.
[110] TNA, WO4/17, 192, 175.
[111] TNA, WO116/1.

The Opposing Sides

The regular infantry were trained to fire in ranks of three, by platoon, volleys of musketry, which had a maximum range of about 100 yards, but were very effective at closer ranges, especially if the men did not fire high. Trained troops could fire two or three volleys per minute. They were also expected to fight at close quarters with fixed bayonets, but hand-to-hand combat was relatively rare.[112]

The cavalry were divided into horse and dragoons. Regiments of horse were more expensive, for they consisted of big men on big horses, trained to engage the enemy cavalry and infantry in close combat with sabres. More commonplace were the dragoons, who began life in the seventeenth century as mounted infantry. They were faster than horse and were used as scouts and to follow up a defeated enemy after the latter had been defeated. In reality, all cavalry played a similar role in the battlefield. Dragoons were also supposed to fight on foot, as the infantry proper did.[113]

How politically reliable the regular forces were was another question. There was concern that some of the officers and men had Jacobite sympathies. Colonel Paul of the Foot Guards had been arrested in the summer of 1715 for having tried to recruit men for the Jacobite cause. In early September 1715, nine men of Honeywood's regiment were found to be disaffected and were arrested; and in the following month, Townshend referred to the 'mutinous behaviour of some of the Invalids' of the Chester garrison.[114] Cornet Sadler of Cobham's dragoons had apparently sympathised with the rioters in July 1715 and was suspended.[115] Some leading Jacobites believed that the army would support them when the time for action occurred.

Finally, there were the civilian forces. It was not uncommon for regular troops and militia to act together on home ground, as they had in the Monmouth Rebellion in 1685. Firstly, there was the County Militia, formed by legislation following the Restoration of 1660. This decreed that landowners supplied men and often horses, the number depending on the annual value of their estates, and paid them; and constables supplied the men with muskets, ammunition and perhaps a sword. They were not uniformed. They would be officered by gentry and nobility, and all would in theory have received a week's training per year. Each county's Lord Lieutenant and his deputy lieutenants had overall responsibility for the militia. They were not obliged to march beyond the county boundaries and were a defensive force.[116] In the 1680s they were seen as

---

[112] Barthorp, *Jacobite Risings*, 25–6.
[113] Barthorp, *Jacobite Risings*, 24–6.
[114] TNA, SP44/118, 27; 333.
[115] TNA, WO4/17, 153.
[116] Jarvis, *Jacobite Risings*, 106–10.

being an adequate police force, to work in support of the regular troops but not as soldiers themselves.[117]

Then there was the posse comitatus. This was the responsibility of the county sheriff. He was able to summon the active men of the county aged from 16 to 60 in the event of civil unrest or any other emergency. Other Whig volunteers, such as those led by Dissenting clergy, were armed with swords, pistols, guns and scythes at the end of sticks.[118]

The regulars were better led, armed and organised than their opponents. Yet their political loyalties were perhaps questionable, and many of the men were but newly raised. However, there was certainly an expectation that they would be able to deal with the Jacobites with ease, Wightman writing, 'those out of Northumberland are the worst that ever were seen, if we can but come fairly at them, I think it no odds but that we must demolish them'.[119] After all, regular troops had smashed Monmouth's rebels at Sedgemoor 30 years previously.

How the forces on each side would perform in the field remained a question which would be impossible to answer until they met. On the face of it, the regular troops seemed to have the advantage of better generals and officers, veteran troops, and proper arms and ammunition.

But, apart from these important tactical considerations, the matter of strategy also loomed high. The Jacobites' over-reaching goal was to unseat George I and replace him with James III and VIII. But they appear to have had no strategy to do so after failing to secure Newcastle, and without this, no concerted effort to forward their aim, except to gather support. At least the regulars had an easy task: to seek out their enemy and destroy them as a fighting force wherever they could be found. This was to prove a severe handicap to the Jacobite army in England.

---

[117] Peter Earle, *Monmouth's Rebels: The Road to Sedgemoor*, London: Wiedenfield and Nicolson, 1977, 82–6.

[118] Ryder, *Diary*, 234.

[119] TNA, SP54/9/83.

ILLUSTRATIONS

Illustration 1   Earl of Derwentwater. Author's collection.

Illustration 2   Thomas Forster, MP. Courtesy of John Nicholls MBE.

Illustration 3   Francis Atterbury. Author's collection.

Illustration 4   Baron George Carpenter. Mezzotint by John Faber Jr, after Johan van Diest (1719 or after). NPG D11252. National Portrait Gallery, London.

Illustration 5   Hoghton Tower. Courtesy of Sir Bernard de Hoghton.

Illustration 6   Richard Towneley. Towneley Hall Museum.

Illustration 7   Sir Charles Wills. Mezzotint by John Simon (published by Edward Cooper, after Michael Dahl, published circa 1700–1725). NPG D19943. National Portrait Gallery, London.

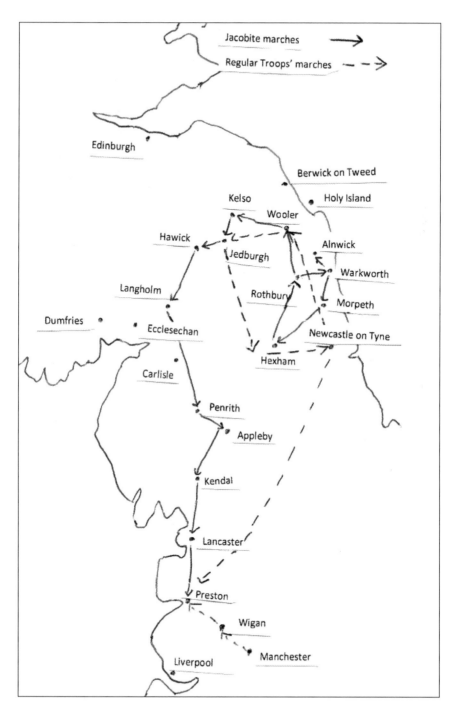

Illustration 8　Map of the North of England. Author.

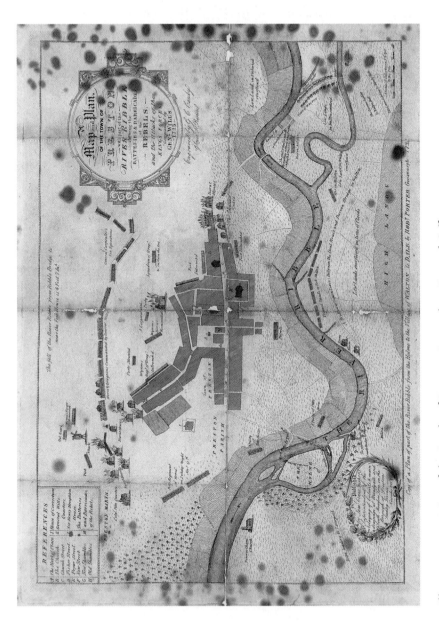

Illustration 9 Map of the Battle of Preston. Lancashire Record Office.

Illustration 10   Re-enactors: Redcoat soldiers, 2013. Author's photo.

Illustration 11 Re-enactors: Jacobites, 2013. Author's photo.

Chapter 6

The Battle of Preston, 12–14 November 1715

The climactic battle of the campaign is inevitably narrated in all histories of the Fifteen, in local histories and in histories of battles in Britain/England, though often based on a narrow number of sources, and described very briefly. Primary sources, written by defeated and embittered Jacobite junior officers and rank and file, attack the decisions of their leaders, while pro-government sources are limited in their descriptions. As to historians, Baynes's account is lengthiest and Szechi's concise account includes the most diverse range of sources. Analysis of the battle, though, is limited. Baynes acknowledged that the attackers had 'a difficult task', but that 'the squabble between Carpenter and Wills draws attention away from the gallantry of Preston's Regiment'.[1] Szechi is critical of Wills, 'the worst commander on the government side', and writes that 'if the Jacobites had responded as aggressively to his botched attacks on Preston as some of them were clamouring to do, he might have gained the special distinction of being the architect of a truly catastrophic defeat'.[2] On the other hand, the Jacobite command is dealt with sympathetically by Gooch: 'it is hardly fair to question Forster's courage because he sought terms when it became apparent he faced overwhelming odds'.[3] What follows is a detailed, well-sourced analytic narrative of the battle and its immediate aftermath.

Preston is one of a handful of places in Britain which witnessed two battles – Falkirk, St Albans and Newbury being the other three. It has the distinction of being the last battle on English soil; some may prefer to award that accolade to Clifton Moor, but the confrontation there in 1745 was more a rearguard action than a battle between two armies. The second battle of Preston was also unusual because it took place almost wholly in a built-up area, whereas the first battle in 1648 took place largely to the east of the town. There was only one other battle during the Jacobite Rebellions of 1689–1746 in which street fighting played a

---

[1] Baynes, *Jacobite Rising*, 117, 204.
[2] Szechi, *1715*, 196.
[3] Gooch, *Desperate Faction*, 84.

significant part. That was at Dunkeld in August 1689, when the numerically superior Jacobite Highlanders were defeated by the defending Cameronian Regiment (later Preston's foot, who, ironically, saw service at Preston in 1715) under Colonel Cleland. The advantage in such fighting belonged to the defenders, for in the said battle 1,200 were able to defeat four times their own number (neither side had artillery).

Although it is difficult to envisage the battlefield of Preston now, given that there are no buildings which survive from the time of the battle and in any case the town has expanded considerably since 1715, contemporary maps make a recreation relatively easy. The town of Preston was built on rising ground and its principal street, running west to east, was Fishergate Street. To the south-east the street led to the road to Wigan, to the west to Liverpool. Friargate Street was the chief thoroughfare leading northwards, towards Lancaster. The first mile of the road towards Wigan was a hedge-lined lane which ended with Ribble Bridge and a little more to the south-east Darwen Bridge. To the west of Fishergate was a marsh bordering on the river. Surrounding the town were enclosed fields, presumably market gardens catering for the townsfolk's food needs. To the south and west of the town was the River Ribble, flowing westwards from Yorkshire and reaching the Irish Sea just to the west of Preston.

Celia Fiennes wrote of Preston a few years before the battle thus:

> Preston stands on a hill is a very good market town … there is a very spacious Market place and pretty Church and severall good houses; at the entrance to the town was a very good house, which was a Lawyers, all stone work … gardens on each side of the house … there was 2 or 3 more such houses in the town and the generality of the buildings especially in 2 or 3 of the great streets were very handsome, better than in most country towns, and the streets spacious and well pitch'd.[4]

Daniel Defoe, writing a decade after the battle, concentrated on the town's social scene:

> Preston is a fine town, and is tolerably full of people … Here's no manufacture, the town is full of attorneys, proctors and notaries … The people are gay here, though

---

[4] Celia Fiennes, *The Journeys of Celia Fiennes*, ed. Christopher Morris, New York: Chanticleer Press, 1949, 187.

not perhaps the richer for that; but it has by that obtained the name of Proud Preston. Here is a great deal of good company.[5]

Preliminaries to Conflict

As we have seen, General Wills was aware of the location of his enemy and had gathered his troops at Wigan on 11 November. Although Forster was informed of Carpenter's movements to his north by the Rev. Paul, he may have been in the dark about those of Wills. As Patten wrote, 'All this while they had not the least Intimation of the Forces that were preparing to oppose them, much less of the Approach of the King's army'. This was because Forster relied on the promises made by the Lancashire Jacobites, who were in sole charge of providing him with local intelligence. They assured him that they would let him know when any enemy was within 40 miles of him. As said, no money was spent garnering intelligence. As with the support promised, Forster was let down again.[6] Certainly some were surprised – Widdrington admitted as much at his trial.[7]

Yet this may not have been so. One source suggests that Derwentwater was informed about their enemies very late on 11 November. According to the Merse officer:

> When this letter was communicated to General Forster, he appeared dispirited, and then, as at all other times, very unfit for such an important command. He had nothing to say, but sent the letter to my Lord Kenmure. His lordship upon reading it, going with other persons of note to Mr Forster's quarters, found himself in bed without the least concern. A council being called, it was thought convenient to detach a party of Horse towards Wigan, as an advance guard, and another party of Foot to Darwin and Ribble Bridges, and the whole army had orders to be in readiness to take the field. But to our great surprise, these orders were countermanded by Forster.[8]

All that we can be certain about is that the Jacobites took no positive action on the day prior to the battle, though since the foot soldiers had only arrived on the previous day, a day's rest was not unreasonable. As ever, the Jacobite leadership was not enthusiastic for a clash of arms – heightened perhaps, by the hope that

---

[5] Defoe, *Tour*, 548.
[6] Patten, *History*, 80.
[7] *Political State*, XI, 1716, 115.
[8] Anon, *A Letter*, 5.

they could have benefitted from support from Manchester and the resources of Liverpool before such a contest would be joined; perhaps hoping that it would be unnecessary, as in 1660.

Forces Involved

It is difficult to ascertain numbers involved in the battle.

Regular Forces under General Wills

    Cavalry
      Brigade 1 – Brigadier Honeywood
        Honeywood's dragoons
        Wynn's dragoons
      Brigade 2 – Brigadier Munden
        Munden's dragoons
        Stanhope's dragoons
      Brigade 3 – Brigadier Dormer
        Dormer's dragoons
        Pitt's horse
    Infantry
      Preston's foot
    Artillery
      None
    Auxiliary forces
      Lancashire Militia, under Hoghton (560 strong)
      'A considerable party' of armed Dissenters under James Wood and Mr Walker (300 strong).[9]

Numbers are difficult to ascertain, and historians differ widely, with estimates varying from 1,600 to 5,000.[10] Clerk erroneously claims that Wills led 1,000 cavalrymen and a company of infantry.[11] One source claims that the combined forces of Wills and Carpenter (who had three cavalry regiments) were 2,500.[12] This would make each of the above units about 250 strong; or allowing for the

---

[9] Rae, *History*, 318n; Ryder, *Diary*, 231.
[10] Barthorp, *Jacobite Rebellions*, 7; Monod, *Jacobitism*, 321.
[11] Clerk, *Memoirs*, 92.
[12] *Political State*, XI, 1716, 167.

cavalry units to be weaker – Carpenter's force was probably only about 600 – and allowing 220 men per cavalry regiment, Preston's foot may have numbered as many as 700 men. Numbers could have been lower. Returns for the regular units of the Duke of Argyle's command in Scotland on 28 October 1715 would certainly indicate so. Argyle's regiments of cavalry numbered between 166 and 174 men each, excluding officers, and the infantry battalions were between 238 and 369 men strong, again excluding officers.[13] It is also worth noting that of Wills's dragoon regiments, all were newly raised; only Pitt's Horse and Preston's Foot were veteran units. Wills's force probably numbered between 1,400 and 1,800. By Continental standards, this was very low (Marlborough had 52,000 troops in his multi-national army at Blenheim in 1704). Even Argyle, who constantly complained about his weak force, had over 3,000 soldiers at Sherriffmuir. As will be seen, the militia and volunteers did not take part in assaults on the town.

Wills's complete command did not take part in the action. As noted, he had an additional two veteran battalions of infantry, Fane's and Sabine's, but did not wait for them to arrive before attacking. Ensign Charles Colville (1691–1775) of the Grenadier company of Preston's foot, wrote, 'indeed I have heard him blamed for not waiting for two old regiments on infantry which he knew well were within a few days march of him'.[14] However, it is uncertain where these battalions were; on 3 November Fane's was at Litchfield and on 12 January Sabine's was at Hereford.[15] Yet a newspaper reported they were two days' march away.[16]

Jacobite Forces under Thomas Forster

    Scottish Forces
      Lowland horse
        Hamilton's troop – 4 men
        Hume's troop – 20 men
        Lockhart's troop – 14 men
        Carnwath's troop – 19 men
        Winton's troop – 15 men

---

[13] TNA, SP54/9/92.
[14] Colville, 'Military Memoirs', 60.
[15] TNA, WO5/20, 116, 182.
[16] *The Daily Courant*, 4388, 16 November 1715.

Scottish infantry
  Mackintosh's battalion – 295 men
  Lord Charles Murray's regiment – 137 men
  Mar's battalion – 36 men
  Strathmore's regiment – 158 men
  Nairn's regiment – 122 men

NB: Drummond's regiment appears to have ceased to exist as an entity by now – presumably all had deserted on entering England and the remnant joined other units.

Unregimented (or in single figure commands) Scots infantry – 328 men

It is important to note that the Scots included men from both the Highlands and the Lowlands.

English Forces
  English cavalry
    Douglas' Troop – 15 men
    Shaftoe's Troop – 16 men
    Hunter's Troop – 14 men
  Organised into tiny commands – 150 men
  Unregimented (mainly Lancastrians) – 549 men

NB: Some of the above would have had horses, especially if part of a gentleman's command from Northumberland or Lancashire, but some would have been on foot.

Artillery
Six cannons of uncertain calibre (probably small) taken from Lancaster with untrained gunners; a sailor in the force, who, according to Patten, 'did not know much how to use them', was in charge.

Totals: 1,026 Scots, 744 English, 12 Irish and one Dutchman. Furthermore, 17 men were thought to be killed in the battle. Grand total of 1,800.[17]

NB: All numbers above are of those who were made prisoner and some were taken after the battle but had not participated in it, such as Shirburn and Molyneux. The actual force would have been numerically stronger.

---

[17] *The Daily Courant*, 16 Nov. 1715; KB8/66.

Again, as with Wills's force, total numbers are impossible to ascertain. Historians are divided, with Monod opining at 2,500 but others cautiously avoiding giving a number.[18]

As for contemporaries, Patten did not even try. The lowest estimate was 1,400 and, as noted above, this was utterly erroneous.[19] A press report alleged they were between 2,000 and 3,000.[20] Rae estimated them at above 4,000.[21] The highest number was quoted in the press and in correspondence between Townshend and Craggs as between 4,000 and 5,000.[22] And a reference in the West Riding Sessions refers to 1,500 men escaping the battle, which if added to the above would make 3,300.[23]

The complete number is the sum of the prisoners taken on 14 November, those killed and those who escaped. Although the first number is approximately 1,783 (based on TNA, KB8/66 and various contemporary published sources), those killed amounted to about 17, and the number of those who escaped the final debacle is impossible to know. Various figures were put forward, as we shall see, but it is impossible to know how accurate these are. Certainly, it would have not been too difficult for numbers of Lancastrians either to have escaped on the night of 12 November when not all escape routes were blocked, or to have melted back into the civil population with the connivance of friends and relatives. But as to the number who did, no answer can be given. Perhaps the true figure might have been about 2,500 – if the Jacobites had about 1,400 when entering England, and over 500 Englishmen from the north-western counties joined, then 2,000 must surely be an absolute minimum number. But we cannot know how many fled before the surrender. Perhaps about 2,500 is a reasonable estimate. However, not all may have been combatants. Many were servants, possibly unarmed.

Compared to the numbers involved in Continental warfare in the early eighteenth century, these numbers are low indeed (there were about 108,000 combatants at Blenheim in 1704, for example). Even when compared to the numbers in other attempts to overthrow the state in early modern England, the numbers are low. Mar had almost 10,000 men under his command, and there were perhaps about 20,000 Jacobites in arms in Scotland.[24] Even allowing

---

[18] Monod, *Jacobitism*, 321.
[19] *Political State*, XI, 1716, 167.
[20] *Weekly Journal*, 255, 19 November 1715.
[21] Rae, *History*, 324.
[22] *St. James' Evening Post*, 73, 15–17 November 1715.
[23] West Yorkshire Archive Service: Wakefield Archives, QS10/13, 112a.
[24] Pittock, *Jacobitism*, 45.

for the less martial nature of England, Monmouth had 3,000 men under his command in 1685.[25]

Even so, with the two armies roughly evenly matched in numbers, or perhaps a slight superiority in numbers for the Jacobites, the advantage lay with the latter, because they were defending positions; conventionally, a 3:1 superiority over the defenders is needed for a successful assault. The odds seemed to be stacked in their favour, despite the difficulties as stated in the previous chapter, if they stood.

At last the two sides were about to fight one another. For the Jacobites, this was involuntarily; after avoiding combat for the past weeks, they now had no alternative but to do so. Retreat against a faster-moving army would result in the loss of most if not all of their force, as infantry would be caught in the open. Wills, on the other hand, was enthusiastic for a trial of strength, as per his orders. With instructions to attack as soon as possible, he did not feel it necessary to await Carpenter's regiments. Furthermore, ambitious for a promotion to lieutenant general, he probably wished to take all the credit for what he may have assumed would be an easy victory over what he imagined, not without some justification, were poorly armed and indifferently led amateurs (Monmouth's irregulars had been routed by regular troops three decades ago). Colville stated the reason as follows:

> I must do that justice to our General, who as I observed before has been blamed for not waiting for more troops, that being posted on the Grenadier Company and having thereby an opportunity of hearing the General's orders and remarks, that when we came to the Ribble Bridge and found the bridge and hollow way not defended, he said that people must surely be in a confusion else they would surely have defended their strong post, and therefore I will attack them and not give them time to think.[26]

Had Wills but known it, troops attacking Preston on two occasions in 1643 had taken one or two hours to take the town. Yet even poor troops can make an effective stand behind cover, especially when led by some decent junior officers.

Day One – Saturday, 12 November

Some Jacobites may have planned to march from Preston on 11 November towards Manchester, but did not do so. However, the march from Preston

---

[25] *ODNB*, 49, 402.
[26] Colville, 'Military Memoirs', 61.

towards Manchester was only postponed until the following day. As preparations were underway on this subsequent day, reports began to come through that Wills's forces were marching towards them. Forster did not believe these at first, but such was their number that he was forced to acknowledge their truth in the end. Already the Rev. Paul, carrying messages to allies in Staffordshire and Leicestershire, had travelled southward and had been stopped by Wills's troopers, but had been allowed to pass.[27]

Wills's troops had to march 11 miles before reaching Darwen Bridge and then Ribble Bridge. Apart from his troops, he also had nine wagons laden with army baggage and these were supplied by four civilian contractors. Once he knew that the Jacobites were still at Preston, he gave the order to march at day break, perhaps at about seven in the morning. He arranged his men prior to the march in the following fashion. A captain and 50 of Preston's foot and the same number of an unspecified cavalry regiment formed the vanguard. Following them were the remainder of Preston's foot. Next were Honeywood's brigade, then Dormer's, and then Munden's at the rear. The baggage wagons followed on afterwards. After a few miles, Wills was approached by James Wood and Mr Walker, two dissenting ministers, and their armed flocks. They offered to help, and Wills agreed to let them accompany his men and that he would allot them a place when they had arrived at Preston. It is probable that the Dissenters acted in this fashion because of their antipathy towards the Jacobites – as previously noted, mobs had destroyed a number of Dissenting chapels in Lancashire in June of that year.[28]

By the time the Jacobites were certain of the danger they were in, a body of infantry had already marched as far as the Ribble Bridge. Two houses stood by the bridge. Forster, with a party of cavalry, rode south and saw the vanguard of the regular army. Patten was sent back with this news to the forces in the town while Forster's men reconnoitred a ford across the Ribble in case it could be used as a means of making a flank attack against the regulars. In the sixteenth century, the bridge was described as being 'a great stone bridge of Ribble, having a very great arches. From Ribble Bridge to Preston half a mile'.[29] Lieutenant Colonel John Farquharson of Invercall had command of the 100 'choice, stout and well-armed Men' of Mackintosh's battalion which were holding the bridge. They were resolute in their task, but were ordered back into the town.[30] According to Clarke, these forces were 300 cavalrymen despatched by Derwentwater.[31]

---

[27] Patten, *History*, 80–81.
[28] Rae, *History*, 318n; LRO, QSP 1091/8.
[29] *VCH Lancashire, VII*, 74.
[30] Patten, *History*, 81.
[31] Clarke, 'Journal', 521.

Apparently this nobleman, on seeing Wills's vanguard, believed that they were on the Jacobite side, shouting, 'they are all for us'.[32]

They were pulled back into the town. This order was criticised by Patten, who remarked, 'This Retreat was another wrong step, and has been condemned on all hands as one of the greatest oversights they could have been guilty of'. He stated that there were no fords nearby and that the bridge could be barricaded and made impregnable to assault.[33] Charles Edward Stuart in 1745, on seeing the town and bridge, also thought it strange 'that they Should have deserted the Bridge'.[34] However, Mackintosh later remarked, that the bridge was untenable because Wills's men could have crossed the river by the fords, the two at Penwrotham and one at Walton-Le-Dale, presumably.[35] His reasoning has been borne out by historians in the following two centuries.[36] If Wills did not know where the other crossing points were, he had enough Lancashire loyalists who would have been able to tell him. Yet troops crossing a ford would be disordered and vulnerable to a counter attack by hostile troops stationed in the vicinity. However, the ultra-defensive and cautious mentality of the Jacobite leaders would not have supported such an aggressive form of forward defence.

Yet the alternative plan, to fight in the town itself, was also criticised, as being 'the maddest resolution that ever man could be capable of, to pretend to keep one open [i.e. unwalled] place without provisions or ammunition'.[37] Indeed, one Jacobite later claimed:

> At first it was resolved to fight them in the fair fields, which … probably would have ended gloriously, for us, for we were all hearty, and well inclined, to the work and the enemy were mostly raw green men and much fatigued … For was it not plain madness for more or equall a number to the enemy and of as good hearts, if not better, to coop themselves up.[38]

On the other hand, infantry are particularly vulnerable, in the open, to cavalry, and the Jacobite commanders were, if nothing else, cautious, as their conduct to date proved.

---

[32] TWAS, CP3/22.
[33] Patten, *History*, 81.
[34] John Murray, 'Memorials of Murray of Broughton, 1740–1747', ed. Robert E. Bell, *Scottish History Society*, 27, 1898, 246.
[35] Patten, *History*, 104.
[36] Baynes, *Jacobite Rising*, 115.
[37] BC, Atholl Papers, 45/12/77.
[38] TNA, SP54/9/107.

Inside the town, 'the Rebels were not idle ... nor did they appear in the least discouraged, but applied themselves resolutely to their Business', and barricades had been erected at the principal streets. There were two on Churchgate to the east of the town. The most easterly, just within the outer limits of the built-up area of Preston, was manned by troops led by Lord Charles Murray. In support of him, near to the parish church, St John's, was a barricade under Brigadier Mackintosh's command. In reserve were the gentlemen volunteers under the direction of Derwentwater, Kenmure, Winton and Nithsdale. They were near to the parish church. Others were stationed centrally in the market place. Derwentwater nominated Patten as his aide and the clergyman rode around the town in this role. The third main barrier was to the north of the town, on Windmill Lane, and was under the direction of Colonel Mackintosh. The final barricade was posted on the west side of town, at the westerly end of Fishergate, and the men there were under the command of Major Miller and Mr Douglas. As well as these four main entry routes into Preston, the by-lanes were also manned.[39] Troops manned the houses near to the barricades, and stood ready in cellars and at windows to receive the enemy.[40] One Captain Innes, with 50 men, was posted in Hoghton's Preston town house 'which was of great service'.[41] Meanwhile, only Carnwath's horsemen and some of the English were mounted; most of those with horses were dismounted.[42]

Cannon were also placed at these barricades. There were two at the Churchgate barricade 'charged with small bullets', perhaps as a form of canister.[43] Presumably there were another two at Windmill Lane and the remaining two at Fishergate. Four cannons were described as 'good' and the other two were of very small calibre. They had been mounted on carriages found at Hoghton's house.[44] That such a competent defence was mounted was probably due to the fact that there was a smattering of officers among the Jacobites who had seen military service, albeit at a junior rank. Richard Shuttleworth encouraged others by 'giving directions how to make the Trenches' and 'pull'd off his coat & work'd amongst the men himself', claiming the guns would be loaded with 80 bullets and would do great execution. Derwentwater offered money to his men to encourage them.[45]

---

[39] Patten, *History*, 83.
[40] Clarke, 'Journal', 521.
[41] *Weekly Journal*, 10 March 1716.
[42] BC, Atholl Papers, 45/12/77.
[43] *Weekly Journal*, 10 March 1716.
[44] Colville, 'Military Memoirs', 60.
[45] Clarke, 'Journal', 521; LRO, DDX2244/1.

Not all believed the defence was efficient. The Merse officer wrote, 'our army was scarcely modelled when the enemy was upon us'.[46] A Lowlander noted that they had managed to 'coop themselves up in a town, which had no wall, and where there was no provisions ... But we were no better used in the defence of the town'.[47] Even more fatally, there was also no overall command or co-ordination of the Jacobite army; as was said in the following year at the trials, 'no orders at all was given but everybody did as he pleased'.[48]

Finally, it is possible that some men were not assigned to any military station. Some may have lacked weapons and/or ammunition. Possibly the 245 servants who accompanied the gentry and nobility did nothing apart from, at most, take care of the horses and any baggage there was. Others behaved less honourably. Patten refers to one (unnamed) Jacobite remaining in an ale house all day.[49]

Wills's men arrived at Ribble Bridge at one o'clock. The Jacobite troops there retreated to the town, so their enemy had an uncontested passage over the bridge and towards the town. Initially, though, Wills was cautious. Perhaps he recalled that Cromwell's troops had been ambushed on their way up along the narrow lane lined with hedgerows from the bridge to the town, as mill stones had been rolled down the slope, narrowly failing to kill the great dictator in 1648. Whatever the reason, Patten claims that Wills 'did indeed expect some Difficulty and Opposition at this Place'. He was doubly certain that an ambush was in the offing once he was aware that the bridge had been abandoned. Therefore, 'he proceeded with Caution, and caused the Hedges and Fields to be view'd and the ways Laid open for his Cavalry to enter'. The infantry drew up in platoons ready for firing upon their enemies prior to crossing the bridge.[50] Finding none were awaiting his troops here, caution turned to optimism and he expected that the Jacobites must have left Preston and be in full retreat to Scotland.[51]

However, he was soon disabused of such notions and prepared for battle. Wills surveyed the town and noted the barricades flung up there, as well as the cannon which had been posted to reinforce these positions. He then made his own dispositions. There was to be a two-pronged attack to storm the barricades and thus take the town. To the south-east of the town, Honeywood was to command Preston's regiment and 50 men (dismounted) from each of the five dragoon regiments, supported by the remainder of Honeywood's dragoons (mounted),

---

[46] Anon, *A Letter*, 6.
[47] TNA SP54/9/107
[48] LRO, DDX2244/1.
[49] Patten, *History*, 87.
[50] Colville, 'Military Memoirs', 60; Patten, *History*, 82.
[51] Patten, *History*, 82.

in case the Jacobites tried to break out. To the north of the town, Dormer was in charge. Under him were the dismounted dragoons of Dormer's and Wynn's regiments, and a dismounted squadron of Stanhope's dragoons. In order, to support this attack, were Pitt's horse and the remaining squadrons of Munden's and Stanhope's dragoons. The auxiliary forces were placed to the south of the Ribble, to prevent any Jacobites escaping in that direction and to prevent any aid coming from Manchester (in retrospect, Wills claimed he wished he had assigned them a more active role).[52] There was to be no attack on the barrier on Fishergate Street, probably because Wills lacked the men to adequately attack three entrances to the town at once and also because the marshy ground there would make it difficult for troops to form up. Some of the troops (the grenadier company of Preston's foot) probably used grenades in the assault, but these were probably of little use; one uncovered in the nineteenth century had failed to explode.[53]

After the troops had got themselves into position, the assault commenced at about two in the afternoon.[54] Honeywood's attack on Brigadier Mackintosh's barrier was met with a murderous fire, not only from behind the barricades but from the cellars and windows of nearby houses. Some of the English Jacobites helped repulse the attack. According to Patten, Hunter 'behav'd with great Vigour and obstinacy at Preston, where he took possession of some Houses during the Attack, and galled that brave Regiment ... making a great Slaughter out of the windows'. Likewise, Douglas: 'very vigorous at the Action at Preston; where he and his men were possess'd of several Houses, and did a great deal of Harm to His Majesty's Forces from the Windows'.[55] So devastating was this musketry that within 10 minutes, according to Clarke, 120 of the attackers had been killed and the remainder obliged to retreat.[56] Another source gives 180 as the casualty figure, including several officers.[57] These figures should be taken as being impressionistic. The very real fog of war caused by the abundance of musket smoke in confined spaces made accuracy impossible, even without any bias. The artillery used by the defenders was less successful, the bullets hitting the sides of houses 'so that no execution was done thereby'.[58] Yet according to

---

[52] Rae, *History*, 319n.
[53] Charles Hardwick, *History of the Borough of Preston and its Environs in the County of Lancashire*, I, Preston: Worthington and Company, 1857, 229n.
[54] Clarke, 'Journal', 521.
[55] Patten, *History*, 49.
[56] Clarke, 'Journal', 521.
[57] BC, Atholl Papers, 45/12/77.
[58] Patten, *History*, 90.

Colville, those Jacobites firing out of houses 'did not hurt us as they durst not look out of the windows to take their aim'.[59]

Apart from the fatalities, many of the rank and file among the attackers were wounded. Edward Cavin a 21-year-old of Wynn's dragoons, with four months' service had been 'shot in the head and left thigh'. Adam Cadwell, from the same regiment and three years his senior, was 'shot through ye body'. Another was Guy Cerlton, aged 28; 'his breast bone broke at Preston his right leg disabled by a sword'. Henry Pawley, 30 years old, of Stanhope's dragoons, was 'wounded at Preston wholly disabled in his left thigh'. Preston's battalion took most casualties. Three suffered eye wounds, one was wounded in both legs, another had part of his right shoulder lost by a cannon ball. There were also arm and hand wounds.[60]

There were many instances of individual bravery on both sides. Regular officers led from the front. Brigadier Honeywood was wounded in the assault.[61] Among those who could not retreat was his fellow, Major John Preston, adjutant to Preston's foot, who had been wounded and would have been killed outright had not Captain Nicholas Wogan risked his own life to try to save that of his enemy. Although Preston died soon after, he acknowledged his enemy's gallantry and subsequent kindness and hoped Wogan would be civilly used after the surrender.[62] Another instance of bravery on the Jacobite side was when a man who carried the gunpowder cask to supply his compatriots at the barrier was told he risked death in taking it there; he still agreed to do so, and was killed in the attempt.[63] It was said, 'During the whole Action Mr Radcliffe was in the midst of the Fire, and expos'd to so much Danger as the meanest soldier then upon Duty'.[64] The Hon. Basil Hamilton, captain on the Jacobite side, 'behaved himself with a great deal of Courage in the Action'.[65]

Forster allegedly appeared at this barrier – the only positive action that anyone accredits him with during the fighting – and exposed himself to hostile fire, and ordered Mackintosh to sally out against the retreating regulars. When Mackintosh refused to do so, Forster threatened him with a court martial for disobeying his commanding officer. Mackintosh explained his reasoning:

---

[59] Colville, 'Military Memoirs', 60.
[60] TNA,WO116/1
[61] Patten, *History*, 85, 101.
[62] Patten, *History*, 50.
[63] Patten, *History*, 102.
[64] Radcliffe, *Genuine and Impartial*, 38.
[65] Patten, *History*, 39.

That if his Foot had sallied out, they might by that means been parted from the Horse, and so left naked to have been cut off: Besides, nothing more frightens the Highlanders than Horse and Cannon. As for obeying Mr Forster, in letting the Horse sally out, he said, if the Horse had attempted any such Thing, they would have gone through the fire of his men; for they were afraid the Horse design'd such a Thing, and would have been made able to have made a Retreat and left them pent up in the Town.[66]

After all, Jacobite infantry caught in the open at Cromdale in 1690 had been routed.

Some of the officers of Preston's regiment learnt that there was an unbarricaded lane in which the adjacent houses were unmanned. They met some resistance there, but pushed it aside. Apparently the Jacobites there had been given orders to withdraw. Captain Innes with 50 Highlanders had garrisoned Hoghton's house, which was nearby, but they were told to withdraw by Forster, though they could probably have held out. This house was a key strategic point, as the Merse officer wrote, 'it did command the head of the Hollow Way that leads from the bridge to the town, and the street in the Mercat Place, and a great part of the neighbouring fields'.[67] This order was initially resisted by Innes: 'at first he refused to obey without a written order'.[68] Even so, in their bid to take possession of it, some of Preston's regiment were killed by musketry from Jacobites in nearby houses. The regulars also secured possession of a house opposite to Hoghton's. The troops in these two houses accounted for 'almost all the Loss the Rebels sustained during the action'. As Colville explained, 'from which we had a full view of the rebels and soon made them quit their post and retire into the church'.[69] Patten blamed Mackintosh for such inept orders to withdraw in his bid to clear Forster of any blame.[70]

Others of Preston's regiment then progressed through the streets and came up against Mackintosh's barrier. Lord Forrester, showing great bravery, reconnoitred the situation in order to note where the Jacobites were posted. He was fired upon, but remained unscathed and, returning to his men, led them against the barrier. A terrible fire from the barricade and adjacent houses caused 'a great many of that old and gallant Regiment' to be killed or wounded. John Hunter's men made 'a great Slaughter' by firing from house windows. Forrester

---

[66] Patten, *History*, 98, 105.
[67] Anon, *A Letter*, 6.
[68] TNA, SP54/9/107.
[69] Colville, 'Military Memoir', 60.
[70] Patten, *History*, 84.

himself was hit several times, though none proved mortal. When his men returned fire, they could do little damage to their opponents who were at least partially concealed by the available cover, and who could fire their well-aimed shots at the attackers with ease. A few shots did strike home, hitting at least three Jacobite officers who later died of their wounds.[71]

Artillery fire was largely ineffectual. The seaman in charge of the two guns facing Preston's regiment 'acted so madly, whether it was that he had too little Judgement, or too much Ale, or perhaps both'. His first shot knocked a chimney down. The second was better, doing 'execution, and oblig'd the Regiment to halt'. And that is all that is known of the cannon fire.[72]

Murray's barrier was also attacked. Although Murray was hard pressed, he and his men made a gallant defence; Patten refers to Murray thus: 'his Courage and Behaviour at a Barrier, where His Majesty's Forces made a bold attack, was singularly brave'. According to one source, 'My Lord Charles Murray ... showed undaunted Courage and killed severall with his own hand'.[73] Others were involved in hand-to-hand fighting, 'close work with sword and pistol ... our gentry attacked the enemy bravely with their broadswords. The dispute lasted a long time'.[74] Murray called for Patten to summon assistance from the reserves under Derwentwater. Patten returned with 50 men. The clergyman was then asked to stand atop the barrier and to view the situation. He was wearing his clergyman's robes and was not suspected of being a Jacobite, and so no one fired at him. He then reported back to Murray. There was then a renewed assault, presumably by the elements of the dismounted regiments of dragoons, for Patten writes that they were 'for the most part, raw, new-listed Men and seemed unwilling to fight, yet the Bravery and good Conduct of experienced Officers, supplied very much that Defect'.[75]

Forrester's men were also fired upon by a flank attack by Derwentwater's volunteers, 'and received the enemy with a very brisk and successful fire'. The Merse officer suggested that artillery be placed in the churchyard to demolish Hoghton's house and for Derwentwater (described as 'brave and undaunted') and Murray to attack. Forster vetoed it, arguing 'the body of the town was the security of the army'.[76] Yet eventually, after suffering losses, the troops were

---

[71] BC, Atholl Papers, 45/12/77.
[72] Patten, *History*, 90–91.
[73] Patten, *History*, 44–5.
[74] TNA, SP54/9/107.
[75] Patten, *History*, 86.
[76] Anon., *A Letter*, 7.

reluctant to renew the assault, one source claiming 'they never durst approach for the dragoons were all raw men and those that came within shott never returned'.[77]

There had been another attack on the south side of the town at four. Here, 300 regulars entered a back street which abutted Churchgate Street. Again, accurate fire on the part of the defenders, who lined gardens, walls and hedges, resulted in, allegedly, 140 regulars being killed.[78]

Although most of the action occurred in the eastern part of the town, there was also fighting elsewhere. Colonel Mackintosh's barrier on the north side of Preston was attacked by Dormer's troops. Mackintosh had nearly 300 men under his command. Again, his men 'made a dreadful Fire upon the King's Forces, killing many on the spot', and again the attackers had 'to make a Retreat'. Dormer received a shot in his leg. Once again, Patten alleges that such a retreat was due to the troops being but newly raised men.[79]

As night drew on, one tactic employed by both sides was to burn property near to the Jacobite barriers. Dormer had Captain Gardiner, Sergeant Johnstoun, Corporal John Marlow and a dozen troopers of Stanhope's to burn houses up to the barricade they had recently attacked.[80] Apparently, eye-witnesses observed that Gardiner 'signalized himself very particularly: for he headed a little body of men … about twelve, and set fire to a barricado of the rebels, in the face of their whole army while they were pouring in their shot, by which eight of the twelve that attended him fell'.[81]

Some houses and barns were burnt near to the entrance of Churchgate street, thus forcing the Jacobites nearby to fall back. According to Colville, some Jacobites were taken prisoner and passed back to the dragoons.[82] The smoke caused by the burning buildings enabled troops to move without being fired upon or to dislodge enemies from their positions. Wills's men were ordered to light up the houses which they occupied. This enabled them to see their targets, but also enabled the Jacobites to see theirs. The ensuing exchanges of musketry thus killed and wounded several on both sides. Orders were then given to extinguish the lights, but these were interpreted as instructions to put more candles in the windows.[83] Trenches were also dug to help keep the regulars' two wings in communication in

---

[77] BC, Atholl Papers, 45/12/77.
[78] Clarke, 'Journal', 521.
[79] Patten, *History*, 88.
[80] Rae, *History*, 320.
[81] Phillip Doddridge, *Some Remarkable Passages in the Life of the Hon. Colonel James Gardiner*, Hedley: Thomas and Cornish, 1812, 95–6.
[82] Colville, 'Military Memoirs', 60.
[83] Patten, *History*, 87–8.

case of attack, and these were supervised by a Lieutenant Robinson.[84] Meanwhile, both armies lay on their arms and there was sporadic fire.[85]

At the end of the day, some properties to the north of the town were also burnt. Had the wind not being blowing northwards, such arson might well have burnt down most of the town.[86] A total of 29 houses, 2 cottages, 10 barns, 4 outbuildings, 2 stables and 1 mill were destroyed; of these, 6 were on Churchgate and nine on Friargate.[87]

Many among the Jacobite command came in for censure. One source claimed, 'our commanding officers, when there was Use for them, either could not be found, or when got, could not command'.[88] Widdrington later confessed that the reason for his inaction was because he was confined indoors due to an attack of gout. According to Patten, 'I could never discover any thing like Boldness or Bravery in him, especially after His Majesty's Forces came before Preston'.[89] Apparently, Forster was similarly confined: 'The maids of Generall Forster's Lodgings will take their Oaths out that he was in Bedd with a sack possett in the hottest time of ye action'.[90] Others among the Jacobite leadership were less than active, Patten asserting that unspecified individuals 'kept themselves warm in a chimney corner during the heat of the Action'.[91] However, among the Jacobite leaders, Derwentwater shone. It was said of him, 'No man of Distinction behaved better than my Lord Derwentwater' by exposing himself to hostile fire, encouraging the men by gifts of money and helping throw up entrenchments for the artillery.[92]

Meanwhile, Mackintosh began to write a letter to Mar, letting him know of the army's success.[93] Others were less confident. Some Jacobites took the opportunity provided by nightfall to escape. According to Rae, 'a great many made their Escape through the secret Passages and By-Lanes into the Country'. Some had escaped via Fishergate, as no troops had been posted to block that route. This was despite the diligence of the soldiers surrounding the town.[94] The militia, too, were said to be 'very serviceable in guarding the Passes and several parties attempting to force their way through them, were either killed, taken

---

[84] Rae, *History*, 320.
[85] Anon., *A Letter*, 7.
[86] Clarke, 'Journal', 521.
[87] TNA, FEC1/246–50.
[88] *Political State*, XI, 1716, 165.
[89] Ware, *Memorials*, 169; Patten, *History*, 61.
[90] TWAS, CP3/22.
[91] Patten, *History*, dedication.
[92] *Political State*, XI, 1716, 165.
[93] Hibbert-Ware, 'Memorials', 136.
[94] Rae, *History*, 324.

or beat back'.⁹⁵ It is impossible to know how many escaped. The West Riding Quarter Sessions thought 1,500 had done so, and searches for escaped Jacobites were also ordered by the Northumberland Quarter Sessions.⁹⁶ Some may have simply dropped their weapons and been sheltered by friends and neighbours in the town itself.

Yet why was this so? The Jacobites had done well to repel their enemies, but had not vanquished them and were aware that Carpenter's men were about to arrive. It seems probable that this civilian army (at least as far as most of the Englishmen were concerned) had been shocked at their first experience of the bloody reality of a battle. They may have expected a peaceful restoration as in 1660, and certainly nothing in the campaign so far would have prepared them for such a rude awakening. After all, the army had had no physical resistance hitherto – the posse had fled at Penrith, and the militia and Stanhope's dragoons had not contested their progress at Lancaster, either.

There were many wounded after the battle. It might have been thought, there being 30 surgeons, doctors and physicians among the Jacobite army, that the wounded men would have been well treated.⁹⁷ The White Bull inn on the market square seems to have been appointed for use as a makeshift field hospital. Treatment seems to have been variable. The Jacobite Captain Peter Farqhuarson, being shot through a leg bone, 'endured a great deal of Torture in the Operation of the Surgeon ... His Leg was cut off by an unskilled Butcher, rather than a Surgeon, and he presently died'. However, several of the regulars who had been wounded and then taken prisoner seemed to be in good spirits, assuring Patten that 'not one Man belonging to the King's Forces but would not die in their Country's Cause'.⁹⁸ Others, though, were downhearted. One source claimed that 'all the prisoners lookt upon the affair as lost'.⁹⁹ Another source noted that least 50 officers and men were taken prisoner following the fighting at Murray's barrier and 'owed the day was lost to them'.¹⁰⁰

Wills's conduct on the first day's fighting later came in for heavy censure by Carpenter. The latter claimed that Wills 'made a rash attack, highly blameable, by loosing so many men to no purpose, before I came up'.¹⁰¹ Certainly, at the end of the first day's fighting, the honours appeared to have gone to the Jacobites.

---

⁹⁵ *The Daily Courant*, 4391, 19 November 1715.
⁹⁶ WAYS: Wakefield, QS10/13, 112A; NRO, QS44/51.
⁹⁷ TNA, KB8/66.
⁹⁸ Patten, *History*, 85, 88–9.
⁹⁹ BC, Atholl Papers, 45/12/77.
¹⁰⁰ TNA, SP54/9/107.
¹⁰¹ *HMC*, Townshend, 170.

Patten remarked, 'Hitherto the Rebels seem'd to have had some Advantage, having repulsed the King's forces in all their Attacks, and maintained all their Posts'.[102]

Some thought that a vigorous counter-attack should have been made. Captain Murray advocated such, as did Derwentwater in one account. As a Lowlander noted, this

> could not have failed of success, for we were uppish and had lost six men, whereas many of the enemy were killed and wounded and were much fatigued, dispirited being mostly raw and new levied troops. But our generals [one account pins this on Forster] positively refused.[103]

Another source elaborates on this theme, claiming that at 11 o'clock, with Murray's men being short of ammunition, a deputation arrived at Forster's quarters, but they found him

> lying in his naked bed, with a sack possett, and some confections by him: which I humbly judge was not a very becoming posture at this time for a general ... everyone is convinced that he failed in almost every point of his prudentials, if not worse.[104]

Why should Wills have instigated frontal attacks on defensive positions? He wrote on the following evening, 'I made such attacks as were necessary to convince the rebels of my being in a condition to reduce them by force'.[105] This sounds like post facto justification, and the following alternative hypotheses are also worth pondering. As a professional soldier, he may well have felt his enemies were amateurs who would not stand against a determined assault (certainly, a lack of offensive spirit on the part of the Jacobites in the campaign to date had been evident). He may also have been ambitious and determined to score off his rival, Carpenter, by gaining a victory without his help. Or he may simply have been zealously carrying out his orders to engage and defeat the enemy as soon as possible. Finally, we might ask whether there was an alternative. Since, lacking artillery and sufficient supplies (which would have taken time to have procured), a lengthy siege was out of the question, the only way to attack the enemy was the assault which was so apparently unsuccessful and undoubtedly

---

[102] Patten, *History*, 87.
[103] TNA, SP54/9/107; Anon., *A Letter*, 7.
[104] *Weekly Journal*, 10 March 1716.
[105] *HMC*, Various Collections, II, 409.

costly, and thus was criticised; but his critics had no other suggestions to offer. And, costly though it was, it did have the effect of reducing morale among some of the defenders, including, crucially, Forster and his coterie. The coup de grace was, though, to come on the following day.

Those who argue that Wills should have waited for reinforcements should bear the following in mind, however. Firstly, Wills did not know how long he would have had to wait for them and then wait for them to become battle-worthy. Secondly, the time spent waiting would have enabled the Jacobites to strengthen their defences. Thirdly, the morale of his waiting troops might have fallen and that of the Jacobites might have risen, believing their enemies were afraid to attack them.

News of the battle was unknown to the outside world on this day, but that one was imminent was common knowledge. Prescott wrote, 'the Warrington post ... brings that this morning the King's Forces marcht from Wigan to attack the rebels at Preston'. Civilians could only await the outcome; Prescott wrote, 'I retreat home', and had a pint of wine.[106]

Day Two – Sunday, 13 November

General Carpenter arrived to the north of Preston with his three regiments of dragoons and a number of volunteer and militia cavalry at either 9 or 10 in the morning.[107] Carpenter's men were probably of limited immediate physical use, because they had marched from Newcastle in but six days, without any halts, and had been in the saddle since early October before that.[108] In the following year, Colonel Molesworth was reimbursed £600 by the Treasury on account of 'the losses sustained by his regiment by horses killed and disabled and other extraordinary expenses in the long and continued marches in a very rigorous season in pursuit of the rebels'.[109] Wills and Carpenter conferred. Wills, as junior officer to Carpenter, offered to relinquish overall command to his colleague. Carpenter generously remarked that 'he had begun the Affair so well, that he ought to have the Glory of finishing it'. He approved of Wills's troop dispositions, but, having inspected them, was disconcerted to find that no one was guarding the road from Preston, which led to Liverpool. Before his own eyes, he could see Jacobites leaving the town by that route. Therefore, he ordered Pitt's two

---

[106] Prescott, 'Diary', II, 473.
[107] *Evening Post*, 980, 15–17 November 1715.
[108] Patten, *History*, 89.
[109] CTB, XXXII, 1716, 18.

squadrons of horse to be stationed there in order to complete the encirclement of the town. One of the cavalry's first acts was to cut down a number of Jacobites trying to flee. One man they killed was a cornet Shuttleworth, who had a green taffeta banner with a buff silk fringe and the sign of a pelican feeding her young. The banner read: 'Tantum Valet amor Regis and Patria' (So prevalent is the love of our King and Country). Carpenter also established a system of communications between the disparate parts of the regular army so that if an attempt to break out was made, those attacked could be reinforced.[110] Cobham's and Churchill's dragoons were posted on the north side of the town and Molesworth's to the south. Wills had established his command post near to the road to Lancaster.[111]

There was some fighting in the morning as a party of dragoons was beaten back, and 'Some few men on both sides were killed this forenoone'. However, a ceasefire was soon agreed on thereafter, at Wills's instigation, in order that they might bury their dead.[112] The arrival of Carpenter's forces may have been decisive. Widdrington later stated that when they had been seen, he 'said very loud before their men that they were all undone, and upon that they consulted to ask termes'.[113] Likewise, according to Patten, 'And now our People began to open their Eyes, and to see that there was nothing but present Death before them if they held out longer and that there was no Remedy, but, if possible, to make Terms'.[114]

Matters were looking black for the Jacobites. Ammunition, which had ever been a problem, was running very low, especially after so much had been expended in the successful defence of the previous day. Provisions, too, were becoming scarce. As ever, the Jacobites were divided as to their best course of action. The Highlanders 'were for sallying out against the King's Forces, and dying, as they called it, like Men of Honour, with their Swords in their Hands'. Charles Radcliffe alleged 'he had rather die with his sword in his hand, like a man of honour, than be dragged like a felon to the scaffold'.[115] This was because, with supplies running low, and with the danger that the enemy might be reinforced, especially with artillery, to be cooped up in a town was to be in a very grave situation indeed. Other actions suggested included burning the houses near the church, and another was to drive the regulars from Hoghton's house.[116] Not all agreed. Forster was persuaded by Oxburgh and Widdrington to parley,

---

[110] Patten, *History*; *St. James' Post*, 131, 5–7 December 1715.
[111] LRO, DDX1788/1.
[112] Clarke, 'Journal', 522.
[113] *HMC*, Townshend, 170–71.
[114] Patten, *History*, 90.
[115] Patten, *History*, 92; Radcliffe, *Genuine and Impartial*, 39.
[116] BC, Atholl Papers, 45/12/77.

convincing their leader that terms would be granted. Presumably they hoped that they would be treated as prisoners of war as in conventional warfare between regular armies, rather than traitors who would face trial and punishment. None of this was apparent to most of the army until the afternoon.[117]

The mental and psychological states of Forster and his coterie are crucial at this point. It would seem that he played little part in the proceedings of the previous day. Having no experience of soldering, his first experience of wholesale death and destruction probably shattered his nerve. He did not like the current situation and wanted to escape it by any means he could. There may have been an element of cowardice here, or at least human weakness. The combination of shock and fear within him were to be crucial. Apparently, the sight of Carpenter's force was decisive:

> the chief prisoners assur'd me [Carpenter] and others that as soon as they saw my detachment from the steeple the Lord Widdrington who was in the churchyard said very loud before their men that they were all undone, and upon that they consulted to ask termes.[118]

Colville agreed with this assessment, writing, that Carpenter's arrival, 'which might have added to their panic and confusion, which we afterwards learnt from themselves had seized them from the beginning'.[119]

Widdrington and Derwentwater, 'solicitous to prevent any further Destruction', were 'instrumental to induce all in arms to submit'. They were confident in obtaining mercy.[120] Oxburgh, accompanied only by a trumpeter, was accordingly despatched at either one or two o'clock to treat with Wills. He was chosen because of his having served in the army and claimed that he had acquaintances in that army which would facilitate their gaining good terms.[121] The Jacobite rank and file had been told that honourable terms were to be accepted and so they remained quiet. Had they known Oxburgh's true mission, they would have shot him as he left Preston.[122] Wills told him that no terms would be forthcoming as he did not have the power to negotiate with them (they were classified as rebels and so could not expect anything more; in any case, when Argyle requested such plenipotentiary powers he was denied them)

---

[117] Rae, *History*, 321.
[118] *HMC*, Townshend, 170–71.
[119] Colville, 'Military Memoirs', 60.
[120] *Political State*, XI, 1716, 113, 115.
[121] Patten, *History*, 92.
[122] Patten, *History*, 92–3.

and that they must surrender at discretion, which only guaranteed that they would not be put to the sword straight away. Oxburgh argued for better terms, but Wills was adamant. If the Jacobites did not surrender in an hour, they would be attacked again. Captain Dalzell was sent to Wills in order to seek terms for the Scots, but received the same answer as Oxburgh.[123]

At his trial, Winton claimed that promises had been made by Wills. He said that he had been 'encouraged by His Majesty's officers to depend on His Majesty's mercy'. Yet the counterclaim was made that 'this deponent gave them no hope of mercy'.[124] A contemporary account stated that Wills 'desir'd them to surrender to the King's mercy and he would represent their case in the most favourable Manner'.[125] Lieutenant Colonel Stanhope Cotton, Wills's ADC, told a Jacobite who asked about this subject while in Preston, 'Sir, that I cannot assure you of, but I know the King to be a very merciful Prince'.[126] Possibly such promises gave Winton and others hopes for mercy. Yet the Jacobites, in the eyes of the law, were deemed rebels and traitors and could expect trial and punishment, perhaps by death. Carpenter later said that such hope 'was very unanswerable by the Rules and Discipline of War'.[127]

Derwentwater and Mackintosh also went, individually, to parley with Wills. According to one source, Wills was threatening and abusive towards them. Derwentwater allegedly said that if there was no help within 12 days they would surrender:

> Upon this Wills swore a great oath and pulls his watch out of his pocket and swore that if they did not surrender within twelve hours' time he would cut every man of them in pieces and swore he would not given them a moment's time longer This he confirmed by the most bitter oaths, curses and execrations in the world, that lord Derwentwater was perfectly terrified that his very lips trembled.

Wills allowed the peer to return to Preston 'for he had a mind he should spread the terror among the rest'. Although Mackintosh could match the soldier in oaths, each claiming to beat the other's forces with a fraction of their own men, even Mackintosh seems to have been impressed by Wills's 'terrible air'.[128] Wills

---

[123] Rae, *History*, 321–2.
[124] *Political State*, XI, 1716, 344, 355.
[125] *HMC*, Var., II, 409.
[126] *Evening Post*, 980, 15–17 November 1715.
[127] Anon., *The Life of the Late Right Honourable George, Lord Carpenter* London: E. Curll, 1736, 25.
[128] Ryder, *Diary*, 173–4.

wrote that evening, 'nor shall I give him any other terms than relying on the King's mercy, to which I imagine they will submit, being sufficiently convinced I have them in my power'.[129]

At three or five, Wills sent Cotton to Preston to receive the Jacobites' answer. Cotton was told that the English and Scots Jacobites were, as ever, in dispute, and that they asked Wills to wait until seven on the following morning. Wills accepted these terms on three conditions: that the Jacobites did not throw up fresh entrenchments, that they did not allow any of their number to escape, and that they offered up hostages.[130] The latter was insisted upon by Carpenter. These terms were eventually agreed to, though at first neither Derwentwater nor Widdrington could be found and Mackintosh was in bed. Carpenter told Dalzell that he wanted two hostages: Kenmure and Derwentwater. Dalzell told him Kenmure would not agree to this, and when Carpenter suggested Mackintosh as an alternative, he was refused again. Carpenter recalled, 'I was unwilling to make great Difficulties, it growing towards night'. They agreed on Colonel Mackintosh. He and Derwentwater went out at eight.[131]

This was shocking news to some of the rank and file; as a Lowlander noted, 'the first knowledge we had of it was when wee saw Colonel Cotton'.[132] Meanwhile, Cotton sent a drummer to all the houses held by the regulars in Preston to let them know that a ceasefire had been arranged and that no more firing was to occur until ordered otherwise. Unfortunately, while Cotton was on this mission, the drummer was shot dead, probably by a Jacobite who was hostile to the idea of surrender; it was only at this time that the army knew what its leaders had been planning for it.[133]

Inside Preston, the disputes between the Jacobites turned violent; 'it was astonishing to see the Confusion the Town was in, threatening, yea, killing one another'. One man was shot and several wounded. Forster was seen as the scapegoat by some and one Mr Murray fired his pistol at him, only for its mark to be wide as Patten struck the pistol. The Scots still wished to fight their way out, to escape or die in the attempt.[134] This seemed a positive step, as one man later wrote, 'if this had been done, we had made a very good Account of them, most of their dragoons being but new levied men'. The bitterness among the rankers towards officers was caught by the same man, who later wrote, 'there were never a handful of men of

---

[129] *HMC*, Var., II, 409.
[130] Patten, *History*, 94–5.
[131] Anon., *Carpenter*, 23.
[132] BC, Atholl Papers, 45/12/77.
[133] Patten, *History*, 93.
[134] Patten, *History*, 96–7.

all occasions, more ready to fight, and never commanding officers as it appear'd, less forward'.[135] Murray was not alone in this desire; 'some were for bringing out Forrester like a publick sacrifice'.[136] Others reproached Forster 'to his face and all he could answer was, that he was sensible of the Incapacity he had for his office, cryed like a child, was sorry for what he had done'.[137]

There was yet another difference of opinion among the Jacobite leadership. The anonymous Lowlander reported, 'yet Witherington pretended by arguments to defend the reasonableness of the capitulation, in fact Mr Bazill Hamiltown with tears declared already we were betrayed'. Lord Murray, Major Nairn, Philip Lockhart, Captain Straton, Derwentwater and Winton 'shewed a great resentment agt the cessation, saying it was downright treacherous', but Earls Nithsdale and Carnwath and Captain Dalziell supported Forster and Widdrington. They alleged the capitulation 'would be fair and honourable', implying that terms would be given to the surrendered.[138]

It seems that some of the English and Scots horsemen, including Derwentwater and his brother Charles, were intending to fight their way out by leaving Preston to the north. They mounted their horses with their men and assembled at the market place. Winton, Lockhart, Nairn and Shafto agreed, arguing that Mackintosh's infantry should flank the hedges on the Lancaster road and the Scots gentry force through the enemy. One account stated that Mackintosh agreed to march his men to join them at the barrier. However, Mackintosh never arrived, and without his men the force felt they were incapable of a successful escape. Another version stated that Mackintosh said 'it was too late to make such an attempt as after hostages were given upon our side'. Carnwath agreed with Mackintosh, claiming the surrender was honourable and necessary. Morale was so low that, that night, despite suggestions to the contrary, all the Jacobite sentries were withdrawn from their posts, except those under Captain Lockhart's command. The regulars saw this as their opportunity to take these posts and make the Jacobite position even more hopeless.[139] One anonymous Jacobite stated, 'This was very choking to us all, but no helping of it, for no sooner had we left our posts than they made themselves masters of them, and of our cannon'.[140] Some were resigned to their fates, 'to it by promises of a fair and honourable capitulation'. They were 'so much surprised by grief they

---

[135] *Weekly Journal*, 10 March 1716.
[136] BC, Atholl Papers, 45/12/77.
[137] TNA, SP54/9/107.
[138] BC, Atholl Papers, 45/12/77.
[139] Anon., *A Letter*, 7.
[140] *Weekly Journal*, 10 March 1716.

would take notice of nothing'.[141] A bitter Jacobite noted, 'I believe this is the first instance of a victorious army after action, yielding themselves prisoners to the vanquished', and Englishman Gabriel Hesketh said 'he was made a prisoner without cause'.[142]

Patten explained why a break-out was not countenanced:

> It is true this might have been attempted, and perhaps many would have escap'd; but it could not have been perform'd without the Loss of a great deal of Blood, and that on both Sides; and it was told them that it would be so, and that if they did get out, they would be cut off by the Country People.[143]

The Jacobite leadership, had, on 13 November, three options. Firstly, they could stand their ground and hope to defeat further attacks by their enemy. Yet with ammunition virtually exhausted this was only to invite defeat. This option was never considered. Secondly, they could have tried to fight their way out. It is impossible to say what the outcome would have been. Some would have escaped; some would have fallen or have been captured. It was a risk and, as seen, the Jacobite leaders were risk averse. So option three, surrender, seemed best, because it was safest in the short term; they would not be killed on the spot. There was no good option, but a choice between three bad possibilities.

It is hard to assess the results of the second option as it was untried. Much would depend on the morale of men on all sides. Despite their exhaustion, a sizable proportion of the Jacobite rank and file felt confident; it is difficult to be certain about the morale of their opponents, who had been bloodily repulsed but who had received reinforcements. Yet the Jacobites were predominantly an army of infantrymen; their cavalry was inferior to their enemies'. Infantry lacking adequate firepower and discipline are vulnerable to cavalry in the open. Forces could make successful escapes; a French army was to escape from Prague in 1742, for example. Yet this had the advantage of a unified command. A successful escape would require, to have any chance of success, a determined and united leadership. This it lacked, and therefore it did not happen.

Despite it being the Lord's Day, there is no reference to Sunday worship. Unbeknown to any at or near Preston, the strategically decisive battle of Sheriffmuir was taking place and Mar's superiority in numbers was not enough to defeat the more skilful Argyle.

---

[141] BC, Atholl Papers, 45/12/77.
[142] TNA, SP54/9/107; TS23/34.
[143] Patten, *History*, 96.

A garbled report of the battle reached Chester later that day, as Prescott recorded:

> Tho the news seems very improbable, it yet prevails, and the Bells go on til about 5 when an Express informs that on Saturday Evening the Kings Forces came to Ribble river, that the rebels maintain'd the pass of the Bridg, that there was a skirmish betwixt 2 parties on the Cawsway wherein several fell & Lord Derwentwater said to bee one of the slain.[144]

Day Three – Monday, 14 November

When the allotted hour of seven arrived, Forster told Wills that the Jacobites were ready to surrender. Mackintosh was of a different view. He told Wills that, as a soldier, he knew that to surrender at discretion was the worst fate of all, and would not do it. He was told that the alternative was for the town to be stormed and for all the defenders to be put to the sword. Kenmure informed him that he and the other Lowland nobles agreed with Forster. Presumably Mackintosh then realised that, with almost half of the Jacobites surrendering, his Highlanders were numerically too weak to continue to effectually resist and that he had to face the unpalatable prospect of surrender. Hostilities were at an end.[145]

Forster was much criticised for the surrender, perhaps not surprisingly as he was commander in chief and so the responsibility was his. Two published accounts, by Jacobites, of the campaign lay the blame squarely on his shoulders, as do two manuscript accounts (all by Scots). Some wondered where his true loyalties lay. Prescott wrote, 'tis from probable reasons suspected that Gen. Forster betray'd his own party'.[146] Thomas Hearne (1678–1735), an Oxford Jacobite, was told by one of the Scots officers at Preston, that

> there was no Treachery in General Foster, or any of the rest, but Cowardice, Foster being a timorous Man, and unwilling to fight, or shew the least part of a General, and so surrendered his Men, whereas had he been all at courageous, the Business had been certainly done for the King.[147]

---

[144] Prescott, 'Diary', II, 473.
[145] Patten, *History*, 96–7.
[146] Prescott, 'Diary', II, 475.
[147] Thomas Hearne, *The Remains of Thomas Hearne*, ed. John Buchanan-Brown, London: Centaur Press, 1966, 240.

His master, whom he met in the following year, did not blame him, and indeed appointed him steward of the exiled Jacobite court household at Urbino, later Palazzo Mutti.[148] Forster appears to have been weak and incompetent, but he was not treacherous. Patten's *History* attempts to refute such allegations. Instead, he lays the blame for the defeat on Mackintosh: 'The Brigadier has got the character of Brave and Bold ... but we all must say, we saw little of it at Preston'; and he blamed 'a Party' for attacking Forster.[149]

In January 1717 there was further discussion about the Jacobite leadership at Preston. Dr Patrick Abercomby informed Mar:

> The avarice, roguery, insufficiency and cowardice of the commanders and others of our people at Preston are perpetually talked of, and asserted with great oaths by not a few here and at St. Germaine. The persons they chiefly exclaim against are the Brigadier, his two brothers and bastard son, Capt. Dalziel etc. The particulars related of them are so infamous that one cannot prevail with oneself to believe them.[150]

There was dissension among their enemies, too, in the moment of triumph; just before they mounted to enter Preston, Carpenter and Wills fell out. Wills took 'on him great command' and so Carpenter, his senior officer, 'us'd him very freely'. Apparently he was even considering placing Wills under arrest, but Carlisle and Lumley prevailed upon him not to do so. If this had occurred, 'itt might have proved fatall to His Majesty's Service', for the Jacobites were still armed and Carpenter even thought that Wills might have ordered the troops under his command to have assisted him against Carpenter. 'So I did not do itt', wrote Carpenter.[151]

Cotton and a number of regular troops entered the town and disarmed the Jacobites. Carpenter and Wills then rode in, in state, with the majority of their forces behind them. Honeywood, with other troops, entered from the opposite end of Preston and they met at the market place, where the defeated and doubtless despondent Jacobites were drawn up. The gentlemen prisoners were placed in the town's inns, The Mitre, The White Bull and The Windmill, under guard while the rank and file were herded into the town's largest public building, the parish church, St John the Divine (many of Monmouth's defeated followers were also housed in a church after Sedgemoor), though 300 of them

---
[148] *ODNB*, 20, 426–7.
[149] Patten, *History*, 98–9.
[150] *HMC*, Stuart Papers, III, 456–7.
[151] *HMC*, Townshend, 171.

were housed in the property of Robert Boyes for two weeks, where they caused £30 worth of damage. Apparently, 'several of the country people were in the disorder and confusion hurried into the church, with the rebels'. In the church, 'they took what care of themselves as they could, ripping all the linings from the seats or pews, and making thereof Breeches and Hose to defend themselves from the extremity of the weather'.[152] According to Major Forrester, the prisoners were 'under closer confinement than the general intended'.[153] Lists of prisoners were drawn up by Major Brown by 22 November and sent to London together with intercepted letters.[154]

However, even at this late stage, one Littleton, a priest, escaped by disguising himself as an apothecary.[155] Francis Legh was concealed by one Mrs Whitehead.[156] One Mr Dickenson also escaped.[157] Simon Fraser had been wounded in the leg and was lying in bed so evaded capture.[158] Some tried to join the Jacobites but did not arrive in time; Mr Gamul was one, apparently, but he returned to Chorley instead.[159] Not all were so fortunate in their escape attempts, for Sydall was taken by dragoons, 'who were, with great Difficulty, dissuaded from hanging him by the way' and was returned to Preston with his neck in a halter.[160]

The prisoners were deprived of their baggage, their money and their linen by the victorious soldiery. It could have been worse; as Forrester wrote, 'it has been lucky for them that I was here, else they would have been very ill used by our people'.[161] There was also some looting of property in the town itself. According to Clarke, 'they with force and armes broke open doers and locks of chambers and closets, and the moneys, plate, goods, and chattels of most of the inhabitants of that towne' were stolen. Even those loyal to King George had their houses pillaged.[162]

Yet such deplorable (in the eyes of Jacobite and civilian commentators) behaviour was hardly unique by the standards of the day. Towns taken after an assault, especially when the attackers had taken considerable losses and where they perceived the civil population was hostile, were often sacked, and the

---

[152] Patten, *History*, 103.
[153] NAS, 220/5/601.
[154] *HMC*, Townshend, 170.
[155] TNA, FEC1/213; Patten, *History*, 103
[156] *Lyme Letters*, 307.
[157] Prescott, 'Diary', II, 476.
[158] *HMC*, Stuart Papers, II, 138.
[159] Prescott, 'Diary', II, 475.
[160] *Flying Post*, 3758, 24 February 1716.
[161] NAS, 220/5/601.
[162] *Political State*, XI, 1716, 166; Clarke, 'Journal', 520–21.

excesses committed by the soldiers should be seen, if not excused, in this context. During the English Civil Wars, Bolton and Liverpool were plundered after they had been taken. Likewise, there was pillage by the victors when Preston changed hands twice in the Civil Wars. Some soldiers saw this as one of the perks of the job and their officers often tacitly accepted such behaviour. Complaint was made by householders and the pillagers were eventually checked by their own officers.[163] We should also note that there were no summary executions, as had occurred to about 100 of Monmouth's followers shortly after their defeat at Sedgemoor.[164]

The horses belonging to the Jacobites were sold and the proceeds shared among the soldiers, though each man did not receive much. Those horses taken by the Jacobites from gentlemen and farmers along their march were, however, returned to their owners.[165]

Lord Carlisle took the opportunity of talking with the English Jacobite peers, 'they being at this time under great dejection of mind'. He suggested that if they gave information about other Jacobites, mercy might be shown. In particular, he asked about Blackett and Durham gentry. He concluded that they did not know much and that they were under Forster's orders. He recommended to Wills that all the tax money taken by the Jacobites along the route of the Jacobite march be returned. He also

> desired him to take particular care, that no innocent person be carryd away when the prisoners are removed, for I am afraid several of the country people were in the disorder and confusion hurried into the church with the rebels, that being the one place where they are at present secured.

James Craggs also talked to them about their involvement in the rebellion.[166]

Because there were insufficient quarters in Preston for all the troops, Carpenter's troops then rode to Wigan to refresh themselves. After all, they had 'chac't the rebels a month, with unusuall difficultys and fatigue' and were in need of good quarters. However, as Carpenter wrote, this made it impossible for him to have arrested Wills, 'tho he deserved it'.[167] The constable of Ribby cum Wray supplied 20 bushels of oats per day for the troops' horses, by warrant of Wills, in the days following the battle.[168]

---

[163] Patten, *History*, 100; Barratt, *Cavaliers*, 188–93; *VCH Lancashire* VII, 75.
[164] Earle, *Monmouth's Rebels*, 175.
[165] Colville, 'Military Memoirs', 60.
[166] *HMC*, Townshend, 169.
[167] Rae, *History*, 323; *HMC Townshend*, 170–71.
[168] LRO, DDX190/108.

Casualty figures were disputed, especially among the regular army. Official figures, as published in the contemporary press and laid down by Rae, recorded that 4 officers and 53 men of other ranks had been killed and a further 92 of all ranks were wounded.[169] The breakdown of these figures is noted in Appendix 3. It suggests that the unit sustaining most casualties was Preston's, with 40 dead and 52 wounded. Pitt's, Honeywood's and Munden's suffered least, with none dead and only a total of 6 wounded. Wynn's suffered 30 casualties and the other two regiments 18 in total. It is also worth observing that 72 horses were killed in the combat, roughly shared in number between the five dragoon regiments, and Pitt's horse suffered none.[170]

Patten claimed that 5 officers and over 200 private men ('how many, it is hard to determine') were killed.[171] Clarke gives a higher figure: 270.[172] An even higher figure was given by the Merse officer: 335 killed and wounded.[173] It was certainly high, with Forrester writing on 16 November:

> We have had our share of it, all the officers that were along with me were either kill'd or wounded save two, with very near 100 of our best men, soe you may believe the loss of soe many brave gentlemen, takes off a good dale of the joy I should have had, in gaining so considerable ane affair ... I escap'd very well myself having only received two slight wounds, one in the face and the other in the hand.[174]

A newspaper reported that 150 of Preston's men had been killed and wounded.[175] Carpenter later wrote that Wills had 'made a rash attack, highly blameable, by loosing so many men to no purpose, (of which you will hear more) except to serve his own ambition by ending it before I came up'.[176] That casualties should have been high is explained thus by Patten: that the attackers were made 'under the greatest Disadvantage imaginable ... being all the time naked, and expos'd to the Fire of the Rebels from Windows, Barriers and Entrenchments'.[177]

How can such differences be squared? We should remember that the official figures would have been compiled under Wills's auspices, and it is commonplace

---

[169] Rae, *History*, 323–4.
[170] *The Flying Post*, 3734, 8–10 Dec. 1715.
[171] Patten, *History*, 102.
[172] Clarke, 'Journal', 522.
[173] Anon., *A Letter*, 7.
[174] NAS, 220/5/601.
[175] *St. James' Evening Post*, 73, 15–17 Nov. 1715.
[176] *HMC*, Townshend, 170.
[177] Patten, *History*, dedication.

for victorious generals to underestimate their casualties – and for the opposing side to exaggerate those of their opponents. Carpenter, who was a professional rival of Wills, can also be assumed to be prejudiced against Wills. On the other hand, Patten, who dedicated his *History* to Wills and Carpenter, had no obvious reason to enlarge on casualty figures; and Forrester's bias is unknown. However, though we can conclude that the official figures are too low, we are no nearer determining an accurate number of casualties. The official figures, however, do indicate that Preston's regiment was in the thick of the fighting, whereas Pitt's horse were kept in reserve and merely had one man wounded and no deaths among horses and men.

As to the Jacobites, the figure was remarkably low. Patten's estimate is of 17 killed and 25 wounded, and Rae agreed with this.[178] Clarke's figure of 18 or 19 dead is similar.[179] The Merse officer gives 35 killed and wounded.[180] The discrepancy in casualty figures should not be surprising. Troops under cover always have fewer killed and wounded than those in the open attacking them, especially when both sides have roughly equal numbers to begin with. Those killed included one Mr Clifton, dying a few hours after being shot in the knee; Thomas Brereton, dying from a 'Vast Flux of Blood' due to a number of wounds; and Peter Farquharson, shot through the leg and dying at an unskilled surgeon's hands. Rank and file killed are not mentioned by name.[181] It is presumed that the dead of both sides were buried in common graves, as was the case during the civil wars; though four officers from the regular army were buried in the churchyard on 27 November.

There was, as noted, dissension among the victorious generals, too. Carpenter was unhappy that 'I find the prints give him all the power and applause, I suppose by his own or some friends direction, and I fear that His Majesty may be under that mistake also'. He wrote to Townshend and Marlborough in order that his share in the victory not be overlooked. After the surrender of the Jacobites he had still wanted to place Wills under arrest, but as he had sent his troops to Wigan could not do so as he had none left to command.[182] The two generals attempted to resolve their differences, though, over quarrels emanating from Spain in 1709, by means of a duel in Hyde Park in the following year, but this was called off by Marlborough's intervention.[183]

[178] Patten, *History*, 102; Rae, *History*, 324.
[179] Clarke, 'Journal', 522.
[180] Anon., *A Letter*, 7.
[181] Patten, *History*, 85–6.
[182] *HMC*, Townshend, 171.
[183] Anon., *Carpenter*, 33.

Civilian losses at Preston are often overlooked. Robert Cotesworth reported to his father in the following year, 'Preston is not so much damaged as to ye outward appearance of the houses as one might have Reasonably expected'.[184] Yet they were not inconsiderable and were valued at thousands of pounds. A total of 221 householders claimed recompense from the Commission of Forfeited Estates in 1718, amounting to £6,241 7s 1d. Some had lost their horses or household goods of corn, hay, shoes, leather, wine and linen. The Jacobites had taken two horses to the value of £17 15s. Others had their property burnt down, either wholly or in part. Joseph Bolton lost a house, valued at £180, and Alice Bolton a barn worth £40. Property in Friargate and Churchgate was especially damaged. The plundering was probably carried on by both sides. Hoghton's barn was destroyed and he lost a great deal of corn, valued at £352. Peploe lost goods to the value of £72 5s and had his barn plundered, to the loss of £35. Forty eight buildings had been burnt down, mostly in Churchgate and Friargate. Finally, the 'Parish Church [was] ... defaced and injured in the seats, floor, windows and several ornaments', and £41 7s 1d was claimed in compensation. A full list can be found in Appendix 4. This damage probably occurred when the Jacobite prisoners were locked into the church after the battle was over.[185] It seems that the theft and damage was caused by both sides, though it is probable that the regulars were more to blame, having greater opportunities. Finally, several civilians – Robert Sergeant, Thomas Seed, Robert Green and the widow Cowell – were 'killed accidentally in the fight in ye towne', presumably by being caught in the crossfire between the two sides.[186]

News of the victory reached London on 15 November. Wills had sent Colonel Maurice Nassau of Grant's foot to relay the news to the court; he received £500 for having done so.[187] The reaction was wholehearted. Liddell wrote on 17 November, 'You see a joy through out the City which can't be well parallel'd and the court shew no less satisfaction. This noble action has nipp'd the designs off our enemys in the budd so they can't expect a plentiful cropp'.[188] Lady Cowper wrote, 'The Surrender of these Prisoners filled the Town with Joy'.[189]

Craggs, on 22 November, wrote to Townshend:

---

[184] TWAS, CP3/22.
[185] TNA, FEC1/245–9.
[186] Henry Fishwick, *History of the Parish of Preston*, Rochdale: James Clegg, 1900, 420.
[187] CTBP, 1716, 18.
[188] Liddell, 'Letters', 200.
[189] Cowper, *Diary*, 57.

> I find this expedition was as fortunate for the conjuncture as any other circumstance because the rebels in two or three days would certainly have been joined by as many thousands well armed and well mounted.[190]

Pulteney wrote on 16 November to Carpenter:

> I write this letter with a very good deal of pleasure because it gives me an occasion to express to you the Joy which I have upon you and Mr Wills success against the King's enemies. I never did question but His Majesty's Forces would be victorious under such commands, and there is not a person in the world takes a greater share in your success than myself.[191]

Patten, in 1717, flattered Carpenter and Wills, writing, 'it was your prudent Management and unshaken bravery, animated by the Justice of the Cause, the Signal Defeat of the day was justly owing'.[192]

It also meant that the Dutch battalions which had been to march to Lancashire, could be diverted towards Hull and thence to Scotland. Other troops could also be sent to Scotland. Confidence in the regime rose with victory over the Jacobites at Preston and Sheriffmuir, too. On 2 November, with undefeated Jacobite forces in both countries, South Sea stock stood at 90⅝–89 and Bank Stock at 118¾–119. By 19 November, with the government looking far more secure, these figures stood at 94½–94¾ and 124¼–124½.[193]

The extent of the victory should not be exaggerated, as Argyle, never optimistic, wrote to Townshend on 19 November:

> I received last night a letter from Mr Carpenter with the good news of the Rebells at Preston being all Prisoners but he makes a Reflection at the end of his letter wch is a very wrong one, he imagines those at Perth may upon this news desire to capitulate. I hope His Majesty's ministers have not been of this opinion, because it would literally very greatly endanger the whole.[194]

More moderately, the Lord Justice Clerk wrote, 'this will putt ane end I hope to the rebellion in England, and must have good consequences as to us'.[195]

---

[190] *HMC*, Townshend, 170.
[191] TNA, WO4/17, 276.
[192] Patten, *History*, dedication.
[193] *The Daily Courant*, 4376, 2 November 1715, 4391, 19 November 1716.
[194] TNA, SP54/10, 64.
[195] TNA, SP54/10, 60.

Battles are rarely decisive. Marlborough's great victories in 1702–1708 are undoubted, but they did not result in the capitulation of France; there were another nine years of warfare between Sweden and her enemies after her major defeat at Poltava in 1709. Though the battle of Preston did not end the rebellion, its significance is that it ended any hope that the Jacobites might make any military headway in the Hanoverian heartland of England. It also strengthened the government's position in Scotland by allowing all the Dutch troops brought over to be sent there, as well as Newton's and Stanhope's dragoons to march northwards. This was a severe blow to the Jacobite cause and a great bolster to that of the government. The Jacobites at Perth began to desert, though whether this was in part because of their inability to achieve victory at Sheriffmuir or news that Inverness had been retaken by loyalist Highlanders is impossible to ascertain. Yet there is no doubting that Preston was a decisive nail in the coffin of the Jacobite cause in 1715.

Chapter 7

The Aftermath of the Fifteen, 1715–1717

Most accounts of the end of the rising have concentrated on the fates of those Jacobites who surrendered at Preston. Traditionally it has been asserted that their punishments were 'savage reprisals' and a recent popular history also makes this assertion.[1] Detailed scholarly studies, though, have argued that this was not the case; punishments had to be made as examples, but clemency was also exercised in order to knit back the civic society that rebellion had wrenched apart, the latter being due in part to the actions of both Tory and Whig elites as well as of the government.[2] This author would agree with this thesis, and adds to it by concentrating on the fates of those in the North West. The fate of the Jacobite prisoners is an important one, but there were other important facets to the North West of England at this time – celebrations for the government's supporters being one, and the continuance of support for Jacobitism being another – showing that the struggle was not entirely over.

Military setbacks did not mark the end of the Jacobite campaign, though they did blunt its offensive capability and in retrospect were the beginning of the end. In Scotland, men began to desert Mar, and Argyle was reinforced with fresh units of regulars as well as the contingent of Dutch and Swiss battalions. The Jacobites had not given up hope, and Mar still retained a force, albeit a diminished one, at Perth. James Francis Stuart arrived in Scotland in December 1715, but without any troops, arms or money. Despite preparations being made to crown him at Scone, the military situation was beginning to look hopeless. Argyle's army advanced from Stirling in late January 1716 and the Jacobites retreated. James and Mar took a ship to France and the Jacobite clans dispersed. The rebellion was over.

---

[1] Baynes, *Jacobite Rising*, 192–5; C. Gold, *The King's Mistress*, Quercus, 2012, 105.
[2] Sankey, *Prisoners*; Szechi, 1*715*, 200–209.

Whigs Triumphant

Whigs had certainly breathed a sigh of relief that the Jacobites were defeated at Preston. They accredited victory to the Almighty. Symson wrote on 23 November, 'Praised be our good and merciful God they were all defeated about 1,500 taken prisoner. Oh that we may praise the Lord for his goodness and that it may please him to quiet all rebellious villains who I hope will meet with their desserts'. He was likewise thankful that the Jacobites had been frustrated in Scotland: 'God be thanked the Duke of Argyll obtained a victory over them in Scotland'.[3] Some were simply relieved. Fellow merchant Stout wrote, 'Almighty Providence preserved us'.[4] The Rev. Booth wrote in his diary, 'Blessed be God who has delivered us from these Popish and Protestant Jacobites one time after another'.[5]

Public celebrations occurred all over the North West of England. Despite initial news of Jacobite success, one of the first celebrations was at Chester, on 14 November. The castle's guns fired and bonfires were lit. Houses and churches were lit up. There were cries of 'No Popery', wild acclamations and 'all imaginable demonstrations of Joy'.[6] The city's elite drank loyal toasts – even Prescott did so.[7] On the following day, he noted, 'The City and the Wiral Militia exercise and exult in their Hatts, wear the Colour of Victory, Green Ribbands'.[8] Nicolson recorded on 14 November that there was 'Good News from Preston' and five days later that there was 'Rejoycing on the good News from Stirling'.[9]

The expenses of Chester's celebrations were approved of by the corporation. Apparently:

> The Treat lately made in the pentice of this city for the entertainment of the Rt. Hon. The Earl of Cholmondeley, Lord Lieutenant and other persons of quality upon the late Defeat of ye Rebels at Preston is approved and the charge thereof allowed by the house out of the treasury of this city.[10]

News of the battle of Sheriffmuir arrived later. On 22 November it was known of in Chester and hailed by the Whigs as a great victory. Allegedly, 5,000

---

[3] Symson, 'Letter Book', 345.
[4] Stout, *Autobiography*, 176.
[5] Crawford, *Diary*, 73.
[6] *St. James' Evening Post*, 447, 19–22 Nov. 1715.
[7] Prescott, 'Diary', II, 473–4.
[8] Prescott, 'Diary', II, 475.
[9] Nicholson, 'Diaries', V, 6.
[10] Bennett, 'Cheshire', 33.

Jacobites had been killed – a gross exaggeration – along with many flags and cannon being captured. Apart from bell-ringing, Prescott noted, 'Hence Joy in the Town inexpressible'.[11]

There was another major celebration at Preston in November 1716, on the first anniversary of the defeat of the Jacobites there. The church bells rang from three in the morning until midnight – doubtless at Peploe's urging – and they would have been rung by teams of bell-ringers in relays. The town flag flew from the church steeple all day. Loyal inhabitants wore orange favours, attended a church service and then enjoyed a banquet at the Black Griffin. The healths of George I, the Prince and Princess of Wales, the late William III and the victorious generals, Wills and Carpenter, were all toasted. Elsewhere, there was a bonfire, there was music and the town was lit up (a similar celebration, sponsored by Hoghton, took place in 1733).[12]

Bells rung throughout the North West to celebrate the defeat of the Jacobites. The accounts for Appleby's churchwardens for 15–16 November read, 'Given in ale to the ringers upon the news and rejoicing of the defeat of the rebels: 2s'. The bell ringers at Kirkby Lonsdale had to wait until 1716, when eight shillings was spent on ringing to mark the victories at Sheriffmuir and Preston. When James Stuart was known to have left Scotland, the bells at Penrith's church rang again, at the cost of two shillings. On 7 June, the day appointed for the official thanksgiving for the victory, the bells of Beetham, Kirkby Lonsdale and Heversham rang.[13] At Carlisle, Stanwix wrote, on hearing the rumour that Forster and Derwentwater had been killed in battle, 'As early as it is, I have ordered the ringing of Bells, and other Rejoicings will follow'.[14]

Liverpool was also the scene of rejoicing. On 29 November, Derby, Hoghton, and the Mayor and Corporation were prominent. There was a 55-gun salute from the cannon mounted on the defences, one shot for each year of the King's life. Toasts were made at the Common Hall and at the Mayor's house to the successful generals, members of the Royal Family and to the town's MPs. A newspaper stated, 'At their entrance in Town was a vast concourse of spectators, supposed to be about 10,000' and 'the Evening concluded with illuminations, ringing of Bells &c and a Ball at Mr Mayor's'.[15]

Loyal addresses were often sent by corporations and counties to the government to emphasise their loyalty and to congratulate the King on the

---

[11] Prescott, 'Diary', II, 475.
[12] *Political State* XII, 1716, 545–6; *Ipswich Journal*, 17 November 1733.
[13] CAS: Kendal, WPR28, 37; WPR19, WPR43/W1; WPR8/W1; Carlisle, PR110/75.
[14] TNA, SP54/10/57.
[15] *The Flying Post*, 3732, 3–5 Dec. 1715.

success of his armies. On this occasion they included Lancaster, Chester, Carlisle, Cheshire and Cockermouth.[16]

Everyone appeared to be Whig. Craggs, on 22 November, wrote, 'now one would wonder where all these disaffected people are gone, for you meet thro all these countys with none that are not ready to live and dye by King George and the Government'.[17]

Very few sermons were published by the northern clergy in the aftermath of the rebellion. Those that were, were geographically unspecific and could have been delivered from any Anglican pulpit in England, and were mainly negative. The Rev. Thomas Baldwin's sermon in Liverpool referred to the terrors which a successful Catholic rebellion would have imposed – a 'yoke more cruel than Egyptian slavery'. George I was praised as being wise and just, protecting his subjects' liberties, in contrast to former Catholic monarchs. He had supported the SPCK, an Act from the previous reign for building another 50 churches, and had given the late Dr Moore's library to Cambridge University. Baldwin argued, 'Tis true, he makes RELIGION his chief care'.[18]

Peploe made much of God's special care for Britain and his deliverance from the spiritual bondage of Catholicism, due to the Reformation and Queen Elizabeth's rescue of England from the Catholicism of her late sister's reign. Catholics were blamed by Peploe for starting the Civil Wars of the previous century. Then there was reference to James II's reign and his attacks on the Protestant establishment – England being saved by the 'happy Revolution'. Peploe stated that all too many people had drunk James III's health and had even supported him more actively. Finally, he praised the happy status quo brought about by a brave king, wise counsels and a loyal army. These, by God's blessing, had crushed the rebellion. God had been merciful.[19]

Dissenting clergy also declared their sense of deliverance in sermons. James Grimshaw, of Manchester, preached there on 8 May about the nation's deliverance from Catholicism and noted that the execution of Jacobites had not been severe. On the anniversary of the Jacobite surrender at Preston, Jeremiah Aldred also preached a sermon on the theme of deliverance, at Cross Street

---

[16] *London Gazette*, 5409, 18–21 February, 5412, 28 February–3 March, 5418, 20–24 March, 5432, 8–12 May, 5443, 16–19 June, 5444, 19–23 June 1716, 5448, 3–7 July 1716.

[17] *HMC*, Townshend, 170.

[18] Thomas Baldwin, *The folly of preferring a Popish King to a Protestant King*, Liverpool, 1716, 13, 6, 8, 9.

[19] Samuel Peploe, *God's peculiar Care in preservation of our Religion and Liberties*, London, 1716, 9–11, 14–15, 19, 23.

Chapel, Manchester. Owen had an anti-Catholic tract printed in January 1716 about the torture devices allegedly found in Catholic premises:

> We have often heard off the cruelty of the Popish Inquisitors in foreign countries, and of the inhuman Tortures which they put those to, who have the unhappiness to fall into their Bloody Hands, but we little thought that ever the good Nature of Englishmen could be so perverted as to be brought to the least approbation of such Practices, and much less to the Use of 'em.

Given the attacks by Jacobites on Dissenters in the previous year, these words are hardly to be wondered at.[20]

For those Tories not favourable towards the Hanoverian Succession and for the Jacobites, such celebrations were an anathema, but, in the light of the Jacobite defeat, they mostly kept their feelings to themselves. Prescott decided to drown his sorrows on 15 November, noting, 'I, in distress, call on Mr Holland about 12, wee go to the Ship and help our Stomacks with a pint of white mixt with Bitter'.[21] Towneley's priest prayed for resignation on 17 and 18 November and, on subsequent days, for the captives.[22]

The Whigs had triumphed and many were rewarded. Peploe, 'who so manifestly distinguished himself for his zeal and loyalty to the government when the rebels enter'd Preston', was rewarded in 1718 by being given the living, following Wroe's death, of the Collegiate Church of Manchester, which was worth £250 per year.[23] Hoghton was given great praise for his role in the suppression of the rebellion by Townshend:

> I cannot omit this occasion of acknowledging the great zeal and firmness you have all along expressed for the defence of the government, and tho' I may have occasioned some loss in your private affairs, I question not but due care will be taken to make you a compensation, and as to my own particular I shall heartily endeavour to represent your case in the truest light.

Similar letters were sent to the magistrates at Carlisle, to Peploe and to Cholmondeley.[24]

---

[20] *The Flying Post*, 26–8 January 1716; Nicholson, 'Lancashire', 78.
[21] Prescott, 'Diary', II, 474.
[22] Nicholson, 'Lancashire', 82.
[23] *The Weekly Journal*, 329, 11 February 1716.
[24] TNA, SP44/118, 133, 241.

There were changes in the composition of the Bench in Lancashire after the Jacobites were defeated. These were made in the Whig interest, of course, but were not to the liking of all Whigs, as Stout reported: 'The nation seems now to be settled and quiet from the late disturbance, and magistrates changed, but not for the better in this town, who pretend to be loyal yet oppress some of the best friends of the King'. Apparently, High Anglican justices had begun to demand money from the Quakers.[25]

Yet, because of the Whig triumph, towns were under the sway of the military and tensions between the soldiery and the civilian population, never good at the best of the times, began to give way to division. Chester was, in the short term, under martial law:

> about 8 the Belman at the Cross near us Reads publicly a proclamacion in the Mayors name, commanding all persons in the City to bee of peaceable and civil behaviour, not to walk about the streets or Rows at unseasonable Hours of the night, nor to use any words or expressions that may tend to disturb the peace or to raise any tumults or Insurrections in this City as they will answer to the contrary at their utmost perils. His Majesties Forces now quartered in this City, having received instruccions to suppress such offenders by Force, introduc'd and obtruded on the City by his Meanes if not against law, yet very contrary to the Recorders great and solemn obligaccions to the City.[26]

These actions were made all the worse because of reports of the actions of the soldiers in Lancashire. On 20 November, Prescott wrote, 'We are disturb'd with Accounts of the barbarous behaviour of the soldiers in their plunder of the popish Gentlemens Houses, especially Standish'. In Preston, 'The soldiers govern, hector and insult the Town'.[27]

There was even a clash between the soldiers and the civil authority. On 19 December, Colonel Fane, in charge of one of the battalions at Chester, put Roger Comberbach, the Recorder, under house arrest. This was because of an alleged argument over provision of fuel for the guards in the castle. Apparently, 'all the Town is alarm'd at the rash and unaccountable behaviour of Fane, but some hear of this strickness with pleasure' because the Recorder had 'bin eminent in his forward execucion of the Laws'. Grosvenor (then Mayor) and the aldermen presented the Recorder's case to the Secretary of State and Fane was superseded

---

[25] Stout, *Autobiography*, 177.
[26] Prescott, 'Diary', II, 474.
[27] Prescott, 'Diary', II, 475.

for his behaviour.[28] Clashes between soldiers and citizens also broke out in 1717.[29] One reason was that, by November 1716, the city felt itself unable to subsist the two regiments being quartered upon it.[30] Yet for lesser periods of time, soldiers were not always unwelcome. Madame Hornby, wife of a Broughton attorney, sent the troops stationed at Preston in December 1715 an ox and a half, several dozen ducks, neets' tongues, white loaves, and bread and ale.[31]

The Plight of the Jacobite Prisoners

The number of captured Jacobites was the largest number of prisoners taken by the state in the memory of man (there had been 1,336 taken in 1685). The Bloody Assizes of 1685 was the only recent precedent, and the Whig judiciary was aware that this had been a propaganda defeat for the victors, including James Stuart's father, James II. Thus comparison will be made between events of 1715 and those of 1685.

For the captured Jacobites, the rebellion was over, but their difficulties were arguably just beginning. Prisoners were still being brought in after the battle. Lord Molyneux and five or six others were arrested at Liverpool.[32] Wills was reimbursed £500 for the subsistence of the prisoners who were initially held at Preston.[33]

Six half-pay officers had been captured with the Jacobites at Preston. As they were subject to military law, their future was short and sharp. Pulteney told Wills that he had the power to try them by court martial and urged him to proceed immediately. He was unhappy that the latter had delayed. 'It is a little unfortunate that any Delay should have happened in the trying of ye prisoners', because Wills already had the power to hold courts martial.[34] The trial was held on 28 November; Major Nairne and Captain Lockhart pleaded not guilty, but all were found otherwise and sentence was carried out on 2 December, when four of them – Nairne, Lockhart, John Shafto and Erskine – were shot. Only the two former were afforded coffins. The other two men, Lord Charles Murray and James Dalzell, were reprieved.[35] In the case of Murray, this was because of

---

[28] Prescott, 'Diary', II, 481–3.
[29] Prescott, 'Diary', II, 580.
[30] TNA, WO4/18, 173.
[31] *St. James' Post*, 131, 5–7 Dec 1715.
[32] *Flying Post*, 3724, 15–17 Nov. 1715.
[33] *Calendar of Treasury Books*, XXIX, II, 1714–15, 864.
[34] TNA, WO4/17, 276.
[35] *Faithful Register*, 21; Ware, 'Memorials', 178–9.

the influence of his aristocratic relations, who had supported the Crown during the rebellion.[36] Dalzell could prove that he had thrown up his commission prior to the rebellion.[37]

On 16 November, Stanhope wrote to Carpenter to tell Wills to send 'all the noblemen, gentlemen, clergy and others of any note' to London. As for the others, he was to 'dispose of them in the castles and prisons of Lancaster, York, Chester and Hull'.[38] Wills was told by Pulteney that he had to discuss the distribution of prisoners with Cholmondeley and Derby.[39] The nobility, some of the gentry (including 11 from the north-western counties) and some of their servants travelled south via Coventry, and pass out of this account.[40] Major Humphrey Bland (1686–1763) of Honeywood's dragoons led the escort and later received £200.[41]

Of the Jacobite leaders, Derwentwater, Kenmure, Oxburgh and three others were executed in London. Forster, Nithsdale, Winton and Mackintosh escaped. Widdrington and Carnwath were discharged in 1717. Towneley and Tyldesley were found not guilty.[42]

There has been less contemporary and historical interest in the majority of the prisoners who were held in the northern gaols. Perhaps this is because none were aristocratic and less evidence survives. About 530 officers and men were despatched to Chester Castle, arriving on 27 November.[43] Prescott wrote in his diary that this was 'a melancholy and shocking triumph, a scene of human Infelicity and mortification'.[44] Yet a newspaper report declared, 'There seemed to be a prodigious number of spectators, who seemed well pleased with the sight'.[45] Another 200, many Highlanders, arrived at Chester on 20 December.[46] Others were sent to Lancaster Castle (the county's gaol) and also to Liverpool; though such was the lack of secure accommodation in the latter, it is likely that the least number were housed there.[47]

---

[36] TNA, SP44/117, 331
[37] Rae, *History*, 326.
[38] TNA, SP44/117, 331.
[39] TNA, WO4/17, 319.
[40] Prescott, 'Diary', II, 476; TNA, SP44/80, 1–18.
[41] *Calendar of Treasury Books*, XXXII, 1716, 200.
[42] Patten, *History*, 114–16.
[43] Prescott, 'Diary' II, 476.
[44] Prescott, 'Diary', II, 481.
[45] *The Daily Courant*, 4401, 1 Dec. 1715.
[46] Prescott, 'Diary', II, 481.
[47] TNA, KB33/1/5.

The Aftermath of the Fifteen, 1715–1717

This was the largest number of prisoners to have been held for treason since the aftermath of the Monmouth rebellion 30 years earlier.[48] It was not the aim of the state to try all these men. Instead, an order of council of 13 December stated that 'the publick peace of the kingdom' decreed 'that a speedy example be made of some of them'. Therefore, the 'gentlemen or men of estates, or such as shall appear to have distinguished themselves by any extraordinary degree of guilt' were to be tried. Of the remainder, they were to draw lots and only 1 out of 20 would be tried. Furthermore, only those men for whom there was plenty of evidence and witnesses against were put on trial.[49] This would result in a relatively small number of men being executed, so time and money, as well as lives, would be saved. The government probably wanted to be seen to be magnanimous and merciful in victory.

Information was gathered in Lancashire in order to provide ammunition for the prosecution, which was to be framed by the Attorney General. Henry Masterman, described by Liddell as 'honest and zealous', was given £300 for collecting such information. He had set off from London on 1 December to do so. Initially he did not have a list of the prisoners, so was compelled to ride around to all the prisons in order to make one.[50] Thomas Molyneux was requested to create a list of prisoners so that indictments could be framed against them and to distinguish which should be tried and which not. Thomas Crisp, county sheriff, claimed £21 for the same service. By the end of December the task had been almost accomplished.[51] Lancashire JPs provided information to William Wall, attorney, and others in December and January. Typically, witnesses stated that they had seen the suspect in arms, with the Jacobites, in Lancashire.[52] Payments were made to reimburse the travel and living expenses of witnesses from both Lancashire and Scotland.[53] Lancashire JPs such as Hoghton and Rigby took depositions in Preston and Lancashire from Jacobite prisoners, soldiers, constables and others throughout December. Men caught up by accident among the prisoners were released on the advice of Lancashire JPs; Alexander Herschlwood, 'a poor innocent man', was one; Robert Wyld and William Gurnall were discharged, too.[54]

---

[48] Sankey, *Prisoners*, xi–xii.
[49] TNA, SP44/118, 155–6.
[50] Liddell, 'Letters', 204.
[51] *Calendar of Treasury Books*, XXXI, 376,, TNA, SP44/118, 138, 148, 160.
[52] *Calendar of Treasury Books*, XXXI, 202, 105–6.
[53] TNA, SP44/118, 175–6; KB8/66.
[54] TNA, SP44/118, 159, 200; KB8/66.

In January 1716 there were 1,259 prisoners (another undated list gives their distribution thus: 222 at Lancaster, 157 at Wigan, 467 at Chester and 446 at Preston). Of these, there was no evidence against 131 gentlemen and 520 plebeian prisoners. There was some evidence against 40 gentlemen and 185 plebeian prisoners and there were a further 383 prisoners against whom there were two or more witnesses. It was decided to try the 40 gentlemen prisoners, 30 of the plebeians by virtue of warrants by the JPs and 25 other plebeians who were deemed of especial guilt.[55] One of the latter was Thomas Sydall, described by Thomas Bootle thus: 'Colonell of the mob at Manchester and being a notorious offender & of great esteem there amongst the disaffected the gentlemen of the county desire he may be there executed for example's sake'.[56] Of the remaining 383 it was decided to lot them with 1 in 20 being put on trial, which produced another 19 men to try. The man who was lotted in the last batch, which numbered fewer than 20, protested at the perceived unfairness, but to no avail.[57]

At the same time, judges Sir Robert Eyre (1666–1735), Sir James Montague (1666–1723), a baron of the Exchequer, and Sir Thomas Bury (1652–1722) were appointed by a Special Commission of Oyer and Terminer, to operate outside the Assize system and to try the prisoners held in the North West. They arrived at Preston on 30 December, travelling via Chester.[58] The trials began at Liverpool on 12 January 1716, and so prisoners to be tried were sent there from Lancaster, Preston and Chester. There was an opening sermon by Peploe. Bury made an address to the Grand Jury. The Grand Jury was summoned, the court seated and Bills of Indictment were found against 48 prisoners. The court was then adjourned for eight days so that the prisoners would have time to prepare their defence.[59]

The Grand Jury found another 113 indictments against them (including at least one man who was in a London prison!).[60] The court reconvened on 20 January and by 9 February, 74 men had been tried (during the Bloody Assizes of 1685, 30 men were tried in one morning alone). Sixteen men turned King's Evidence and were held apart from the others. Of those tried, men from Lancashire were represented out of all proportion (30 out of 74), probably because there were more witnesses to testify against them.[61]

---

[55] TNA, KB33/1/5/54, 65.
[56] BL. Stowe Mss 750, f157r.
[57] TNA, KB33/1/5/54.
[58] *The Flying Post*, 3738, 17–20 Dec. 1715 and 3743, 29–31 Dec. 1715.
[59] Rae, *History*, 378; *Political State*, XI, 1716, 168.
[60] *Flying Post*, 3752, 19–21 Jan. 1716.
[61] *Political State*, XI, 1716, 169; Rae, *History*, 378–9; Earle, *Monmouth's Rebels*, 171.

Little is known about the trials, in contrast to those of the noblemen and gentry tried in London, who were deemed of more importance and thus newsworthy, and for whom lengthy accounts were recorded. Scant detail was reported here. Those tried first were the men 'against whom the Proofs were very full, with some aggravating circumstances'. It would seem, from the evidence of two cases, that the trials proceeded thus. Witnesses for the prosecutions were arraigned against the prisoners, but were examined in court without knowing the testimony of their predecessors. The witnesses gave their testimonies to show that the accused had been in the company of the Jacobites in Lancashire. In the case of Richard Shuttleworth, those witnesses against him included fellow Jacobites such as Edward Shafto and one Calderwood, Fishwick, his servant, Budsworth, gaoler of Lancaster, and nine others. They testified that Shuttleworth had been in company with the Jacobite rebels. Similarly, with Muncaster, witnesses swore that he had been with the Jacobites. In Muncaster's case, William Winder, constable of Garstang, recalled that Muncaster had forced him to provide beef for the Jacobites.[62] A Mr Birch told Lady Petre, 'They being Scotch evidence agst them [the Chorleys] of very mean credit as I hear', and Chorley 'took some frivolous exceptions against his indictment in vain'.[63]

Although prisoners did not speak in their own defence, they had those who did; and often witnesses were brought in their defence. It was alleged in Muncaster's case that he had been with one Butler at a farm near Garstang on 9 November, but on the following day had been forced to accompany the Jacobites to Preston and 'he had not it in his power to get away'. Mary Frelfal, a maid, agreed with this testimony.[64] On the behalf of some of the Scots, it was argued that they had been forced into rebellion by fire and sword, but this was dismissed unless they had tried to escape; Faille Ferguson had gone along under guard and had refused a lieutenant's commission, and thus was acquitted.[65]

One newspaper noted, 'The prisoners have with them for their Advices, two or three of your Newgate Sollicitors, who cause them to give the court a great deal of needless Trouble by tedious challenges of the Juries and the like'. Another commented that the lawyers (such as Mr Arden of Sloppach) 'take up much time to little Purpose and do their Clients more Hurt than Good'.[66] One lawyer may have been Henry Tyrer of Ormskirk, attorney, who later tried to persuade

---

[62] LRO, DDX2244/1, *St. James' Evening Post*, 102, 21–4 January 1716.
[63] LRO, DDPT 14 Birch to Petre, 28 January 1716.
[64] LRO, DDX2244/1.
[65] *Flying Post*, 3756, 28–31 Jan. 1716.
[66] *Weekly Journal* 4 Feb. 1716; *Flying Post*, 3760, 7–9 February 1716.

a witness to withdraw his statement against his client.[67] Sydall's trial was also remarked upon. At first it was thought 'he is so sick, and looks so pitifully, that some think he will save the hangman a labour'. It was alleged that his illness was caused by the drink he had been sent by friends in Manchester to prevent him from making revelations against them. In any case, 'his trial was comi-tragical', with witnesses recalling his words uttered in public. He was not the only prisoner to be ill and on trial.[68]

Most were found guilty and sentenced to death, with seven acquittals. The latter included one man who had been forced into the rebellion and had been under guard throughout. As noted above, those most likely to be executed were those against whom there were said to be 'aggravating circumstances'. These included Richard Shuttleworth, who was alleged to have said 'He hope to see the streets run with Hereticks' Blood as fast as if it had rained for four days'. Sydall was also too prominent a Jacobite to be left unhanged, and likewise James Blundell, a former churchwarden.[69] Generally speaking, though, even if a man alleged that he had been forced into the rebellion, it was said that he could have deserted as others had.[70] Two men who had been found guilty died before the sentences could be carried out.[71]

The executions occurred in a number of towns throughout Lancashire. There were 12 at Preston (five on 28 January, seven on 9 February), five at Wigan (9 February), five at Manchester (on 11 February), four at Garstang (on 16 February), four at Lancaster and four at Low Hill, near Liverpool (on 25 February). In total, 34 men were hanged, with the first five being drawn and quartered.[72] A graphic account of the first five executions was noted by John Lucas, a Leeds schoolmaster. After being taken to Sandy Hill, a half mile from Preston on the road to Lancaster, on sledges with ropes around their necks and arms:

> When they were hung so long that they were concluded dead, they were cut down, then stripped, laid on their backs, and their privy members being cut off were thrown into a great fire made there for the purpose, then they were turned upon their faces and their heads being chopped off, they were turned over again and their bellies ripped open to their hearts, their bowels, their livers and lastly

[67] TNA, KB8/66.
[68] *Flying Post*, 3756, 28–31 January, 3758, 2–4 February 1716.
[69] Rae, *History*, 378–9; *Political State*, XI, 1716, 69.
[70] *Flying Post*, 3756, 28–31 January 1716.
[71] *Flying Post*, 3767, 23–5 February 1716.
[72] *Faithful Register*, 27–8.

their hearts thrown into the fire, then their arms, legs & thighs were chopped off, which with the trunks of their bodies and heads were putt into coffins.[73]

The sheriff's bill came to £132 15s 4d, half of which went to the two hangmen.[74]

There would have been more executions, had not the original sentences been countermanded. Prescott noted on 2 February that expresses had arrived from London to the judges that they stop some of the executions. Apparently, 17 were to have been hanged at Manchester – as noted, this number was vastly reduced.[75]

Most prisoners did not repent their actions before they were executed. One who did was Roger Muncaster, speaking at Preston on 28 January: 'I am brought hither to be a miserable and dismal spectacle to you all. The Crime I am accused of, Condem'd and brought hither to be executed, bears no meaner, or less infamous title, then Rebellion, a Crime prohibited by the Laws of God and Man'. He begged God's pardon for such behaviour.[76] Muncaster's last speech appeared in much of the press. Yet as Rae wrote, most were not penitent.[77] One Captain Straton, a Jacobite, wrote to Mar in March 1716 that 'all of them, save one, died justifying what they had done'.[78] When Alexander Drummond was executed, he underwent his ordeal 'with a becoming Courage and Resolution and drew a Great deal of Compassion from the Spectators'.[79]

Three of those hanged had the further indignity of having their heads struck up on public places as a reminder to others – Richard Shuttleworth's head was displayed on Preston Town Hall as 'a terrible example to all passengers'.[80] Sydall's was placed on the market cross at the Exchange in Manchester.[81] The remains of one corpse was erected at Lancaster, one at Garstang and another at Preston. As Robert Cotesworth remarked, in June 1716, 'There was Gallawayes [sic] and heads put up at every Towne wee came at'.[82]

These executions did not pass without protest. John Molyeneux of Pilkington, a watchmaker, accosted a group of soldiers on 11 February. He said, 'Oh you are all King George's soldyers and you have been murdering today and Butchering five men and putting them out of their way'. Five days later, Robert Sholwerdine, an

---

[73] LLSL, Diary of John Lucas, 86–7.
[74] Anon., 'Sheriff's expenses', *Lancashire and Cheshire Historical Society*, XII, 1859–60.
[75] Prescott, 'Diary', II, 490.
[76] *Weekly Journal*, 329, 11 February 1716.
[77] Rae, *History*, 380n.
[78] *HMC*, Stuart Papers, II, 9.
[79] *Faithful Register*, 31.
[80] Leeds Library, Diary of John Lucas, 86–7.
[81] *Faithful Register*, 32.
[82] TWAS, CP3/22; *Faithful Register*, 32.

innkeeper of Manchester, shouted 'Down with the rump' and 'You are nothing but Rebells and nothing but a parcel of Rebells' several times, and added, 'Damn ye Presbyterians, what can you do att us you can but cut off my members and set them up ahead as you have done with Sydalls'. He was in an inn at Buckley and also drank 'confusion to ye Presbiterians and down with the rump'.[83]

Other Jacobites were put on trial at the Assizes held at Preston in September 1716. Thirty were sent from Chester on 8 September and another 58 on the 20th.[84] Thirteen were tried on 21 September and eight on 23 September. Four were convicted after a trial, four pleaded guilty; nine were acquitted, two were cleared, even though there was clear proof against them, three were acquitted through want of proof, and another three were held over for trial in the following year. It was noted that more of the prisoners should have been found guilty, but 'the Juries were grown stiff; and notwithstanding they had been Eye Witnesses of, and even felt the dismal Effects of the late unnatural rebellion, yet they acted like the Juries of Surrey, thought fit to break up the Assizes'. Perhaps they felt that enough men had suffered for their part in the rebellion and that only a few more should face the ultimate punishment. Of those found guilty, three were due to hang at Lancaster and two at Preston, all being drawn but not quartered, and all on 2 October, but in the event all took place at Preston. Four of those hanged, who were all Lancastrians, 'persons of mean character', said nothing. John Bruce, the Scot who was hanged, was defiant to the last, declaring in a paper given to the sheriff:

> I am not asham'd of that cause for which I Die, but rejoice that I am worthy to be a sacrifice for the vindication of the undoubted Rights of my Lawful and Natural liege Lord, King James the Third, and the expiring Liberties of my Dear Country.

Although a Protestant, Bruce affirmed his belief in the hereditary succession of monarchs. In late March 1717, 194 Jacobite prisoners were sent from Lancaster to Chester, but there is no record of any trials; indeed, 49 men were discharged at this time.[85]

It is interesting to note that relatively few of the men from the North West chose to be transported – 19 in all. Yet a far higher percentage of the north-western men were executed – 21 out of 39 in total, and all of these were from Lancashire. Yet none of the north-western men who were sent to London for

---

[83] TNA, PL27/2.
[84] Prescott, 'Diary, II, 533, 536.
[85] *Weekly Journal*, 29 September, 13 October 1716, 16 March 1717.

trial were executed. They were either acquitted in 1716, such as Tyldesley and Towneley, or were discharged in the following year. It was probably thought that this large number of Lancastrians hanged in Lancashire would make the deepest impression on that county and prove a grim warning to all those considering rebellion, as had occurred, albeit on a far larger scale (about 250 executions), in the South West in 1685.[86]

As said, it had never been the intention of the Crown to initiate wholesale execution. As early as 22 November, Stanhope told Wills, 'You may easily imagine that the King's clemency will incline him to pardon the greatest part of the common sort'. He told Wills that the prisoners should petition for transportation to the American colonies for a period of seven years.[87] Yet, 'the King is inclined to shew mercy to the bulk of the prisoners, and yet would not have them remaining in the country in order to create new disturbances, it is expected they should comply with the terms of transportation'.[88]

Those not tried were told to formulate a humble petition to the Crown, confessing their guilt and pleading that their lives be spared. This meant that those who did would be transported to the American colonies by ships belonging to Liverpool merchants, there to serve in the colonies as indentured labourers for seven years.[89] By early February, over 300 at Lancaster, and others at Chester, had availed themselves of this opportunity.[90] According to another source, most of the 300 prisoners at Lancaster and 600 at Chester did petition as told.[91] Some refused to petition for transportation: 206 in all – and of these, 26 were from Lancashire.[92] Jacobites complained at this treatment, alleging 'by cruel usage [the prisoners] had been forced to sign indentures of slavery and others who had hitherto refused still treated with the greatest barbarity'.[93]

These prisoners were to be taken good care of and delivered to the merchants 'in a fair state of health'. Any who were ill were 'as soon as possible [to be] taken out of their places of confinement, in order to have the benefit of the air ... within the castle walls ... with proper Guards so as to prevent their making escape'. They were to be given 'proper medicines', 'administered them by physicians and apothecaries' in order 'to prevent any contagious distempers getting among

---

[86] Earle, *Monmouth's Rebels*, 175.
[87] TNA, SP44/117, 339.
[88] TNA, SP44/118, 186.
[89] Rae, *History*, 379–80.
[90] *Flying Post*, 3761, 9–11 February 1716.
[91] *Political State*, XI, 1716, 173.
[92] TNA, KB33/1/5/14–15.
[93] *HMC*, Stuart Papers, III, 548.

them'. About 44 men were deemed to be too ill for transportation, and these may have been released in order to stop contagion affecting their fellows.[94] Those who were only temporarily ill 'may be fit for transportation when they recover'.[95]

Major Solomon Rapin, of Dormer's dragoons, was in charge of the prisoners at Lancaster in March. He was told that the Attorney General had prepared pardons for the prisoners on whom death sentences had been passed, as long as they agreed to be transported. Those who refused to sign the petition would be given another opportunity to do so. Seventeen refused. Rapin was told, notwithstanding, to deliver them to the merchants to be transported.

On 28 February 1716, Sir Thomas Johnson (1664–1728), a Whig MP for Liverpool, had been awarded the contract to transport the prisoners across the Atlantic. He was given 40 shillings per head to do so.[96] On 20 March he received £1,000 in part payment.[97] Transportation began on 30 March and was completed by 31 July. Ten ships carried 639 men to South Carolina, Jamaica, Virginia, St Christopher's and Barbados (almost all were Scots; only 16 men from the North West were transported). In detail, 95 were sent on the *Scipio* to Virginia on 30 March; 81 on the *Wakefield* on 21 April to South Carolina; 47 went on the *Two Brothers* to Jamaica on 26 April; 104 on the *Susannah* to South Carolina on 7 May; 80 on the *Friendship* on 24 May to Virginia; 30 on the *Hockenhill* on 25 June to St Christopher's; 126 on the *Elizabeth and Anne* to Virginia on 29 June; and 56 on the *Godspeed* to Virginia on 28 July. One man went on the *Africa* to Barbados on 15 July. The final batch was of 18 men went on the *Anne* to Virginia on 31 July.[98]

However, of the men on the *Elizabeth and Anne*, 10 were bought off at Liverpool, one for £40 and one for £50, and another four were bought off at Cork, the ship's first staging post. One man died at sea. Seven or eight men paid the captain five guineas in return for special treatment on board ship. On arrival in the colony, they petitioned the governor to the effect that it was illegal to transport men unless they had been convicted in court or they had consented to transportation.[99] Others escaped from the *Hockenrill*, when the prisoners

---

[94] TNA, SP35/5, fol.54r; SP44/120, 24–5.
[95] TNA, SP44/120, 8–9.
[96] *Calendar of Treasury Papers*, V, 196.
[97] *Calendar of Treasury Papers*, V, 200.
[98] *Calendar of State Papers Colonial, America and the West Indies, 1716–1717*, 29, London, 1930, ed. Cecil Headlam, 167–73.
[99] Norman Shaw, 'Jacobites transported to Virginia', *Notes and Queries*, 12th series, X, 1922, 361–2.

took over the ship, and sailed to freedom in France after selling the cargo in the Americas.[100]

The common men seemed, largely, content to admit their guilt, sign the petition for mercy and then be sentenced to seven years' transportation. Yet the gentlemen prisoners in Chester Castle, to a man, refused. They would agree to being transported, but refused to beg for mercy, presumably deeming it beneath their honour.[101] The prison officials threatened them, fed them on bread and water, and cast them into a dungeon.[102] According to Sir Hugh Paterson, 'They cry out very much here against the present violent measures in England, and I believe such instances of barbarity and cruelty can scarce be given even in the reigns of Nero or Oliver Cromwell'.[103]

Treatment aboard the ships which sailed from Liverpool was objected to. On one ship, a prisoner later remarked

> You can't imagine the bad treatment we had from the master while he had us in his power, having all been kept in irons except one and myself, who had bought our freedom. However, as to everything else, we all fared alike, our meat being a salt hough of beef for five, and a biscuit to everyone once a day, and an allowance of stinking water as red as blood, being kept in claret casks. Our beds were in every way answerable to our diet. This and the insults we suffered every hour from the master and crew, added to the unspeakable misfortunes we suffered from a long imprisonment.[104]

A number of prisoners escaped. Given the initial number of 1,783 and then the subsequent figure of 1,259 (in late December 1715), even allowing for 200 being sent to London, that leaves just over 300 unaccounted for. These men probably escaped, perhaps due to lax security or/and Jacobite sympathisers. There was a steady seepage of escapes after this. Two men bribed a guard to be allowed to escape from Chester.[105] As had been the case in London, there were a number of escapes from the northern gaols thereafter. Five or six escaped from Chester Castle in January.[106] In late February, another 28 got away from Chester.[107] A total

---

[100] *HMC*, Stuart Papers, III, xxxvi, 305.
[101] *HMC*, Stuart Papers, II, 232; Haydon, *Anti-Catholicism*, 83.
[102] *HMC*, Stuart Papers, II, 232.
[103] *HMC*, Stuart Papers, II, 233.
[104] *HMC*, Stuart Papers, III, 305.
[105] Prescott, 'Diary', II, 489.
[106] *Weekly Journal*, 309, 21 January 1716.
[107] *Flying Post*, 3769, 28 February–1 March 1716.

of 22 men escaped from Wigan in late November.[108] A number of Lancashire gentlemen, listed as prisoners, are recorded as being alive in 1717 or afterwards, though are not recorded as being discharged, but clearly were, pointing to the fact that record-keeping and survival was, as ever, less than perfect.[109]

John Walker was one escapee. He had been drinking with John Groves, a private in the Royal Welsh Fusiliers, who was one of the guards in Liverpool. Walker offered him £10. The two left on 15 February 1716. Another was John Hothersall, who escaped and was hidden by his sister, Anne Lecknby.[110] A dramatic escape was made in early January 1716:

> a Highlander (a brisk young Fellow) as they were marching to Leverpool, took an Opportunity of steeping out of the Ranks, and vaulting over a five-barr'd gate, made his escape in the Face of the Soldiers; 7 or 8 shot after him, but mist him; It was in vain for any of them to think of pursuing him, for he ran and jump'd over the Hedge and Ditch with Great Swiftness.[111]

Some prisoners died in the northern gaols; the exact number is unknown. At least 43 are known not to have survived Lancaster Gaol.[112] Between January 1716 and July 1716, 22 prisoners died at Liverpool – at least they are recorded as being buried, and presumably most or all were Jacobite prisoners, not common felons.[113] Many died in Chester, as Lady Otway observed: 'So much sickness now in our castle that the dye in droves like rotten sheep and be 4 or 5 a night throne into the castle ditch ffor graves'.[114]

Apart from poor sanitation caused by overcrowding, these deaths were also due to the severe weather that affected Britain in the winter of 1715–16, when even the Thames froze. In February 1716, Prescott wrote, 'Contagious and fatal distempers, Fever Flux & small pox spread among the prisoners in the Castle'. John Rutherford, a prisoner, wrote, 'A fever raged amongst us while few hath escaped, and hath brought several to their graves'.[115] The bad weather persisted for some months. In December, Prescott noted there had been 'A very sharp and

---

[108] TNA, SP35/5, fol. 209r.
[109] *VCH Lancashire*, III–VIII.
[110] TNA, WO71/122; *VCH Lancashire*, VII, 64.
[111] *Bristol Post Man*, 28 January 1716.
[112] *Faithful Register*, 399–400.
[113] Liverpool Record Office, 283 PET 1/1.
[114] HMC Xth Rep. App. IV, 352.
[115] Prescott 'Diary', II, 491; Griffiths, 'Diary', 49.

severe frost with wind and snow'.[116] Two months later, he recorded, 'Frost hard and bearing'.[117]

The magistrates were concerned about illnesses being contagious and wrote in a letter to the government, on 17 February, 'many of them ill of a spotted fever. The contagion of which has infected some of the soldiers in both regiments ... We have a Melancholy Prospect of this Malignant Distemper getting to a Height and spreading among us'.[118]

Lady Otway wrote, 'The feavour and sickness increaseth dayly, is begun to spread Much into the Citty, and many off the guard solidgers is sick, it is thought by infection'. Just before the trials it was stated that 165 were ill.[119]

The conditions in which the prisoners in the northern gaols found themselves account for these deaths. Robert Cotesworth, son of William Cotesworth, was touring Lancashire in early 1716 and reported to his father in June:

> We saw the greatest Misery at Lancaster yt ever wee saw before. All yt ever could go in Cartes or Ride on Horse back they carried to ship of at Leverpoole yt rest wch were about 34 (most of 'em Scotchmen) lie in a kind of a Dark hole under ground and are so weak yt they cannot help one another. Some of them are spotted wth ye fever. We saw one of then lying Dead wrapt in his plaid.[120]

Yet the officials were not wholly inhumane. Between 4 March and 20 August 1716, £181 was spent on medical bills for between 50 and 60 prisoners held there.[121]

Exact figures for the ultimate disposal of the prisoners of the rebellion are unknown. Certainly, numbers of those escaping or dying in custody, which have been quoted above, are probably underestimates. Some who remained in gaol after 1716 were probably pardoned through the Act of Grace passed that year. Part of this contemporary lack of interest can perhaps be garnered from the attitude of the writer of *The Faithful Register*, who commented about the transportees, 'who being generally of the common sort, makes it very little necessary to mention them further'.[122]

Each prisoner was allocated four pence per day for food and drink. This was to consist of a pennyworth of small beer, a penny for cheese and tuppence for

---

[116] Prescott, 'Diary', II, 481.
[117] Prescott, 'Diary', II, 492.
[118] Bennett, 'Cheshire', 39.
[119] HMC Xth Rep. App. IV, 352; TNA, KB33/1/5/8.
[120] TWAS, CP3/22.
[121] *Calendar of Treasury Books*, XXXI, 315, 372–3.
[122] *Faithful Register*, 403.

bread. One of the contractors was William Stout. He bought about two or three hundredweight of cheese per week, at about 12s or 14s per hundredweight. He concluded that the prisoners were 'a profit to the country' as the supply of food to both prisoners and guards brought about £3,000 of business to local merchants.[123]

Initially conditions were poor. Lady Otway wrote, 'They are almost starved for want of some covering'.[124] Captain Straton wrote that they were 'crowded like beasts in a fold, having a raging fever amongst them, and daily dying with ill usage and want of necessities, little or no distinction made betwixt the best gentlemen and the meanest sort'.[125]

Yet for some, life was fine, even in captivity. Robert Cotesworth noted, 'We saw a great number of ye Gentlemen Rebells at Liver[pool] they have money in abundance are not at all daunted and are Drunck every Night'.[126] It seems that Lord Molyneux must have given his parole for he was 'prisoner at large' in Liverpool.[127] Prescott visited Scottish prisoners in Chester Castle in March 1716 and noted, 'Wee are civilly treated by the Scottish gentlemen in that room, with Tea and fine Brandy'.[128] Stout wrote, 'Besids the King's allowance, they had supplys privetly from the Papists and disaffected, so as to live very plentyfully'.[129] Prescott noted on the day after the prisoners arrived at Chester that Dr Arthur Fogg (1669–1739), Vicar of St Oswald's Church, Chester, was collecting money for their succour and Prescott contributed five shillings. Others brought food and clothing to the prisoners.[130] Francis Towneley 'left ye little he had for relief of sufferers'. John Gillibrand told Lady Petre the response of the prisoners to such alms: 'Poor prisoners send up daily Prayers to Heaven for blessings here and hereafter on you & yours. Something yet undistributed but in 4 or 5 days I go to Liverpool where too many objects of pity are to be found'.[131]

Not all were sympathetic towards the prisoners. Some potential donors were insulted.[132] Prescott wrote, 'All conversations are full of the necessarys of the prisoners and the severities of the Guards in not permitting charitable exhibitions to bee brought to them'. The Mayor and Recorder acted likewise

---

[123] Stout, *Autobiography*, 176.
[124] HMC Xth Rep, IV Appendix, 352.
[125] *HMC*, Stuart Papers, II, 9.
[126] TWAS, CP3/22.
[127] *Faithful Register*, 403.
[128] Prescott 'Diary', II, 499.
[129] Stout, *Autobiography*, 176.
[130] Prescott, 'Diary', II, 476.
[131] LRO, DDPT 14, Gillibrand to Petre, 22 April 1716.
[132] Prescott, 'Diary', II, 479.

against the would-be donors.[133] Yet not all of the guards were surly; Prescott noted in May 1716 that 'The Capt. Shows great humanity which is gratefully acknowledged by the Captives'.[134]

Many prisoners were in good spirits, at least in January 1716. John Ashton told how

> I hath several times heard ye Pretender's health drunk amongst ye said prisoners by the name of King James the third with a general huzza of all ye greatest part of ye prisoners ... scarce a glass of beer or water is drunk amongst ym without saying God bless King James the third.[135]

Liddell had seen a letter from Masterman and reported, 'The Preston prisoners have bin very uppish ever since their confinement on what account I know not; they say Marr will be able to release them but those are distant views'. After Pierson had been questioned, he refused to swear to it and Masterman deemed him 'a harden'd obdurate sinner and that nothing can be made of him'. Not all shared these views; Philip Hodgson 'is the most dejected; he plainly says we shall be buoy'd up with hopes off a pardon till we are hang'd'.[136]

Whigs reported the spirits of the prisoners to be fine. When prisoners were taken from Chester to Liverpool to stand trial, it was reported that they 'seem to go with great courage'.[137] Those at Chester Castle 'appear very confident in their Behaviour, and seem to divise the Fate which is likely to attend them'. It was thought that their spirits were high because they were receiving encouraging letters from sympathisers from outside, especially from Scotland. Some were delivered by a woman from Liverpool. When some of these were opened, she was seized and sent to Liverpool.[138]

By the spring of 1717, some prisoners at least were being allowed considerable latitude. Lord Charles Murray, who had avoided the death sentence in 1715, was one. Prescott recorded that Murray was visited by his daughter, Lydia. Murray was much sought after by Mrs Suzy and Bell Bunbury.[139]

Some Whigs were sympathetic to the plight of prisoners known to them. They included Symson, despite the fact that he had written, that once the

---

[133] Prescott, 'Diary', II, 481.
[134] Prescott, 'Diary', II, 509.
[135] TNA, KB8/66.
[136] Liddell, 'Letters', 213.
[137] *Weekly Journal*, 309, 21 January 1716.
[138] *Weekly Journal*, 329, 11 February 1716.
[139] Prescott, 'Diary', II, 569, 570.

Jacobite prisoners were in custody 'they will meet with their desserts'.. He was approached by Mrs Sanderson, a friend of his late wife. Her husband had been gaoled at Lancaster and she wished to save his life. She wrote, 'I know none can assist him more nor indeed so much as you'. Symson contacted William Shaw of Preston and asked him to intercede, and Sanderson's life was saved.[140] Alexander Drummond 'was a young Man of most comely personage and grew great compassion from most people'. Therefore, 'It was him for whom some young Women of the better sort at Leverpoole hazarded their Fame by appearing before the Judges to intercede for his Life and thereby involving themselves in a suspicion of countenancing his Crime'. They were unsuccessful.[141]

Some prisoners remained in gaol for a long period of time. On 1 November, despite the transportations, escapes, deaths and executions, there were still 201 prisoners at Lancaster, 12 at Chester and 7 at Liverpool.[142] At Chester, nearly £300 was spent on subsistence for prisoners there between 1 May and 29 July 1717. After the latter date, the remaining prisoners, now further reduced to 194 men, were discharged.[143] Prescott recorded on 29 August 1717, 'Wee pass in the road, on this side of Frodsham, thoro a considerable number of the prisoners this morning discharged by virtue of the Act of Pardon, cheerfully returning to their Country, Scotland & Northumberland'.[144] It is difficult to summarise the fates of the prisoners. With 194 being released in 1717, 639 were transported, 39 were executed, at least 65 died in captivity and about 44 were released due to illness; and of the remainder, just under 300, some escaped, some died, and any men acting as witnesses for the Crown would also have been released. Alas, the names of most of the latter three groups are not given. The known fates of men from the North West are detailed in Appendix 2.

There were also trials in Carlisle of Scots prisoners taken from Scottish gaols in December 1716, though none of them was convicted. Nicolson took a close interest in these trials, but none of the other leading Whigs from the North West did. James Lowther evaded serving on the grand jury. Nicolson complained of others' non-attendance:

> Neither of our temporal lords in the Commission (Earl of Carlisle and Lord Lonsdale) are in the country. The former has indeed liv'd long in Yorkshire; but his friends here hop'd that (on this occasion) his lordship would have

---

[140] Symson, *Letter Books*, 346, 425–6.
[141] *Faithful Register*, 31.
[142] TNA, SP41/5, f61r.
[143] *Calendar of Treasury Papers*, V, 227; TNA: PRO, SP35/9, fols.158r–159r.
[144] Prescott, 'Diary', II, 588.

countenanced them with his presence. The latter left us just as the judges were upon the confineds of the county.[145]

Perhaps they were tired of the judicial process and wanted to live in peace? Yet Nicolson was magnanimous; he entertained some prisoners, feeding them with powdered beef and cabbage, visited others and found they joined him in loyal prayers for George I and the established Church.[146]

Yet even after the Act of Grace of July 1717, the imprisonment of Jacobites taken in rebellion was not quite over. Robert Scarisbrick, John Gregson and John Ashton had escaped imprisonment, but surrendered themselves in July 1717 and were sent to Newgate. In March 1718 Scarisbrick was held at Lancaster and was tried at the County Assizes. He was finally released in September 1718.[147] Another long-term prisoner was Richard Shuttleworth (not to be confused with his namesake who was hanged), who in April 1718 'hath been for a considerable time and still is a prisoner' at Lancaster Castle; he was ordered to be released.[148]

Catholics and Jacobites

The reactions of Catholics and Jacobites in the North of England varied considerably in the aftermath of the defeat of their cause.

At first, some were buoyed up by rumours of success elsewhere. Prescott recorded on 31 January that one Mr Yates told of 'Lord Marrs success, Argyle defeated, the Swiss cut in peeces'.[149] Two days later, there was news that 'a bloody Battle was decided on Marrs part'.[150] What actually happened was that Mar was not successful in battle; indeed, there was no battle. Argyle's army advanced and Mar's retreated before dispersing in utter and ignominious defeat.

For others, flight seemed the best and safest option. There was certainly an exodus of Catholics and others from Lancashire after the surrender at Preston. Robert Cotesworth remarked:

---

[145] William Nicolson, 'Eight Letters by William Nicholson', ed. Henry Paton, *SHS Miscellany*, I, 1894, 523.
[146] Sankey, *Prisoners*, 122–3.
[147] Blundell, 'Great Diurnall', 207n, 226–7, 240; *Weekly Journal*, 16 March 1717.
[148] TNA, SP44/80, 73.
[149] Prescott, 'Diary', II, 490.
[150] Prescott, 'Diary', II, 490.

> There is not one Roman Catholick left in Lancaster ... Every Town wee came at there were about 12 Gentlemen that kept coaches at Preston before the Rebellion about six of 'em are fled nobody knows where to and there is not one Roman Catholick left at Preston, tho' ye Towne Swarmed wth them before.[151]

One such Lancashire Catholic gentleman was Blundell. Initially, after hearing news of the defeat of the rebellion, he spent six days in the priest's hole in his house. On 24 November, he rode southwards to London, reaching the city on 2 December. After staying here a leisurely few months, he sailed to Flanders in March. While in London he met several other Catholic gentlemen from Lancashire. It is to be regretted that Blundell was so laconic and guarded in his entries that the specific danger he was in is not mentioned.[152] George Hilton, a Jacobite gentleman who had escaped after the battle of Preston, went into hiding near to his home in Westmorland, and was never found by the authorities.[153] Yet we should not overestimate the flight of the Catholics – and most of those who fled returned. Peploe recorded there being 643 Catholics in Preston in 1717.[154]

As has been noted, some of those who remained sympathised with the plight of Jacobite prisoners and tried to alleviate their sufferings. At Warrington, Tories, especially women, gave them ale, bread and other food.[155] At Chester, there were those who wished to give the prisoners food and clothing, too.[156] On 6 March, Prescott recorded giving his son a pound to give to the prisoners there.[157] It was claimed that £2,000 was sent to the captive Towneley in London by friends in Lancashire.[158]

There was another way in which Jacobite and Catholic landowners in England suffered. This was by the offices of the Forfeited Estates Commission, a body set up by Act of Parliament in 1716 to ascertain Catholic and Jacobite land ownership and to confiscate those lands belonging to families who had rebelled. This law applied to both England and Scotland, and the county in England in which it had most impact was, of course, Lancashire. Francis Foot, Solicitor and Clerk of Discoveries, was sent to Preston in August 1716 and the office for the

---

[151] TWAS, CP3/22.
[152] Blundell, 'Great Diurnall', 152–3, 153n, 161
[153] *The Rake's Diary*, xxix.
[154] Haydon, 'Peploe', 76.
[155] *The Flying Post*, 3730, 29 November – 1 December 1715.
[156] Prescott, 'Diary', II, 479.
[157] Prescott, 'Diary', II, 496.
[158] Nicholson, 'Lancashire', 82.

Commissioners was established at one Mrs Hewson's house in September. They stayed there until November, when they relocated to Newcastle.[159]

The Commissioners met with mixed receptions in Lancashire. Leading Whigs helped them. Peploe drew up a complete report of 'estates granted to superstitious uses in and around Preston' by listing estates where there were priests. Others were influenced by the rewards given by the Commissioners, and so men informed on Catholics they bore grudges against. Those informers, such as William Turnor of Brindle, who began their stories but refused to conclude them were gaoled.[160]

It was not all plain sailing for the informants. Richard Hitchmough, an informer, had his house raided and garden destroyed one night in July 1717. William Shepherd, a former servant of Molyneux, tried to bribe an official, though without success.[161]

Not all the information provided was successfully pursued. A raid on Westby Hall, seat of the Cliftons, in March 1716 was hardly a triumph. Some Catholic regalia was found, but the priest had absconded before the search party arrived. Attempts to carry away goods found there were hindered by local people.[162]

Attempts were certainly made by landowners to make the Commissioners' work difficult for them. Fields were left unploughed or open and tenants departed, so it was difficult to ascertain the real value of the land. Catholics petitioned for delays in registering their estates, in order to give themselves time to remove timber from their lands and to devalue it in other ways. Estates were conveyed into the hands of trustees. Tenants of the Standish estates were backward in revealing their leases, and when these were shown tried to use fraudulent practices in order to alter the sums mentioned therein. Friendly Protestant landowners became trustees of Catholic lands. The Leybourne lands were transferred to the nominal ownership of Thomas Gillow. John Leybourne had participated in the rebellion whereas Gillow had not. In 1717, tenants of the Scarisbrick estates near Ormskirk locked the Commissioners' agents out and laughed at them.[163] Alexander Butler, Richard Butler's brother-in-law, tried to save the latter's estates by having them assigned to him by a deed of gift, and Mr Curwen, another relation, acted as a trustee to the Rawcliffe estates, though both stratagems ultimately failed.[164]

---

[159] *Forfeited Estates Commission*, London, 1968, 3.
[160] Purcell, 'Jacobite Rising of 1715', 419, 423.
[161] Purcell, 'Jacobite Rising', 420.
[162] Purcell, 'Jacobite Rising', 425–6.
[163] Purcell, Jacobite Rising', 425–9.
[164] Gillow, *Biographical Dictionary*, 5, 365.

However, the Commissioners' men were not always deceived and often spotted the tricks that were being used against them. Many Jacobites lost their lands. Twenty-four Catholic and one Protestant Jacobite landowner had their lands confiscated and sold after 1715; another 10 had their estates taken from them but not sold.[165] The Dalton estate was forfeited and was only bought back at the cost of £6,000. The Carus family seat, Halton Hall, was sold. The estates of the Butlers, the Leybournes and the Heskeths were also all confiscated and sold. The Chorley estates were sold for £5,500 to one Abraham Compton. John Robinson and John Edsforth had estates at Myerscough and these were confiscated. Albert Hodson's estate was sold, but a friend bought it back for him in 1723.[166] The widow of Robert Kellett (who had died in Newgate on 28 May 1716) was desperate as his being outlawed led to her estate being confiscated. She complained in 1718 that she would 'be destitute of all manner of subsistence, and even the common necessaries of life, without Grace or Favour'. The outlawry was reversed.[167]

For the government, this had been relatively successful, and was in contrast to the ineffectiveness of the Commissioners in Scotland. The Whig establishment in the northern kingdom, armed with Scottish property laws, were protective of their fellow Scots and acted to delay the work of the Commissioners. They were so successful that when the Commission was disbanded in 1724, they had barely scratched the surface in Scotland.[168]

Priests were also pursued, as noted above. The Rev. Thomas Rawdon, chaplain at Leighton Hall, had to make his escape with what little he could carry and travelled via Kendal to Yorkshire. Others were less fortunate. The Rev. James Swarbrick was arrested at Richard Gillow's house in Singleton and was sent to Lancaster Castle, where he died in 1716, and the Rev. James Gerard died at Liverpool. Several others were apprehended, too, but were all eventually released.[169] Newly appointed JPs adopted a more severe line against Catholics in other ways. They encouraged soldiers to plunder Catholic homes.[170]

Yet not all was forlorn for the Jacobites. Even in defeat, the Jacobite cause made some converts. One such was Prescott, who was not a Jacobite in 1714, but by 1716 he was. Proof of his changing attitudes is witnessed in his outrage at the lot of the Jacobite prisoners, but confirmation came on 10 June 1716. He

---

[165] Blackwood, 'Lancashire Catholics', 47, 58–9.
[166] Tyldesley, *Diary*, 28, 39, 42, 60; Hardwick, *Preston*, I, 241; *VCH Lancashire*, VII, 141, VIII, 179.
[167] TNA, SP44/360, 103.
[168] Sankey, *Jacobite Prisoners*, 138–49.
[169] LRO, RCFE2/1.
[170] Purcell, 'Jacobite Rising', 429–30.

recorded, 'Mrs Midleton & Mrs Lloyd come over silently to celebrate this Birth Day of King James 3. The Health is not drunk by name, wee invent the best within the compass'.[171]

Despite defeat, some Jacobites were not downhearted. Verbal Jacobitism was alive and well in parts of Cheshire. On 6 December 1715 at a pub in Brereton, John Comberbach, on being asked to drink the King's health, 'said the Pretender was King James' son and by all the gentlemen was the Right Heire to ye Crown and would have it'. Three weeks later, Thomas Burton in Lancaster declared, 'King James the third of England and of Ireland the 8th was the lawful King and we shall quickly have him'. In June 1716, Daniel Horden of Gawsworth was said to have cried, 'Down with ye Rump and God bless King James the Third'. Peter Swaine, a yeoman, was near Congleton church in the following month and 'Cryed down with the Rump'. Apparently, 'it was his frequent practice to use seditious words with other scandalous and reflecting words against the government'.[172]

Verbal abuse could turn into something else. In Manchester in 1716, two officers were shouted 'hem' at. After several such cries, one officer replied, 'Cuckoo', to which a passing tradesman commented, 'I know of no cuckold but King George'. On being pursued he shot one of his pursuers in the eye.[173]

At Chester on the night of 9 August 1717, shortly after the prisoners had been released, three of them showed their defiance:

> being joined with several disaffected persons of this Neighbourhood, [they] appear'd in the streets with Musick playing their beloved Tune, The King shall enjoy &c ... They proclaimed the Pretender by the name K.J.3d. and drank his Health as such; cursing His Majesty with all the Royal Family.

They also shouted 'Down with the Rump' and threatened passers-by and loyal Whigs, ordering them to pray for the Stuarts. Eventually, their antics were ended by a gang of young Whigs putting them to flight.[174]

John Hardman, a Lancashire miller, vowed, 'If I ever be released I will make the best of my way to the Earl of Mar to assist King James III'.[175]

Jacobites could also fight back against those who had informed against them. Edward Shafto, who had been a trial witness, later stated that his behaviour 'hath so exposed him to the malice of the Tory faction in the north that his son

---

[171] Prescott, 'Diary' II, 513.
[172] Bennett and Dewhurst, *Quarter Sessions*, 205.
[173] Ryder, *Diary*, 330.
[174] *Political State*, XIV, 1717, 214–15.
[175] LRO, QJ1/1716.

in law, who entertained him, was threatened to be turned from his farm, if he harboured him'.[176] Liddell reported in June 1716 that support for Jacobitism was as strong as ever in Northumberland and 'the other gentleman assured him that itt was the like in Lancashire and other adjacent countys'.[177]

The restoration attempt had been defeated, but Jacobitism remained a political force, even in public. Jacobite drinking clubs in Lancashire and Cheshire remained, though their members were as discreet as ever. Yet in 1745, support for the Jacobite cause in England was far less than it had been in 1715 and the almost complete lack of gentry support was noticeable. This was probably in part because the Lancashire Jacobites had been badly stung – either by execution or by loss of estates.

Conclusion

The aftermath of the rebellion brought differing fates to different groups of people in the North of England. Most affected were those in Lancashire and Cheshire, because that was where the fighting had occurred and where the prisoners were held thereafter. Whigs could celebrate their victory by public demonstrations of their loyalty to George I and his government, with sermons, loyal addresses and other festivities.

Yet for the captured Jacobites, matters were grim; a few were executed, some had their estates confiscated and others were transported. Others, though, held on to their lands, through a variety of means. As for other Jacobites and Catholics, their morale varied; some fled the country, but others continued to snipe at their enemies in Lancashire. The Whigs acted against them in various fashions; Symson helped a Jacobite prisoner, while Peploe helped harry local Catholics. By the time of the Act of Grace in the summer of 1717, the last obvious vestiges of the rebellion were over, except for memories. Civil society was beginning to knit itself together again.

---

[176] *Calendar of Treasury Books*, XXXI, III, 1717, 720.
[177] Liddell, 'Letters', 238.

Postscript in 1745

Thirty years after the attempt to restore the Stuarts, another Jacobite campaign tried again to do just that. There were a number of resonances to the Fifteen, and a number of men who were involved in both struggles.

The Jacobite army, larger and more confident, took the same route from Scotland: Penrith, Appleby, Kendal, Lancaster and Preston. At the latter, John Murray of Broughton noted:

> Next day, the whole Army halted, & the Chevalier mounted on horse back to take a view of the ground where the two former actions had happened, and after having been shown the dispositions that were made in the year 1715 here, and the passes to the town described as well as possible by some gentlemen then in the Army who had been there made prisoners, he seem'd to think it Strange that so fair an occasion of fighting Gll Wells had been let Slip, or that they Should have deserted the Bridge and made so easy a Capitulation when the Town was Cappable of making so good a defense.[1]

Well aware of this,

> Preston, so fatale to the Scots that they never could get beyond it, but Lord George Murray, in order to evade the freet (or suspicion which the Highlanders are full of) cross'd the bridge and quarter'd a great many of the men on that side of the water.[2]

Some of those strongly opposed to the Jacobites in 1715 were also so in 1745. Captain James Gardiner, now a colonel of dragoons, led his men at the battle of Prestonpans on 21 September 1745, but was killed and died a hero's death. Major Humphrey Bland was now a major general and was the architect of victory at Culloden. Samuel Peploe, now Bishop of Chester since 1724, preached against

---

[1] Murray, 'Memorials', 246.
[2] Lord Elcho, *A Short Account of the Affairs of Scotland, 1744–1746*, Edinburgh: The Mercat Press, 1907, 327n.

the Jacobites at his cathedral. Hoghton organised the county militia as he had previously, but they were forced to disband, lacking regular military support. Henry Pelham was no longer a dragoon captain but the King's first minister. The Rev. James Fenton, still Vicar of Lancaster, whose behaviour in 1715 was equivocal, was a firm supporter of the Hanoverian dynasty and had to flee from the Jacobites' approach.[3] Fewer of those in the North West of England participated in the 1745 rebellion on the Jacobite side – perhaps 200 at most. Virtually none of the gentry participated, but some members of the same families as before did so. The son of Thomas Sydall, a wigmaker of Manchester and married, joined the Jacobite army in November 1745 and became the adjutant of the Manchester regiment, formed of most of the few English recruits, about 200–300 strong. Captured at the siege of Carlisle in the following month, he was tried, found guilty of high treason and hanged, drawn and quartered. As his father's had done, his head adorned a spike in Manchester. Francis Towneley, nephew of Richard Towneley, joined the Jacobites and headed the Manchester regiment, but was not so fortunate as his uncle in 1716 and suffered the same fate as Sydall.[4] John Daniel joined the Jacobites in 1745, as did his father in 1715.[5] But these were very much the minority.

---

[3] Oates, *Jacobite Invasion*, 38–9.
[4] Oates, *Jacobite Invasion*, 62, 64–5, 101.
[5] Walter Blaikie, ed., 'Origins of the Forty Five', SHS, 2nd series, 2, 1916, 167–224.

Conclusion

The struggle in the North of England in 1715 was part of a wider struggle taking place throughout Britain in 1715–16. Because it began later than the contest in Scotland and ended sooner, and involved fewer combatants, it has often been relegated as an episode of lesser significance. Clearly, its climax did not lead to an end of the rebellion, as Argyle, naturally concerned as ever for his own command, was quick to observe to his political masters.

Yet history is, by its nature, written retrospectively. The author is possessed of the knowledge of what happened subsequently, which was denied to contemporaries. We know that the Jacobite campaign in England was lost by the Jacobites and that it was of relatively short duration. Contemporaries did not know what the outcome would be. The concern in London, to say nothing for those on the front line in the North of England, was far from insignificant.

That a fairly small Jacobite force, which had lost much by Scottish desertions before its descent into England, could march through three northern counties with minimal opposition caused shock waves in London. That it did so was not the fault of the county community, ill equipped as they were to counter a military threat unaided by sufficient numbers of regular troops.

A military decision was necessary, which in itself would be taking a risk. The government's major advantage at the outset was that it had possession of a small professional army, added to by a number of further units raised in the summer of 1715. Wielded effectively, it could crush the rebellion at its birth. Decisive battles were possible; those at Preston in 1648, Worcester in 1651 and Sedgemoor in 1685 had all resulted in the forces attempting to overthrow the status quo being defeated before their campaigns could gain the momentum that the Parliamentary armies had gained from 1642 to 1646. Failure, though, could lead to a lengthy civil war with an unpredictable outcome, a paralysis of prosperous commerce and effective foreign policy, and even the risk of external intervention. The stakes were high. For the Jacobites, failure could also mean death, especially for those in positions of authority.

Active support for the Jacobite cause had not been inconsiderable in Northumberland and Lancashire. Yet it was less than had been anticipated by the Jacobite leaders. They also faced unexpectedly rapid resistance being formed against them in Newcastle, which prevented their seizing a major town as Mar had done a month ago at Perth. With both sides reinforced, a clash near Kelso loomed. The divided Jacobite leadership, faced with a number of options, decided to avoid a clash of arms.

Yet they retained the initiative and brushed aside those local levies in the north-western counties. Initially unbeknown to them, regular troops were marching towards them as they marched southwards through Lancashire, hoping for an uninterrupted march to towns which had much potential in terms of recruits and wealth (Manchester and Liverpool respectively). It came as a rude shock that their enemies were so close at hand. The decision to fight was then forced on the Jacobites by the regulars. A conclusion, one way or another, was at hand.

The Battle of Preston was important, as well as bloody. Despite this, it has often been overshadowed by events 30 years later. It was the last time a significant military encounter took place on English soil. The fighting at Clifton in 1745 was a rear-guard action, resulting in relatively few casualties, and though both sides claimed victory, it was hardly decisive in the history of the campaign. This cannot be said of Preston. On 14 November, the Jacobite danger in England was ended as a military presence. The state could now focus on its enemies in Scotland, who, coincidentally, had suffered a strategic setback at Sheriffmuir on the day before.

This is not to say that the outcome at Preston was pre-ordained. There was little to choose between the sides in numbers and only part of the regular force were seasoned veterans, though they did have the edge in experienced officers throughout their forces. Yet the Jacobite army, though poorly led at its highest echelons, was capable of fighting bravely, well and successfully, in relatively well-prepared positions. Their victory, though, was only a very short-term one. Firstly, they lacked the ammunition for a drawn-out defence. Secondly and more importantly, they were saddled with a leadership that was willing to compromise for the sake of human life. An all or nothing gamble of offensive action or a fighting retreat was not for them. In acting the way they did, they gave their enemy the victory and delivered many of their followers to transportation, death in gaol, or occasionally death on the gallows or block.

In this the regulars had been fortunate. The rank and file and officers up to brigadier level had fought as bravely as their opponents, and had taken many casualties. Whether they would have continued to do so had the fighting continued is another question, as they were not put to the test. Wills had taken a considered gamble in his attack, and one which had failed in the short term, but his resolve was unbroken. The fortuitous arrival of Carpenter with his force was more a psychological than a physical aid to victory, but of crucial significance for all that. Once negotiations had begun, the old splits in the Jacobite army reopened and this time, unlike on the previous occasions, proved fatal. A Jacobite victory was possible but, given the state of their army's leaders, was highly unlikely; the dissension between Wills and Carpenter was nothing compared to theirs.

The importance of the battle's result and the destruction of the Jacobite army in England was that, with an important (and, compared to Mar's army in Scotland, more immediate) threat removed, the government received an important fillip in confidence. Conversely, their opponents in England and elsewhere felt their hopes falter and thus did not act against the government. Troops could be, and were, diverted to Scotland to finish the job that Argyle had begun at Sheriffmuir by managing to halt the Jacobite advance. Mar was now increasingly isolated as his army began to dwindle and the balance of force tipped away from him. Preston did not herald the end of the rebellion, but it was a powerful signal that Nemesis could not be far away. Before Preston there was the potential for a Jacobite victory; afterwards, that chance was no more.

Then there was the long-term impact. Although Jacobitism in Lancashire survived, in 1745, when the larger and more successful Jacobite army marched through the county, even fewer men joined it than had in 1715. This lack of support was a factor in causing the retreat from Derby, and so eventual defeat. The difference can be explained by the dichotomy between Jacobitism as a political, religious and social phenomenon, and the all-or-nothing commitment of taking part in a military campaign. The military result at Preston that made possible the confiscation of estates after 1716 probably served as a brake on active Jacobitism among the gentry in 1745, and with that, among their tenants. Thus the low turn-out in 1745 can be partly, at least, explained by the draconian deterrent that had been visited upon their recent forebears in and after 1715. As a Catholic apologist later wrote, 'The forfeitures of property which succeeded the execution of some of the principal Catholic rebels, was a great blow to the interest of the body, but fortunately the blood then spilt was a lesson to the rest of the party, which has proved highly useful to their posterity'.[1] It was this long-term effect, as well as the surrender at Preston, that was decisive. Thus Lancashire Jacobites found it more congenial to toast the 'King over the water' than to buckle on their swords and summon their dependents to battle. As noted, Thomas Forster complained of their lack of support in 1715 – what would his shade have thought, witnessing the even smaller turn-out of 1745?

The result of the battle of Preston was thus of significance for three points. In the short term, it led to the end of the Jacobite threat in England in 1715. In the

---

[1] John Berington, *The State and Behaviour of the English Catholics*, London, 1780, 89.

medium term, it helped quicken the defeat of the Jacobites in Scotland. Finally, because of the measures taken against the English Jacobites in the rebellion's aftermath, it served to dampen their descendants' ardour for further military action in 1745. Although a small battle in terms of numbers of participants, it proved to be of decisive importance as well as being the final battle fought in England.

Appendix 1
Jacobite Rioters

All from Manchester, unless otherwise stated.

Attack on Monton Chapel

Thomas Husworth, bricklayer
William Chorleton, tape weaver
James Williams, taylor
Jonathan Slater, husbandman
John Coppock, husbandman

LRO, QJ1/2/10, pp. 522–3

Thomas Sydall, blacksmith
Thomas Toogood, bricklayer
Samuel of Knutsford, husbandman
John Whalley, husbandman
John Wilding, husbandman/weaver, Salford
John Atkinson husbandman
Robert Atkinson, weaver
Thomas Hall, husbandman
William Ward, shoemaker
Abraham Boom
Robert Atkinson

TNA, PL28/1, pp. 234–8

Attack on Manchester Chapel

Peter Cottrell, labourer

Henry Croft, labourer
Jonathan Greenwood, labourer
Thomas Hardman, husbandman*
John Whittington, husbandman, Salford.
John Greenhaigh, husbandman/tailor*
John Garstang, husbandman*
William Barton, patten maker
William Hilton, weaver/husbandman*
Samuel Boardman, calendar man
George Williamson, husbandman*
John Clayton, pattenmaker*
*denotes also in TNA listing

LRO, QJ1/2/10, pp. 522–3

Abraham Boomer, weaver
Simon Kearsley, dyer
George Bent, fustian cutter
Richard Walker, joiner
Richard Haworth, bricklayer, Salford
James Wilkinson, labourer, Salford
Joseph Meadowes, shearman
John Fallow, badger
Jonathan Nightingale, tanner
John Anderson, fustian cutter
James Birch, junior, shoemaker
George Haywood, weaver
Josiah Ellen, feltmaker
Joseph Holde, tailor
Jeremiah Holden, tailor
Charles Smith, shearman
Francis Wood, weaver
Francis Goodall, husbandman
James Bradshaw, shoemaker
Thomas Pollett, weaver
John Pollett, husbandman
James Gartside, grocer
Thomas Hardman, husbandman
James Robinson, fustian cutter

Jonas Mann, cabinet maker

TNA, PL28/1, pp. 234–8

Rioters on 28 May (Manchester?)

Richard Jebb, chapman
Benjamin Naylor, Mercator
John Holebrook, pharmatopola?
Samuel Barber, glovemaker
John Barlow, dyer
Thomas Evans, dyer
Hammet Kirkes, merator

TNA, PL28/1, p. 236

Appendix 2
Jacobite Prisoners

Jacobites of North West England

Cheshire

Name	Parish	Trade	Company/Troop	Religion	Fate
Gordon, Roger	Middlewitch	Chapman			
Lucas, John	Presbury	Chapman			
Legh, Francis	Lyme	Gentleman		Protestant	Escaped
Turner, William	Stockport	Servant			Transported 29 June 1716

Cumberland

Name	Parish	Trade	Company/Troop	Religion	Fate
Barton, John	Pranton	Servant			
Bell, Thomas	Kirkandrew	Carpenter	Hunter		
Betty, Charles	Whicham	Labourer	Talbot		
Bready, John	Wetheral	Servant	Talbot		Discharged
Dalton, Charles	Oarby	Gentleman	Widdrington's		Marshalsea/Newgate
Farne, John	Wetheral	Labourer	Owgan		Discharged
Farnworth, John	Wetheral	Labourer	Owgan		Discharged
Garrick, George	Denton	Gentleman	Dalziel/Carnworth		
Graham, George	Arthrid	Gentleman	Dalziel/Carnworth		
Hamilton, Oliver	Whethan	Servant	Talbot		Died

continued

Name	Parish	Trade	Company/Troop	Religion	Fate
Harrington, Robert	St. Corbells	Shoemaker	Douglas		
Linnott, William	Whictam	Gentleman	Dalziel/Carnworth		
Moses, Michael	Whicham	Labourer	Owgan		Discharged
Mattay, Edward	Wetheral	Servant	Errington		
Nevill, Charles	Wetheral	Servant	Shaftoe		
Pesrodd, John	Wetheral	Servant	Harrison		
Rideley, Alex	Denton	Servant/Weaver			
Salkeld, Roger	Whitehall	Gentleman		Catholic	Escaped
Sands, William	Whitehaven	Gentleman			
Stuby, Robert	Wetheral	Servant			Transported 29 May 1716
Tinker, Edward	Wetheral	Servant			Discharged
Willson, John	Wetheral	Carpenter	Talbot		Discharged
Willson, William	Wetheral	Servant	Owgan		

Lancashire

Name	Parish	Trade	Company/Troop	Religion	Fate
Abbott, R	Myerscough	Husbandman		Catholic	
Abbott, Richard	Lancaster	Farmer	Tinsley		Tried 21/23 Sept. 1716 Acquitted
Abram, William	Walton	Weaver			
Alkinson, John	Kirkham	Servant			Discharged
Allanson, John	Preston	Esquire		Protestant	
Allen, Nathan	Preston	Carpenter		Protestant	
Anderton, Sir Francis	Lostock	Baronet		Catholic	Newgate Discharged
Anderton	Barton			Protestant	
Anderton, Hugh		Esquire		Catholic	
Anon	Croston	Servant			
Appleton, James	Burnley	Servant		Catholic	

Appendix 2: Jacobite Prisoners

Arkwright, William	Preston	Yeoman		Catholic	Tried 20 Jan. 1716
Ashton, John	Littlewood			Protestant	
Ashton, Roger	Ashton	Yeoman		Protestant	
Ashton, John	Bralo	Invalid			
Atkinson, John	Corkham	Servant			
Atkinson, William	Walton	Webster		Catholic	
Atrish, William	Lancaster	Gentleman	Langdell		
Baccus, John	Cartmell	Servant		Catholic	
Barker, Robert	Kirkham				
Barlow, Anthony	Preston	Gentleman		Catholic	
Barlow, Thomas	Preston	Gentleman		Catholic	
Barnes, Francis	Preston	Glazier		Protestant	
Barrow, Edward	Weeton	Husbandman			
Barrow, John	Westby	Gentleman		Catholic	
Barton, Edward	Myerscough	Husbandman		Protestant	
Barton, Hugh	Claughton	Yeoman		Catholic	Tried 21/23 Sept. 1716 Acquitted
Barton, Thomas	Claughton	Husbandman		Catholic	
Barton, William	Kerome	Servant	Shaftoe		Discharged
Beswick, Edward	Manchester	Chapman		Protestant	
Bickerstaff, Robert	Leighton	Husbandman		Catholic	
Billing	Constable	Gentleman		Protestant	
Bilborrow, Richard	Ashton	Husbandman		Catholic	
Birches, Richard	Preston	Joiner		Catholic	Tried 4 Feb. 1716
Birches, Thomas	Preston	Joiner		Catholic	
Blackbourne, Richard	Lancaster	Gentleman			Tried 8 Feb. 1716 Acquitted
Blackburn, John	Salwick	Husbandman		Catholic	
Blackburn, Richard	Bleasdale	Gentleman		Catholic	
Blackwell	Halergrain			Protestant	

continued

Bleasdale, John	Brockhall	Gentleman		Catholic	
Bressell, Len	Goosnargh	Labourer			
Blue, Luke	Walton	Webster		Protestant	
Blundell, James	Standish	Tanner			Tried 26 Jan. 1716 Executed 10 Feb. 1716, Garstang
Bolton, William	Bleasdale	Yeoman		Catholic	
Bradley	Ashton	Husbandman		Catholic	
Brayes, William	Corkram	Gentleman			Tried 24 Jan. 1716
Brindle, Henry	Walton	Husbandman		Catholic	
Brockholes, William	Claughton	Gentleman		Catholic	
Brockholes, John, b. 1692, m. 1712	Claughton	Gentleman		Catholic	Died 1719
Brown, James	Fishwick	Taylor		Catholic	Tried 24 Jan. 1716 Executed 10 Feb. 1716, Wigan
Browne, John	Blackburn	Weaver			Tried 29 June 1716
Bryerley, Tomas	Fishwick	Hatter		Catholic	
Bryers, Thomas	Preston	Yeoman		Catholic	
Bryes	Latham	Yeoman		Catholic	
Bryes	Broughton	Husbandman			
Burn, James	Fishwick	Tailor		Catholic	
Butler, Richard	Rawcliffe			Catholic	Died 1 Jan. 1716, Newgate
Butler, William	Myerscough	Gentleman		Catholic	Tried 20 Jan. 1716 Executed 28 Jan. 1716, Preston
Calvert, Thomas	Walton	Husbandman			
Cardwell, William	Myerscough	Servant			
Caroling, Richard	Preston	Innkeeper		Catholic	

Appendix 2: Jacobite Prisoners

Carrdene, Thomas	Haulton	Esquire			
Cartmell, John	Bishbourne	Husbandman		Protestant	
Cartmell, Thomas, b. 1693	Garstang	Gentleman			Tried 24 Jan. 1716 Executed 14 Feb. 1716, Garstang
Cartmell, Thomas	Bishbourne	Husbandman		Catholic	
Carus, Charles	Halton	Gentleman			Tried 2 Feb. 1716 Transported 29 June 1716
Carus, Thomas	Halton	Gentleman		Catholic	
Caton, James	Brockhall	Husbandman		Catholic	
Catterall, William	Myerscough	Husbandman		Catholic	
Charles, Thomas	Lancaster	Seaman			
Charnley, William	Blackburn	Weaver			Tried 21/23 Sept. 1716 Executed 2 Oct. 1716
Charnley, William	Walton	Husbandman		Catholic	
Chorley, Charles, b. 1684	Chorley	Esquire		Catholic	Tried 21 Jan. 1716 Died in gaol
Chorley, Richard, b. 1660	Croston	Gentleman		Catholic	Tried 21 Jan. 1716, Executed 9 Feb. 1716, Preston
Clarke, Thomas	Lancaster	Seaman			Discharged
Clarkson, John	Singleton			Catholic	
Clayton, John	Preston	Gentleman			
Clayton, William	Brindle	Husbandman		Catholic	
Clifton, George	Preston	Gentleman		Catholic	Outlawed
Clifton, Thomas	Lytham			Catholic	
Clifton, Thomas	Lytham			Catholic	
Comebach, George	Elson	Husbandman		Catholic	
Comerall, John	Preston	Ironmonger		Protestant	

continued

Core, William	Burnley	Servant			
Cottam, Oliver	Bishbourne	Gentleman		Protestant	
Coupland, Robert	Lancaster	Taylor	Butler	Protestant	
Cowe, Henry	Burnley	Labourer			
Cowling, George	Chorley	Husbandman		Catholic	
Cowp, George, b. 1675/91	Walton	Weaver		Catholic	Tried 21/23 Sept. 1716 Acquitted
Cowp, James	Walton	Weaver		Catholic	Discharged
Cowp, Lawrence	Walton	Weaver			
Cowp, Richard	Ribbleton	Husbandman		Catholic	
Cowp, Thomas	Walton	Weaver		Catholic	Tried 20 Jan. 1716 Executed 28 Jan. 1716, Preston
Cowper, Henry	Curedale	Webster		Catholic	
Cowper, James	Whittington	Tailor		Catholic	
Cowper, Robert	Curedale	Husbandman		Catholic	
Coxe, Edward	Walton	Shoemaker		Catholic	
Craven, James	Thurnham	Husbandman		Catholic	
Crinchley, John	Myerscough	Husbandman		Catholic	
Croston, Richard	Preston	Gentleman		Protestant	
Dale, Thomas	Walton	Innkeeper		Catholic	
Daniel, John	Broughton	Yeoman		Catholic	
Daniel, Robert	Ashton	Gentleman		Catholic	
Danver, James	Walton	Webster			
Daronson, James	Blackburn	Weaver			
Darwen, Matthew		Husbandman		Protestant	
Darwen, Thomas	Walton	Webster		Catholic	
Darwen, William	Walton	Webster		Catholic	
Davies, Richard	Clayton	Gentleman			
Dewhurst, Roger	Walton	Husbandman			
Deyes, Richard	Wallay	Servant			
Dockeda, James	Claughton	Husbandman		Catholic	

Appendix 2: Jacobite Prisoners 203

Duckworth, Edward	Ribbleton	Smith		Catholic	
Duckworth	Whittingham	Husbandman			
Eastham, Edward	Cuerdale	Husbandman		Catholic	
Eastham, Leonard	Walton	Husbandman		Catholic	
Eaton	Lugg	Gentleman		Catholic	
Eaton	Lugg	Gentleman		Catholic	
Echston, Christopher	Croston	Glover		Catholic	
Edmondson, Richard	Broughton	Gentleman	Tinsley		
Ellis, John	Catterall	Yeoman		Catholic	
Ethersham, Matthew	Preston	Husbandman		Protestant	
Faircroft, James	Wigan	Weaver			
Fenwick, John	Myhills	Gentleman			Discharged
Fidler, John b. 1666, m. 1691	Woodplumpton	Husbandman		Catholic	
Fidler, Joseph	Ashton	Husbandman		Catholic	
Finch, James	Walton	Husbandman		Catholic	Tried 27 Jan. 1716 Executed 10 Feb. 1716, Wigan
Finch, John	Blackburn	Weaver			
Finch, John, b. 1695	Walton	Webster		Catholic	Tried 2 Feb. 1716 Executed 11 Feb. 1716, Manchester
Fisher, John	Goosnargh	Webster		Catholic	
Fisher, William	Standish	Farmer			
Forster, Robert	Burnley	Servant			
Frame, Bartholomew	Cressen	Servant			
Francis, John	Burnley	Jersey comber			
Gardener, Luke	Whittingham	Servant			
Garner, William	Broughton	Farmer			
Gartledge, James	Manchester	Chapman		Protestant	

continued

Gerard, James	Blackburn	Yeoman			Died, Lancaster
Gerard, James	Walton	Husbandman		Catholic	
Gerard, James	Haighton	Gentleman		Catholic	
Gibson, Charles	Preston	Gentleman		Protestant	Died 1731?
Giby, Henry	Preston	Servant			
Gill, Henry	Castell	Servant			Transported 7 May 1716
Gillow, Richard	Singleton	Husbandman		Catholic	Died at home
Goose, Thomas	Catterall	Yeoman		Catholic	Tried 28 Jan. 1716 Executed 14 Feb. 1716, Garstang
Gore, William	Burnley	Servant			
Gradwell, William	Preston	Gentleman		Protestant	
Grayston, William	Upper Wyresdale	Husbandman		Catholic	
Green, John	Myerscough	Labourer			
Green, Thomas	Myerscough	Husbandman			
Green, William	Preston	Esquire		Protestant	
Gregson, James	Preston	Shoemaker		Protestant	
Gregson, James	Preston	Husbandman		Catholic	
Gregson, John	Ribbleton	Gentleman		Catholic	Alive 1717
Guest, Martin	Chorley	Sadler			
Gurnall, Richard	Myerscough	Husbandman		Catholic	
Hall, Joseph	Goosnargh	Husbandman		Catholic	
Hammond, George, b. 1698	Burnley	Husbandman		Protestant	Transported 7 May 1716
Harris, John, b. 1698	Burnley	Weaver			Transported 15 July 1716
Harris, John	Burnley	Husbandman		Protestant	
Harris, William, b. 1679	Burnley	Shoemaker		Catholic	Tried 26 Jan. 1716 Executed 11 Feb. 1716, Manchester
Harrison, James	Claughton	Webster		Catholic	

Appendix 2: Jacobite Prisoners

Hartley, James	Walton	Carpenter			Discharged
Hartley, James	Cuerdale	Husbandman		Catholic	
Hast, Richard	Preston	Servant			
Haunton, Robert	Charnock				Escaped
Hays, Charles	Croston	Servant			Discharged,
Hays, Robert	Claughton	Webster		Catholic	
Helson, Thomas	Charnock	Husbandman		Protestant	
Hesketh, Cuthbert, b. 1692	Goosnargh	Gentleman		Catholic	Marshalsea
Hesketh, Gabriel, b. 1666, m. 1691	Goosnargh	Gentleman		Catholic	Marshalsea
Hesketh, William, b. 1696	Singleton	Gentleman		Catholic	Died 1735
Hesmantall, Ellis	Chorley	Husbandman		Protestant	
Heyes, Charles	Cresen	Servant			Discharged
Hodgkinson, Henry	Preston	Gentleman		Catholic	
Hodgkinson, Luke	Preston	Gentleman		Catholic	
Hodgson, Albert	Leighton	Esquire		Catholic	Marshalsea
Hodgson, Evan	Walton	Husbandman		Catholic	
Hodgson, Robert	Walton	Husbandman		Catholic	
Hodgson, Thomas	Walton	Husbandman		Catholic	
Hodgson, William	Singleton	Husbandman		Catholic	
Hodkinson, Richard	Goosnargh	Servant		Catholic	
Hodkinson, Barthlomew	Maseo	Servant		Catholic	Discharged
Hodson, Richard	Blackburn	Weaver			Discharged
Hodson, Robert	Singleton	Husbandman		Catholic	
Hodson, William	Walton	Weaver			Discharged
Holland, Richard	Walton	Yeoman			
Hord, John	Lancaster	Servant			Transported, 7 May 1716
Houghton, Robert	Thurnham	Gentleman		Catholic	

continued

Hoghton, William	Croxteth			Catholic	
Hothersall, John	Hothersall			Catholic	
Howard, William	Standish	Carpenter			
Hudson, George	Walton	Webster		Catholic	
Jackson, Thomas	Preston	Butcher		Catholic	Tried 24 Jan. 1716 Died Jan. 1716
Jackson, Thomas	Preston	Husbandman		Catholic	
Johnson, Richard	Thornbush	Servant			
Johnwood, Roger	Pleasington	Labourer		Protestant	
Kellett, John	Walton	Husbandman		Catholic	Died 1716, Newgate
Kellet, Robert	Lostock	Gentleman		Catholic	
Kemp, George		Gentleman		Protestant	
Kilshaw, Thomas, b. 1691, m. 1716	Croston	Weaver			Discharged
Kitchen, John	Preston	Silversmith		Catholic	
Lane, John	Cartmell	Carrier			Discharged
Langdale, Jordan	Samlesbury	Esquire		Catholic	
Lawrence, Edward	Corkram	Servant		Catholic	
Leybourne, John	Natesby	Esquire		Catholic	Marshalsea
Mather, Thomas	Fulwood	Weaver			Discharged
Mailer, John	Wigan	Weaver			
Malley	Myerscough	Husbandman		Catholic	
Malley, Richard	Myerscough			Catholic	
Malley, Thomas	Leighton	Husbandman		Catholic	
Mason, William, b. 1678	Stonyhurst			Catholic	
Mastoe, Nicholas	Preston	Servant			Discharged
Mateley, William	Manchester	Silk dyer	Forster	Catholic	
Mather, Thomas	Fulwood	Husbandman		Protestant	
Maudsley, Henry	Myerscough	Yeoman		Catholic	
Mayfield, John	Latham	Gentleman		Catholic	Alive 1722
Mercer, George	Deane	Servant			

Miller, William	Broughton	Husbandman		Catholic	
Molyneux, Viscount				Catholic	Discharged
Muncaster, Roger	Piling	Gentleman/attorney		Protestant	Tried 20 Jan. 1716 Executed. 28 Jan. 1716, Preston
Moore, William	Cartmell	Yeoman			
Morris, William	Lostock	Groom			Discharged
Moxall, John	Brindle	Carpenter		Catholic	
Naike, Thomas	Croston	Weaver			
Nailer, Alex	Wigan	Weaver			
Nailer, Thomas, b. 1658	Croston	Glover			
Newby, Edward	Cartmell	Servant			Discharged
Newsham, Henry	Brockhill	Husbandman		Catholic	
Newton, Jona	Winch	Mason			Transported 7 May 1716
Oram, Roy	Townley	Gentleman		Protestant	
Ord, John	Lancaster				Transported 24 June 1716
Orde, William	Mitton	Farmer			
Orm, John	Preston			Protestant	
Park, Thomas, b. 1695	Croston	Husbandman		Catholic	
Parker, Edward	Gressingham	Gentleman		Protestant	
Parkinson, Christopher	Nether Wyresdale			Catholic	
Parkinson, James	Singleton	Yeoman		Catholic	
Parkinson, John	Myerscough	Husbandman		Catholic	
Parkinson, Richard	Broughton	Barber		Catholic	
Partington, William	Walton	Husbandman		Catholic	
Pateson, William	Singleton	Yeoman		Catholic	
Perkinson, William, b. 1694	Blackburn	Weaver			
Piling, James	Burnley	Weaver			

continued

Pilling, James	Burnley	Labourer		Protestant	
Pleasington, James	Natesby	Apothecary		Catholic	Transported 24 June 1716
Pleasington, John	Natesby	Gentleman		Catholic	
Pleasington, Robert	Natesby	Gentleman		Catholic	
Porter, Joseph	Burnley	Jersey comber/labourer			Tried 27 Jan. 1716 Executed 11 Feb. 1716, Manchester
Porter, Joseph	Burnley	Husbandman		Protestant	
Postlewhaite, Richard	Preston	Barber		Protestant	
Prockter, John	Walton	Weaver			Transported, 30 March 1716
Procter, John	Goosnargh	Husbandman		Catholic	
Prokter, Roger	Brindle	Husbandman		Catholic	
Prue, Roger	Eidsforth	Gentleman			
Randford, Nicholas	Croston	Husbandman		Catholic	
Randford, Richard	Wigan	Servant			Discharged
Randford, William	Standish	Miller			
Richardson, Michael	Garstang	Smith	Talbot		
Richardson, Nicholas	Garstang	Smith	Talbot		
Rigby, James	Standish	Husbandman		Catholic	
Rigby, Joseph	Preston	Husbandman		Catholic	
Rigby, Richard	Walton	Husbandman		Catholic	
Robinson, Ben	Padiham	Husbandman		Protestant	
Robinson, Benjamin	Pagaine	Smith			
Robinson, Philip	Lancaster	Servant			Discharged
Robinson, Philip	Natesby	Husbandman		Catholic	

Appendix 2: Jacobite Prisoners

Robotham, John	Claughton	Servant			Tried 24 Jan. 1716 Executed. 9 Feb. 1716, Preston
Robson, Edward, b. 1668	Ormskirk	Joiner			
Rothwell, R	Samlesbury	Husbandman		Catholic	
Rowbotham, Henry	Preston	Husbandman		Catholic	Tried 24 Jan. 1716 Acquitted
Rowbotham, John	Claughton	Husbandman		Catholic	
Ryley, John, b. 1668/1687/1692	Burnley	Servant			Transported, 30 March 1716
Sagar, Stephen	Burnley	Smith		Protestant	
Salter, Robert	Preston	Hatter		Protestant	
Sanderson, James	Plumpton	Husbandman		Catholic	
Scarisbrick, Robert	Scarisbrick	Esquire		Catholic	Acquitted 1718
Scott, Thomas	Wigan	Gentleman			
Sagar, Stephen	Burnley	Joiner			Tried 26 Jan. 1716 Executed 11 Feb. 1716, Manchester
Sergent, Henry	Lancaster	Servant			Transported 7 May 1716
Shafto, John	Garstang	Servant			
Sharrock, Lawrence	Preston	Shoemaker		Catholic	
Shaw, John	Lancaster	Servant		Catholic	Discharged
Shepherd, Roger	Stonyhurst	Husbandman		Protestant	
Shirborn, Richard	Preston	Gentleman		Catholic	Outlawed
Shirborn, Nicholas	Stonyhurst	Gentleman		Protestant	Discharged Died 1717
Sturzaker, John	Bleasdale	Yeoman		Catholic	
Shuttleworth, George	Aston	Labourer			

continued

Shuttleworth, Nicholas, b. 1687	Padiham	Gentleman		Protestant	
Shuttleworth, Ralph	Burnley	Gentleman		Protestant	
Shuttleworth, Richard	Garstang	Gentleman		Catholic	Tried 20 Jan. 1716 Executed 28 Jan. 1716, Preston
Shuttleworth, Richard	St. Michael's	Sailor			
Shuttleworth, Richard	Preston	Gentleman		Catholic	Died 1748–9
Shuttleworth, Richard	Rawcliffe	Gentleman		Catholic	
Shuttleworth, Richard, son	Rawcliffe	Gentleman		Catholic	
Shuttleworth, Thomas	Ashton	Husbandman		Catholic	Tried 21/23 Sept 1716 Executed 2 Oct. 1716
Shuttleworth, William	Ashton	Husbandman		Catholic	
Shuzzak, John junior	Bleasdale	Husbandman		Protestant	
Siddall, Thomas, b. 1667/1670, m. 1700/1704	Manchester	Smith			Tried 27 Jan. 1716 Executed 11 Feb. 1716, Manchester
Simpson, James	Burnley	Weaver			Transported 7 May 1716
Singleton, George	Broughton	Servant			
Slater, James				Protestant	
Slater, William, b. 1694	Burnley	Labourer		Protestant	
Slater, William	Burnley	Servant			
Smith, John	Litham	Husbandman		Catholic	
Smith, William	Singleton	Husbandman		Catholic	
Southwold, John	Ribbleton	Gentleman		Catholic	
Standish, Ralph	Standish	Esquire		Catholic	Newgate Died 1752

Stanley, Thomas	Preston	Esquire		Catholic	Alive 1717
Stephenson, James	Cartmel	Bricklayer			
Studdard, Benjamin	Burnley	Weaver			Transported 7 May 1716
Studdard, Bernard	Burnley	Labourer		Protestant	
Studdard, Joseph	Burnley	Weaver		Catholic	
Studdard, Joseph	Burnley	Labourer		Protestant	
Sumner, John	Kerom	Frazier			
Swarbrick, George	Singleton	Husbandman		Catholic	
Swarbrick, James	Singleton	Husbandman		Catholic	
Swarbrick, John	Singleton	Husbandman		Catholic	
Swarbrick, John senior	Westham	Yeoman		Catholic	
Swarbrick, James	Kirkham	Gentleman		Protestant	Alive 1717
Sykes, Edward	Wyresdale	Yeoman		Protestant	Tried 24 Jan. 1716, Acquitted
Tasker, John	Walton	Husbandman		Catholic	
Tauson, John	Broughton	Husbandman		Catholic	
Tayler, Theophilus	Standish			Catholic	
Taylor, William	Myerscough	Servant			
Taylor, William	Myerscough	Husbandman		Catholic	
Thelfor, John	Garstang	Servant			
Thirselar, Thomas	Broughton	Servant	Tinsley		
Thorp, George	Fishwick	Husbandman		Catholic	
Thorp, Ingleby	Preston	Gentleman		Protestant	
Thorp, Lawrence	Fishwick	Husbandman		Catholic	Tried 21/23 Sept. 1716 Acquitted
Thorp, Samuel	Croston	Husbandman		Protestant	
Threfall, Cuthbert	Bilsburrow	Yeoman		Catholic	
Tiby, Henry	Preston	Weaver			

continued

Tildesley, Edward	Myerscough	Esquire		Catholic	Marshalsea Acquitted
Towneley, Richard b. 1687	Townley	Esquire		Catholic	Marshalsea Discharged
Trafford, John jun, b. 1689	Croston	Gentleman		Catholic	Died 1760
Traves, Charles	Myerscough	Labourer		Protestant	
Traves, John	Myerscough	Labourer		Protestant	
Troutbeck, William	Ribbleton	Tailor		Catholic	
Turner, George	Walton	Husbandman		Catholic	
Turner, Lawrence	Michell	Farmer		Catholic	Discharged
Tyrer, Henry	Ormskirk	Gentleman			
Wadsworth, Joseph	Claughton	Gentleman		Catholic	Tried 24 Jan. 1716 Executed 14 Feb. 1716, Garstang
Wadsworth, Robert	Hiaghton	Gentleman		Catholic	
Wadsworth, William	Haighton	Gentleman		Catholic	
Wakesley	Elson	Husbandman		Catholic	
Walker, John	Corkram	Servant			
Walker, John	Lancaster	Skinner			
Walker, John	Scotforth	Collarmaker		Catholic	
Walker, Robert	Forton	Yeoman		Catholic	Tried 21/23 Sept. 1716 Acquitted
Walmsley, Charles	Preston	Gentleman		Catholic	
Walmsley, Henry	Preston	Gentleman		Catholic	Tried 21 Jan. 1716 Acquitted
Walmsley, Richard	Preston	Gentleman		Catholic	Tried 21/23 Sept. 1716 Acquitted
Walmsley, Richard	Walton	Husbandman		Catholic	
Walmsley, Robert	Goosnargh	Servant		Catholic	
Walmsley, Robert	Blackburn	Servant			

Appendix 2: Jacobite Prisoners 213

Walmsley, Robert	Myerscough	Husbandman		Catholic	
Walmsley, Thomas	Preston	Gentleman		Catholic	Alive 1718
Walmsley, Thomas	Bilburrow	Innkeeper		Catholic	Tried 27 Jan. 1716 Acquitted
Walmsley, William	Latham	Husbandman		Catholic	Transported 28 June 1716
Walton, Thomas	Windor	Gentleman		Catholic	
Walworth, William	Kirkham	Farmer			
Wamsley, Charles	Showley	Gentleman			
Wansley, Henry	Showley	Gentleman	Widdrington		
Ward, William	Manchester	Shoemaker			Tried 21 Sept 1716
Wareing, John	Aughton	Husbandman		Protestant	Tried 21/23 Sept. 1716 Acquitted
Wareing, John	Brindle	Husbandman		Catholic	
Wareing, Thomas	Brindle	Husbandman		Catholic	
Warren, Edward	Chorley	Esquire		Protestant	Died 1720
Wearing, Richard	Kecon	Taylor	Thorp		Discharged
Wenklow, Henry	Ribchester	Labourer			
Wenklow, John	Ribchester	Labourer			
Westby, Cuthbert	Burn in Thornton	Gentleman		Catholic	
Westby, John	Burn	Esquire		Catholic	Died 1728
Westby, Thomas	Burn in Thornton	Gentleman		Catholic	Died 1729
Whalley, William	Walton	Whitesmith		Catholic	Tried 28 Jan. 1716 Executed 10 Feb. 1716, Wigan
Whitehead, Thomas	Claughton	Gentleman		Protestant	Alive 1724
Whittingham, Henry	Whittingham	Gentleman		Catholic	
Whittingham, Richard	Whittingham	Gentleman		Protestant	

continued

Name	Parish	Trade	Company/Troop	Religion	Fate
Whittinghan, Richard	Ribbleton	Husbandman		Catholic	
Wild, Robert	Bury	Weaver			
Wilkinson, John	Lancashire gaol	Apothecary			Escaped
Williamson, Nicholas	Ingell	Yeoman		Catholic	
Wilson, Henry	Preston	Farmer		Catholic	Transported 24 May 1716
Winckley, Edward	Walton	Gentleman		Catholic	
Winckley, Henry	Alston	Yeoman		Catholic	
Winckley, John	Alston	Husbandman		Catholic	Tried 21/23 Sept. 1716 Executed 2 Oct. 1716
Winder, John	Preston	Gentleman		Protestant	
With, Richard	Preston	Farmer			
Woods, John	Poulton	Husbandman		Protestant	
Woof, William	Cartmell	Yeoman			Transported 30 Mar 1716
Worswick, Robert	Walton	Husbandman		Catholic	
Worthington		Stoneman		Catholic	
Wright, Duncan	Preston	Barber		Protestant	
Wyke, James	Walton	Husbandman		Catholic	
Wyke, John	Walton	Husbandman		Catholic	
Wyke, Peter	Walton	Husbandman		Catholic	

Westmorland

Name	Parish	Trade	Company/Troop	Religion	Fate
Chamber, Joseph	Witherslack	Yeoman			Transported 7 May 1716
Gibson, Joseph	Kirby Lonsdale	Servant			
Hilton, George	Hale	Gentleman		Catholic	Escaped

Sanderson, Alexander	Heversham	Labourer			
Thornburgh, Francis	Kendal	Gentleman			Escaped
Wilson, John	Morlan	Gentleman			

Appendix 3
British Army Casualties

Fatal Casualties

Unit	Field Officers	Captains	Lieutenants	Cornets/Ensigns	Others	Total
Pitt*	0	0	0	0	0	0
Wynn	0	0	0	0	6	6
Honeywood	0	0	0	0	0	0
Munden	0	0	0	0	0	0
Dormer	0	0	0	0	3	3
Stanhope	0	0	0	0	7	7
Preston*	2	0	1	0	37	40
Total	2	0	1	0	53	56

*denotes unit from Irish establishment

Wounded

Unit	Field Officers	Captains	Lieutenants	Cornets/Ensigns	Others	Total
Pitt	0	0	0	0	1	1
Wynn	0	1	1	1	21	24
Honeywood	0	0	0	0	5	5
Munden	0	0	0	0	0	0
Dormer	0	1	0	0	4	1
Stanhope	0	0	0	0	3	3
Preston	2	2	1	4	43	52
Total	2	4	2	5	77	90

Horses Killed and Wounded

Unit	
Pitt	0
Wynn	15
Honeywood	12
Munden	12
Dormer	16
Stanhope	17
Total	72

Flying Post, 3734, 8–10 Dec. 1715.

Wounded

Brigadier Honeywood, 'a contusion on the shoulder by a musket shot'.
Major Bland, 'slight wound in the Arm'.
Lord Forrester, lieutenant colonel, of Preston's Foot, 'two or three Wounds'.
Major Preston, 'shot through the body a little above the Breast'. Died 13 November
Captain Ogleby, 'a wound in his side'.
Major Lawson, 'likewise wounded'.
Brigadier Dormer, 'a contusion in his Knee'.

Patten, *History*, pp. 101–2.

Captain Robert Ferguson, William Sinclair (grenadier company) and Lieutenant William Elphinston of Preston's killed; possibly another died of wounds. *St. James Evening Post* 83, 15–17 Nov. 1715
Captains Robert Preston and William Westerdean and two unnamed lieutenants were buried at Preston churchyard on 27 November.

Preston Parish Registers

Disability Pensions granted 1716

Wynn's Dragoons

Edward Cavin (21 years), 4 months' service, 'shot in the head and left thigh at Preston', 1716.
Adam Cadwell (24 years), a year and 9 months service, 'shot through ye body at Preston', 1717.
Guy Cerlton (28 years), 'his breast bone broke at Preston his right leg disabled by a sword and very well recommended', 1718.

Stanhope's Dragoons

Henry Pawley (30 years), 15 years' service, 'wounded at Preston wholly disabled in his left thigh', 1716.

Dormers' Dragoons

Thomas Johnstone (41 years), 25 years' service, 'Shot in the left shoulder bruised in ye left side', 1716.

Pitt's Horse

Thomas Chatterton (52), 15 years' service, dismissed, recommended as Invalid, 1716.
John Certs, (49), 21 years' service, 'shot through small of ye left leg at Preston is now a running sore', 1718.

Preston's Foot

Samuel Wallace (51 years), 21 years' service, wounded in both legs, 1716.
Donald McKenzie (48 years), 15 years' service, lost a piece of his right shoulder by cannon ball, 1716.
David Rosse (52 years), 23 years' service, 'almost blind shot in the left eye', 1716.
Alexander Russell (36 years), 14 years' service, 'shot in the left eye', 1716.
John Dickson (38 years), 8 years' service, 'shot in the belly and left leg', 1716.
John McCalle (44 years), 18 years' service, 'lost his left eye', 1716.
Duncan McDougal (36 years), 14 years' service, 'shot through the left arm', 1716.

Donald McClean (50 years), 17 years' service, 'shot through left hand at ye battle of Preston, disabled him and cut on ye left arm', 1718.

William Lownes (50 years), 17 years, service, 'shot on ye joint of the right arm, wounded on ye left leg at Preston', 1718.

Robert Niscoll (37), 7 years' service, 'a great rupture on ye right side got at Preston', 1719.

TNA,WO116/1

Appendix 4
Civilian Losses

Damage to Civilian Property in Preston

1   ? Henley £54
2   Christopher Dawney £5 10s
3   Agnes Bolton £60 15s
4   Isabell Bostock £15
5   Henry Wareing 39s
6   George Drinkwater £12
7   Matthew Sharples £28 10s
8   Thomas Greenhaigh £13 10s
9   James Moor £13 6s
10 Richard Etherington £9 9s
11 Thomas Woodburne £10
12 Elizabeth Wilding £2 12s 6d
13 Thomas Leach £12
14 Henry Thompson £18 7s
15 Robert Holme £17 5s
16 Willaim Walmesley £6 14s
17 John Arkwright £10
18 Grace Bostock house £60 and goods £9
19 John Whalley house and outbuildings £65 19s
20 William Charnock barns, outhouses and goods £24 12a
21 Margaret Fleetwood £6 10s 6d
22 Thomas Sherrington cloths, goods, linen, bedding £18 16s
23 John Claughton corn, hay £27
24 George Slayer £4 16s
25 Edward Panber £9 10s
26 Thomas Livesey £3 burnt goods £2 destroyed.
27 John Greenshaigh £13 8s
28 Anne Hotch, widow house and goods burnt £38
29 Jennett Radcliffe £11

30	Elizabeth Goodshaw house £7 2s
31	Thomas Ward innkeeper £5 10s
32	Richard Myers house in Churchgate £76 corn £27 10s
33	Richard Abram goods £10 10s
34	Christopher Pearson £22 10s
35	Hannah Smith £10
36	Robert Gurnell £22 10s
37	William Walmsley £4
38	John Barber house and goods £40 14s 8d
39	William Ryder goods £3 £28 10s
40	Richard Wilkinson goods £70
41	Willaim Walmsley £41
42	Thomas Anderton £30
43	John Kay corn 47s
44	Henry Heaton £6
45	John Maitland £4
46	Agnes Patten £140
47	Thomas Johnson linen, cloth £5
48	Richard Pedder cloth £5
49	Richard Suddall £42 15s
50	Willliam Wall 2 houses Churchgate £100
51	Nicholas Heslett £15
52	Thomas Hodgkinson £10
53	Alexander Osbaldeston £60
54	William Beasley £19
55	Mary Osbaldeston £95
56	Nicholas Starkie House and stables £482
57	Richard Bentinshall £30
58	Richard Casson £30
59	William Lemon £50
60	William Arkwright £40
61	William Gradwell Barns £211 Goods £171
62	Henry Parr £20
63	John Winckley £60
64	Henry Newsham 2 cottages and goods £47
65	Richard Gwen £25 5s 9d
66	Elizabeth Tomlinson £20
67	Mrs Mary Stanley £35
68	Sir Edward Stanley £55

Appendix 4: Civilian Losses

69 Sir Henry Hoghton Barn and corn £352
70 William Jackson House in Churchgate £9 10s
71 Mrs Elizabeth Stanley £26
72 Roger Welchman £70
73 Edward Stanley House in Churchgate £116
74 James Drinkwater £8
75 Frances Garstang £18
76 Robert Clark £15
77 Thomas sill £15
78 Cutt Nixon £8 8s 6d
79 John Singleton £48
80 John Cumbrall 5 houses and 1 barn £125
81 Edward Smith house and barn in Friargate £140
82 James Green Barn and goods £120
83 Henry Barnes £24
84 John Colly Cash, goods and corn £19 7s
85 Thomas Molyneux Esq. House in Churchgate £56
86 John and William Richardson £23
87 William Markow £8
88 William Richardson £27
89 John Richardson £27
90 Thomas Nock £30
91 Ellen Farnworth £23
92 William Rowe £4
93 Hugh Walker Barn, corn, hay £40
94 Alice Forshaw 30s
95 Samuel Peploe Goods £72 5s Plundered barn £35
96 William Hobson barn £5
97 Elizabeth Settle linen £11
98 Benjamin Cardwell £9
99 John Nock goods from Friargate £14
100 Robert Winder goods £2
101 George Tirson £3 2s
102 Francis Heardley barley in Friargate burnt £9
103 Thomas Walley £12 14s 4d
104 Katherine Atherton kilns in Friargate £15
105 Thomas Walne linen, hay, cloth £7
106 Thomas Kilsham £28
107 Anne Bradley £4

108 Thomas Linsham Goods £12 4s 6d
109 Astell Hodges property in Friargate £13 6s
110 William Hayhurst 5 houses, outhouse, barn in Churchgate and Friargate £200
111 John Hayhurst £5
112 Alice Bolton barn burnt £40
113 Robert Foggy wheat and barley £12 5s
114 Richard Ireland 30s
115 Robert Chaddock £40
116 Francis Maddock £9
117 William Hodgkinson £8
118 Edward Manwaring £5
119 Joseph Bolton house and papers £180
120 Joseph Curtis hay, wine, liquor, linen and goods £40
121 Henry Vincent £7
122 George Taylor £28 9s 6d
123 Henry Judland £7
124 Katherine Richardson £4
125 Mary Thorpe 15s
126 William Astley £2 3s
127 William Salter £8
128 James Smith £5 5s
129 Alice Rishton £21 1s 6d
130 Thomas Astley £3 5s
131 Rudolph Cooke £3 2s 6d
132 Margery Blanklegde £7
133 James Parkinson £10 19s 11d
134 Margaret Parr £4
135 Henry hays corn and hay Fishergate £8
136 Larori Salter corn and hay £5 10d
137 Robert Read £3 10s
138 Richard Translaigh Friargate £6
139 Armet Heslington goods £14
140 James Aldred £27
141 James Cattan 20s
142 Thomas Lettmore shoes and leather 25sd
143 Elana Greenwood £10
144 Edward Burton house £9 5s
145 Thomas Sander £62 10s

146	Ewin Hodgkinson £5 5s
147	John Salter corn and hay £49 7s
148	Jeremiah Wilson £11 7s 5d
149	Joseph Drinkwater cash £6
150	Thomas Anderson? ?
151	Thomas wood, £51 14s 6d
152	William Entwhistle, goods, £51 1s 6d
153	Richard Linesay, ditto, £2 10s
154	Richard Shakeshaft corn, goods, £8 10s
155	Richard Sharp, wigs and hair, £31
156	Thomas Aspinall, cash to Jacobites, £6 17s
157	Michael Postlewhaite cash by Jacobites, £14 1s 2d
158	John Hodgson goods, £30 19s
159	Richard Norlett, goods £21 7s
160	Edmund Churcholm, horse by jacobites, £12
161	Willaim Gratson, horse by acobites, £5 15s
162	Michael postlewhaite, goodsm £40
163	George Rishton, goods £15
164	Mary Woods, goods £15 3s 6d
165	Robert Heathm goods, £2 3s
166	Margaret Salter, beds and linen, £3
167	Ewan Ware, goods, £21 10s
168	Edward Lucas, books, clothes, £3 3s
169	Thomas Dolphin, goods £5
170	Thomas Sudell, goods burnt £5
171	Richard Gradwell, goods and corn, £24
172	Seth Jolly, goods, £2 16s
173	Robert Boyes £30, house used for prisoners 2 weeks.
174	Henry Bayley, goods, £5
175	Henry Fisher, £3 15s
176	Thurston Welch, £4 12S
177	Robert Pilkington, £11 6s
178	Elizabeth Walmsley, goods, £20
179	Hugh Barton, goods £2
180	Henry Shippard, house and goods burnt, £14
181	Edward France, barley burnt, £3 13s
182	David Brown, barley £5 2s
183	Edward Farnworth, goods, £30
184	John Lamplugh, goods, £4

185 Ellis Guest, goods, £3
186 Edward Haydock, hay, ale goods, £16
187 John wade, goods, £68
188 Richard Myers £31 19s 11d
189 John Newsham, goods, £9
190 John Thornton, hay and straw, gods £30
191 Ann Tomlinson, stable, mill and goods £30
192 John Silcock, Goods, £4
193 Jennett Seed, ditto, £5
194 John Parr, ditto, £15
195 Nicholas Brammell, ditto £19
196 John Poole, ditto, £7
197 Nathaniel; Aspden, ditto, £10
198 William Goodshew, ditto, £5 10s
199 Margaret Ridding, goods, £3
200 Elizabeth Preston, goods, £4
201 John Mitton, goods, £2 5s
202 Thomas Marsden, £1 15s
203 John Ryley and John Handkinson for William Johnson, property £15 10s
204 Anne Croole, goods, £7
205 John Walker, lead etc. £3 10s
206 George Clarke, £17 clothes, sheets, napkins, hay brass candlesticks and £1 16s 6d excise from Jacobites
207 James Greene goods £16
208 Christopher Knutt barley, kiln £5 12s 6d
209 Thomas Addison, hay £3 10s
210 Liver Wilson hay, corn £25
211 Thomas Becconsall barn Friargate £8
212 Hugh Harmon barley £4 8s
213 The Parish Church ... defaced and injured in the seats, floor, windows and several ornaments' £41 7s 1d
214 James Bolton 2 houses, barn outhouse £100
215 Richard Bray, goods, £35
216 James Prokter, ditto, £1 7s 8d
217 Richard Dickinson, horse and money, £7
218 Stephen Elliott, wood and goods burnt, £3
219 Jon Melling, wood, £35
220 Alexander Hudson, goods, £30
221 Timothy Ethough, goods, £20

222　James Derbishire, burnt and lost goods £3
223　Francis Bramwell goods, apparel £3
224　Mercy Copper, goods and money 40s
226　Anne Hatch, goods, burnt by regulars, £30

TNA, FEC1/246-250

Selected Bibliography

Manuscript Collections

Blair Castle
Atholl Papers 45/12/77

Bodleian Library
MS Eng. Misc e331

British Library, London
Additional Manuscripts, 37993, 63093
Stowe Mss 748, 750

Cheshire Record Office
AF/49g/50
DSS1/3/88/6

Chetham's Library
MUN. A2.137

Cumbria Archives: Carlisle
CA2/3
PR110/75

Cumbria Archives: Kendal
WPR18W1, 19, 28, 43/W1, WQ/0/2

Durham University Library Archives and Special Collections
Clavering Correspondence

Hertfordshire Record Office
D/EP F195

Lancashire Record Office
DDPT 14
DDX 198/108
DDX2244/1
PR2956/2/1
PR3360/4/1/1
PR3168/7/9
PR2566
PR183
PR3360/4/1/1
RCFE2/1

Leeds University Library Special Collections
Townshend Papers

Manchester Central Library
L1/21/4/21 and 42/1/10

The National Archives, Kew
ASSI 41/1 Northern Assizes
CHES 24 Palatinate of Chester
KB8 and 33 Court of King's Bench
PL28/1 Palatinate of Lancashire
SP35 State Papers: Domestic
SP44 Secretaries of State
SP54 State Papers: Scotland
TS23/34 Treasury Solicitors
WO War Office: 4/7 17, 5/20, 71/122, 116/1

National Archives of Scotland, Edinburgh
GD45/1/201
GD220/5/601

Northumberland Record Office
ZCE10/2

Printed Primary Material

Anon., *A Compleat History of the Late Rebellion*, London: W. Hinchliffe, 1716.

Anon., *The History of all the mobs and insurrections in Great Britain, from William the Conqueror to the Present Time*, London, 1715.

Anon., *A Letter about the Occurrences from and at Preston*, Edinburgh, 1718.

Anon., *The Life of the Late Right Honourable George, Lord Carpenter*, London: E. Curll, 1736.

Anon., 'Sheriff's expenses', *Lancashire and Cheshire Historical Society*, XII, 1859–60.

Anon., *A True and Exact Copy*, Manchester, 1715.

Baldwin, Thomas, *The folly of preferring a Popish Pretender to a Protestant King*, Liverpool, 1716.

Bennett, Benjamin, *A Memorial of the Reformation...*, London: John Clark, 1721.

Berington, Joseph, *The State and Behaviour of the English Catholics from the reformation to the year 1780*, London: R. Faulder, 1780.

Blundell, Nicholas, 'The Great Diurnall of Nicholas Blundell', II, 1712–19, ed. Frank Tyrer, *Record Society of Lancashire and Cheshire*, 1970.

Calendar of Treasury Books and Papers, 1716, London: HMSO.

Calendar of Treasury Books, XXIX, 1714–15, London: HMSO.

——, XXXII, 1716, London: HMSO.

——, XXXIII, 1717, London: HMSO.

Clarke, Peter, 'Journal of Several Occurrences from 2nd November 1715 in the Insurrection Begun in Scotland and Concluded at Preston in Lancashire', in *Miscellany of the Scottish Historical Society*, vol. 1, Edinburgh: T. and A. Constable, 1893.

Clavering, James, 'Some Clavering Correspondence', ed. Edward Hughes, *Archaeologia Aeliana*, XXXIV, 1956.

Clegg, James, 'The Diary of James Clegg of Chapel en le Frith', 1708–55, III, ed. Vanessa Doe, *Derbyshire Record Society*, V, 1981.

Colville, Charles, 'Military Memoirs of Lieutenant General the Hon. Charles Colville', ed. J.O. Robson, *Journal of the Society for Army Historical Research*, XXV, 1947.

Cowper, Mary, *Diary of Mary, Lady Cowper*, ed. Spencer Compton, London: John Murray, 1865.

Dalton, Charles, *English Army Lists*, VI, London: Eyre and Spottiswoode, 1904.

——, *George I's Army*, London: Eyre and Spottiswoode, 1930.

——, *List of Half Pay Officers*, London: Private circulation, 1900.

Defoe, Daniel, *Daniel Defoe: A Tour around the Whole Island of Great Britain*, ed. Pat Rogers, Harmondsworth: Penguin, 1970.

Doddridge, Phillip, *Some Remarkable Passages in the Life of the Hon. Colonel James Gardner*, Hedley: Thomas and Cornish, 1812.

Estcourt, John Edgar and Payne, John, eds., *The English Catholic Non Jurors of 1715; being a summary of the register of their estates with genealogical notes*, Farnborough: Gregg, 1969.

Faithful Register of the Late Rebellion, London. T. Warner, 1717.

Fiennes, Celia, *The Journeys of Celia Fiennes*, ed. Christopher Morris, New York, Chanticleer Press, 1949.

Fitzherbert-Brockholes, D., ed., 'A Narrative of the Fifteen', *Lancashire and Cheshire Historical Society*, II, 64, 1912.

France, R.S., ed., 'Registers of the Estates of Lancashire Papists, 1717–1788', I, *Record Society of Lancashire and Cheshire*, 1945.

Griffiths, Nehemiah, 'Diary of Nehemiah Griffiths', ed. J.C. Bridge, *Journal of the Chester and North Wales Archaeological and Historic Society*, 1909.

Hearne, Thomas, *The Remains of Thomas Hearne*, ed. John Buchanan-Brown, London: Centaur Press Ltd, 1966.

Hibbert-Ware, Samuel, 'Memorials of the Rebellion of 1715', *Chetham Society*, V, 1845.

Hilton, George, *The Rake's Diary; The Journal of George Hilton*, ed. Anne Hillman, Kendal, Curwen Archives Trust, 1994.

Historical Manuscripts Commission, Calendar of the Stuart Papers, I–III, London: HMSO, 1902–1920.

——, Manuscripts of the Earl of Carlisle, London HMSO, 1897.

——, Manuscripts of J.J. Johnstone Esq., of Annandale, London: HMSO, 1897.

——, Manuscripts of S.H. Le Fleming Esq., of Rydal Hall, London: HMSO, 1896.

——, Manuscripts of the Marquess Townshend, London: HMSO, 1887.

Hoghton, Henry, 'A Calendar of the deeds and papers in the possession of Sir James de Hoghton, baronet of Hoghton Tower, Lancashire', ed. J. Lumby, *Record Society of Lancashire and Cheshire*, 88, Chadwyck Healey, 1936.

Jarvis, Rupert, 'Customs Letter Books of the Port of Liverpool, 1711–1813', *Chetham Society*, 3rd series, 6, 1954.

——, *The Jacobite Risings of 1715 and 1745 compiled from documents in the possession of the Cumberland County Council*, Cumberland: Cumberland County Council, 1954.

Liddell, Henry, 'The Letters of Henry Liddell to William Cotesworth', ed. Joyce Ellis, *Surtees Society*, 197, 1987.

Maxwell, James, *A Narrative of the Expedition of Prince Charles Edward Stuart to Scotland in 1745*, Edinburgh: T. Constable, 1841.

Murray, John, 'Memorials of Murray of Broughton Sometime Secretary to Prince Charles Edward, 1740–1747', ed. Robert Bell, Edinburgh, *Scottish Historical Society*, 27, 1898.

Lyme Letters, 1660–1760, ed. Lady Newton, London: William Heinemann Ltd, 1936.Nicolson, William, 'Diaries of Bishop Nicolson', ed. Bishop of Barrow in Furness, *Cumberland and Westmorland Archaeological and Antiquarian Society Transactions*, new series, V, 1905.

——, *Letters on various subjects; literary, political and ecclesiastical, to and from William Nicolson*, London, 1809.

Oldmixon, John, *The History of England during the reigns of the royal houses of Stuarts*, London: J. Pemberton, 1730.

Patten, Robert, *History of the Rebellion*, London: J. Roberts, 1745.

Peploe, Samuel, *God's peculiar Care in preservation of our religion and liberties: A sermon preached at Lancaster Assizes the 24th of March 1716*, London: A. Eaton and D. Birchall, 1716.

Prescott, Henry, 'The Diary of Henry Prescott, LL.B., Deputy Registrar of Chester Diocese, II', ed. John Addy and Peter McNiven, *Record Society of Lancashire and Cheshire*, 132, 1994.

Radcliffe, Charles, *A Genuine and Impartial Account of the remarkable Life and Viccssitudes of fortune of Charles Radcliffe, Esq.*, ed. Gerard Penrice, London, 1747.

Rae, Peter *History of the Late Rebellion rais'd against ... King George by the friends of the Popish Pretender*, Dumfries, 1746.

Ryder, Dudley, *The Diary of Dudley Ryder, 1715–1716*, ed. William Matthews, London: Methuen, 1939.

Sanderson, Thomas, *The Life and Literary Remains of Thomas Sanderson*, ed. J. Lowthian, Carlisle, 1829.

Shairp, Walter and Craggs, 'Jacobites and Jacobins: Two Eighteenth Century Perspectives. The Memoir of Walter Shairp: The Story of the Liverpool Regiment during the Jacobite Rebellion of 1745 and The Writings of the Cragg Family of Wyresdale', ed. Jonathan Oates and Katrina Navickas, *Record Society of Lancashire and Cheshire*, 3rd series, 25, 2006.

Sinclair, John, *Memoirs of the Insurrection in Scotland in 1715*, ed. Walter Scott, Edinburgh: Abbotsford Club, 1845.

Stout, William, *The Autobiography of William Stout of Lancaster, 1665–1752*, ed. John Marshall, Manchester: Manchester University Press, 1967.

Symson, Joseph, *An Exact and Industrious Tradesman, The Letter Books of Joseph Symson, 1711–1719*, ed. S.D. Smith, Oxford: Oxford University Press, 2003.
Thoresby, Ralph, *Letters of Eminent Men to Ralph Thoresby*, II, Colburn, 1832.
Tyldesley, John, *The Tyldesley Diary: the personal record of Thomas Tyldesley during the years 1712, 1713, 1714*, ed. John Gillow, Preston: A. Hewitson, 1873.
Walpole, Robert, *The Memoirs of the Life and Administration of Sir Robert Walpole* I, ed. William Coxe, London, 1798.
Warrender, George, Warrender Letters of 1715, ed. Walter Dickson, *Scottish Historical Society*, 3rd series, 25, 1935.
The Bristol Post Man, 1716
The Daily Courant, 1715
The Flying Post, 1715–1716
The Ipswich Journal, 1733
The London Gazette, 1714–1716
The Original Weekly Journal, 1715 and 1716
The Post Boy, 1714
The St. James' Evening Post, 1715–1716
The Weekly Journal, 1716–1717.

Secondary Works

Arnold, Ralph, *Northern Lights: The Story of the Lord Derwentwater*, London: Constable, 1959.
Barratt, John *Cavaliers: The Royalist Army at War, 1642–1646*, Stroud: Sutton, 2004.
Barthorp, Michael, *The Jacobite Rebellions, 1689–1745*, London: Osprey, 1982.
Baskerville, S.W., 'The political behaviour of the Cheshire clergy, 1705–1752', *Northern History*, XXIII, 1987.
Baynes, John, *The Jacobite Rising of 1715*, London: Cassell, 1970.
Bennett, J.H.E., 'Cheshire and the Fifteen', *Journal of the Chester and North Wales Archaeological and Historic Society*, ns 21, 1915.
Blackwood, B.G., 'Lancashire Catholics, Protestants and Jacobites during the 1715 Rebellion', *Recusant History*, 22/1, 1994.
Cruickshanks, Eveline, ed., *Ideology and Conspiracy: Aspects of Jacobitism, 1689–1759*, Edinburgh: John Donald, 1981.
Cruickshanks, Eveline, Handley, Stuart and Hayton, David, *House of Commons, 1690–1715*, II, Cambridge University Press, 2002.
Duffy, Christopher, *The '45*, London: Cassel, 2003.

Earl of Egerton, 'The Cheshire gentry in 1715', *Cheshire and North Wales Archaeological Society Journal*, XV, 1909.

Earle, Peter, *Monmouth's Rebels: The Road to Sedgemoor, 1685*, London: Weidenfeld and Nicolson, 1977.

Gillow, J., *A Literary and Biographical Dictionary of the English Catholics*, New York: Burt Franklin, 1969.

Gold, Claudia, *The King's Mistress*, Quercus, 2012.

Gooch, Leo, *The Desperate Faction? The Jacobites of North East England, 1688-1746*, Hull University Press, 1995.

Gooderson, P., *A History of Lancashire*, London: Batsford, 1980.

Green, P.G., 'Charity, morality and social control, clerical attitudes in the diocese of Chester, 1715-1795', *Lancashire and Cheshire Archaeological Society*, 141, 1992.

——, 'Samuel Peploe and the ideology of anti-Catholicism among the Anglican clergy in early Hanoverian England', *Lancashire and Cheshire Historical Society*, 145, 1996.

Hardwick, Charles. *History of the Borough of Preston and its Environs in the County of Lancaster*, Preston: Worthington and Company, 1857.Haydon, Colin, *Anti-Catholicism in Eighteenth Century England, c. 1714-1780*, Manchester: Manchester University Press, 1993.

——, 'Samuel Peploe and Catholicism in Preston, 1714', *Recusant History*, 20/1, 1990.

Hilton, John Anthony, *Catholic Lancashire: A Historical Guide*, Wigan: North West Catholic Historical Society, 1981.

Hodson, Howard, *Cheshire, 1660-1780: Restoration to Industrial Revolution*, Chester: Watergate, 1978.

Holmes, Geoffrey, *The Making of a Great Power, England, Late Stuart and Early Georgian England: 1660-1722*, Harlow: Pearson, 1993.

Holmes, Geoffrey and Szechi, Daniel, *The Age of Oligarchy, Pre Industrial Britain, 1722-1783*, Harlow: Pearson, 1992.

Jarvis, Rupert, *Collected Papers on the Jacobite Risings*, Manchester: Manchester University Press, 1971.

Kirk, John, *Biographies of the English Catholics in the Eighteenth Century*, London: Burn and Oates, 1909.

Lenman, Bruce, *The Jacobite Risings in Britain, 1689-1746*, London: Eyre Methuen, 1980.

Lord, Evelyn, *The Stuarts' Secret Army, English Jacobites, 1689-1752*, New York: Pearson, 2004.

Lole, F.P., 'A Digest of the Jacobite Clubs', *Royal Stuart Society Paper*, LV, 1999.

McCord, Norman and Thompson, Richard, *The Northern Counties from AD1000*, London: Longman, 1998.

Monod, Paul, *Jacobitism and the English People, 1689–1788*, Cambridge University Press, 1989.

Nicholson, A., 'Lancashire in the Rebellion of 1715', *Lancashire and Cheshire Archaeological Society*, III, 1885.

Oates, Jonathan, 'The aftermath of the Jacobite Rebellion of 1715 in Northern England', *Northern History*, XLIV, 2008.

——, 'The armies operating in the North of England in 1715', *Journal of the Society for Army Historical Research*, 2012.

——, 'Cumberland and Westmorland in the Jacobite Rebellion of 1715', *Transactions of the Cumberland and Westmorland Archaeological and Antiquarian Society*, VI, 2006.

——, *The Jacobite Invasion of 1745 in North West England*, Lancaster University, 2006.

——, 'Jacobitism and popular disturbances in Northern England, 1714–1719', *Northern History*, XLI: 1, 2004.

——, 'Responses in the North of England to the Jacobite Rebellion of 1715', *Northern History*, XLIII, 2006.

——, 'Responses in Newcastle to the Jacobite Rebellions of 1715 and 1745', *Archaeologia Aeliana*, 5th series, 2003.

Oxford Dictionary of National Biography, 2004.

Phillips, Colin and Smith, John, *Lancashire and Cheshire from AD 1540*, London: Longman, 1998.

Pittock, Murray, *Jacobitism*, Basingstoke: Macmillan, 1998.

Plumb, John, *The First Four Georges*, London: Fontana, 1956.

Purcell, P., 'The Jacobite Rising of 1715 and the English Catholics', *English Historical Review*, 1929.

Reid, Stuart, *Like Hungry Wolves: Culloden Moor the 16 April 1746*, London: Windrow and Greene, 1994.

Roberts, John, *The Highland Wars: Scotland and the Military Campaigns of 1715 and 1745*, Edinburgh: Polygon, 2002.

Sadler, John, *Culloden: The Last Charge of the Highland Clans: 1746*, Stroud: Tempus, 2006.

Sankey, Margaret, *Jacobite Prisoners of 1715: Preventing and Punishing Insurrection in Early Hanoverian Britain*, Aldershot: Ashgate, 2006.

Sedgwick, Romney, *History of Parliament: The Commons, 1715–1754*, London: HMSO, 1970.

Speck, William, *Stability and Strife, England 1714–1760*, London: Edward Arnold, 1977.

Stevenson-Sinclair, Christopher, *Inglorious Rebellion: The Jacobite Risings of 1708, 1715 and 1719*, London, 1971.

Szechi, Daniel, *The Jacobites: Britain and Europe, 1689–1788*, Manchester: Manchester University Press, 1994.

——, *1715: The Great Jacobite Rebellion*, London: Yale University Press, 2006.

Tayler, Alistair and Henrietta, *1715: The Story of the Rising*, London: Thomas Nelson and Sons. 1936.

Victoria County History of Cumberland, II, ed. James Wilson, London: Archibald Constable and Co. Ltd, 1905.

Victoria County History of Lancashire, IV, V, VII, VIII, ed. William Page, London: Constable and Co. Ltd, 1911–1914.

Wardle, A.C., 'Sir Thomas Johnson and the Jacobite Rebels', *Lancashire and Cheshire Historical Society*, 91, 1939.

Williams, J.A., 'The distribution of Catholic chaplains in the early eighteenth century', *Recusant History*, 12 1973.

Index

Appleby 63, 68, 76–9, 84, 100, 187
Argyle, John Campbell, Duke of 2, 27, 34, 42–5, 47, 59, 118, 127, 145, 149, 157, 159–60, 181, 189, 191
army, Jacobite
    artillery 82, 115–17, 128, 133, 135, 138
    casualties 141, 155
    cavalry 44, 48–9, 85, 113, 115–16, 127–8, 131, 148–9
    infantry 44, 48–50, 85, 113–16, 125, 128, 131, 148–9
    leadership 9, 46, 48–9, 109–11, 113, 125, 134, 140, 190
    numbers 2, 6–7, 33–4, 40–41, 44–5, 50–51, 55, 71, 85, 98, 127–30
    officers 111–13
    rank and file 34, 97–103, 197, 215
    recruitment 7, 29–33, 39, 78, 80–81, 84–7, 95, 98
    tactics 114
    weaponry 40, 44, 86–7, 113–17
    see also individual leaders
army, regular 1, 25–7, 33, 60, 67, 72, 74, 76, 95
    artillery 120, 126
    casualties 135–9, 154–5, 217–20
    cavalry 25, 33, 45–7, 90, 120–21, 126–7, 152
    infantry 25, 120–21, 126–7
    leadership 117–18
    numbers 126–7
    officers 118–19
    reliability 23, 121
    tactics 121
    weaponry 45, 120
    see regiments and individual officers

bell ringing 5, 13, 15, 18, 20–24, 68, 79, 87, 93–4, 150, 161
Berwick 30, 35, 38–9
Blackett, Sir Willia 37, 39–41, 153
Blundell, Nicholas 14, 26, 66, 88–9, 108, 182
Bolingbroke, Henry St. John, 1st Viscount 24, 30, 104

Carlisle 11–15, 25–6, 60–63, 66–7, 76, 78, 105, 107, 161–2, 180, 188
Carlisle, Charles Howard, Earl of 16, 26, 62–4, 68–9, 90, 92, 105, 151, 153, 163, 180
Carpenter, Lieutenant General George 2, 36, 44–9, 52–3, 73, 82, 88, 90–92, 96, 117–20, 123, 125–7, 130, 141–7, 151, 153–5, 157, 161, 166, 190–91
Catholics 6–7, 11, 14, 18, 25–6, 29–30, 33, 38, 55–7, 62–6, 68, 78, 80–81, 84–6, 89, 94, 97–8, 100–101, 103, 105, 108–10, 116, 162, 181–4, 186, 191, 198–214
Cheshire 7, 12, 14–18, 24–6, 57–60, 65, 68, 80, 91–2, 94, 98, 100–101, 103–4, 106, 162, 184–6, 197
Chester 11, 15–18, 20, 25, 59–61, 65, 67–8, 87, 90, 92–5, 105, 118, 121, 150, 160, 162, 164–6, 168, 172–3, 175–6, 178–80, 182, 185, 187
Cholmondeley, Hugh Cholmondeley, Earl of 26, 93–4, 106, 160, 163, 166
Church of England clergy 6, 13, 15, 20–21, 26, 33–4, 40, 56, 59, 67–8, 73, 77, 79, 84, 88, 93, 101, 103–5, 107–8, 160, 162–3, 178, *see also* individual clergymen

churchwardens 5, 68, 103, 170
Clarke, Peter 73–5, 80, 82–4, 87, 131, 135, 152, 154–5
Colville, Ensign Charles 119, 127, 130, 136–7, 139, 145
constables 5, 21, 26, 32, 62–3, 65–6, 80–81, 102, 153, 169
Cotesworth, Robert 156, 171, 177–8, 181
Cotesworth, William 4, 32–3, 35–8, 40, 52, 177
Cumberland 5, 7, 12–13, 16, 23, 26, 57–9, 62–5, 72–3, 76–8, 84, 94, 96, 98, 103, 105, 107, 113, 197–8

Derby, Edward Stanley, 10th Earl of 16, 61, 65, 106, 161, 166
Derwentwater, James Radcliffe, 3rd Earl of 2–3, 32, 40, 45, 58, 75, 86, 89, 110–11, 113, 125, 131–3, 138, 140, 142, 145–8, 150, 161, 166
discharges 170, 172–3, 180, 197–9, 201–3, 205–9, 211, 213
dissenters 6–7, 14, 18–22, 57, 59, 84, 102–3, 105–8, 122, 126, 131, 162–4
Dormer, James, Brigadier 118, 126, 131, 135, 218
Dumfries 41, 47, 49–50, 75
Dutch forces 25, 157–9

Edinburgh 27, 36, 41, 43–4, 47, 60
Eecapes 152, 175–6, 180, 197–8, 205, 214–15
executions 101, 165–6, 170–73, 180, 186, 197, 200–204, 207–10, 212–14

Fenton, Dr James 83–4, 188
Forrester, George, Lord 119, 137–8, 152, 218
Forster, Thomas, 2, 7–8, 32–5, 38–9, 41–3, 46, 51, 53, 71, 77, 79, 91, 109–11, 123, 125, 127, 131, 136–8, 140, 142–5, 147–8, 150–51, 153, 161, 166, 191
  criticism of, 7, 9, 97, 109–10, 137, 142, 147–8, 150–51

Gardiner, Captain James 119, 139, 187
George I, King of Great Britain 2–3, 6, 9, 12–14, 15, 17–18, 20, 23–4, 26, 30–31, 34, 37, 47, 58–9, 62, 71, 86, 88, 105–8, 119, 122, 152, 161–2, 181, 184–6
Glasgow 47, 49

Hexham 39–42, 44, 52
Hilton, George 84, 100, 182, 214
Hoghton, Sir Henry 17, 65, 81–2, 92, 106–7, 126, 156, 161, 163, 167, 188, 223
Holy Island 30, 38
Honeywood, Brigadier Phillip 118, 126, 131, 134–6, 151, 218

Jacobitism 2, 10, 58, 94,
  rioting 2, 4, 15, 18–22, 27, 30, 37, 59–60, 62, 84, 102–3, 193–5
  verbal 2, 6, 13, 15, 22–3, 37, 58–9, 81, 94–5, 103, 171–2, 179, 185–6
James II, King of Great Britain 2, 11–12, 56, 64, 101, 105–6, 109, 111, 162, 165
James Stuart 2, 12–13, 17, 20–21, 24, 30–31, 34, 39–40, 42–3, 58–60, 62, 67, 71, 74, 86–7, 95, 101, 104, 122, 151, 159, 161, 165, 172, 179, 184–5
Johnson, John 4, 35–7, 40, 45, 52
Justices of the Peace 5, 16–17, 22, 26, 32, 65, 77, 80–82, 94, 109, 167–8, 184

Kelso 42–5, 48–9, 51–3, 95, 116, 190
Kendal 13, 15, 61, 64, 71–2, 76, 78–80, 184, 187, 215
Kenmure, William, Viscount 41, 43, 45, 51, 53, 111, 125, 133, 147, 150, 166
Kirkby Lonsdale 64, 68, 72, 78–9, 107, 161, 214

Lancashire 5–7, 11–14, 15–17, 22, 26, 40, 47, 50, 55–8, 60–61, 63, 65, 67–9, 78, 80–81, 84–6, 88–9, 91, 94–8,

100, 103, 105, 108, 110, 125–6, 128, 131–2, 157, 164, 167–70, 172–3, 176–7, 181–3, 185–6, 189, 191, 198–214
Lancaster 14, 23–4, 57, 61, 72, 81–7, 88, 90, 95–6, 98, 104, 116, 124, 128, 141, 148, 162, 166, 168, 170–73, 176–7, 180–82, 185, 187–8, 198–9, 201–2, 205, 207–9, 212
Liddell, Henry 33, 36–8, 40, 156, 167, 179, 186
Liverpool 13, 15, 24, 27, 57–8, 85, 89, 91–2, 108, 124–6, 143, 153, 161, 165–6, 168, 170, 173–6, 178–80, 184, 190
London 13, 15, 21, 25–6, 31–4, 36, 60, 64, 67, 72, 90, 93, 95, 108, 152, 156, 166–9, 172, 175, 182, 189
Lonsdale, Henry Lowther, Viscount 63–5, 67–9, 72–4, 75, 106, 180
Louis XIV, King of France 11, 24, 30–31, 111
loyalism,
    addresses 14–15, 61–2, 161–2, 186
    public displays 13–15, 18, 24, 26, 37, 59, 61, 93, 159–61, 186
    see also bellringing

Mackintosh, William, of Borlum 42–3, 48, 51, 111, 113–14, 116–17, 128, 131–3, 135–7, 140, 146–8, 150–51, 166
Manchester 18–22, 24, 55, 58. 60, 80, 85, 88, 90–91, 93, 101–3, 126, 130–31, 135, 162–3, 168, 170–72, 184–5, 188, 190, 193, 203–4, 206, 208–10, 213
Mar, John Erskine, Earl of 2, 26, 32–4, 37, 41–3, 44–5, 47, 51, 55, 60–61, 97, 110–11, 113, 129, 140, 149–51, 159, 171, 179, 181, 185, 190–91
Marlborough, John Churchill, Duke of 16–17, 59, 91, 117, 127, 155, 158
militia 25–6, 35–7, 49–50, 55, 62–6, 72–5, 78–9, 81, 85–6, 88–90, 92–3,

96–7, 102–3, 107–108, 121–2, 126–7, 140–41, 143, 160
Monmouth, James Scott, Duke of 31, 50, 85, 110, 121–2, 130, 151, 153, 167
Morpeth 34, 36, 39
Munden, Richard, Brigadier 118, 120, 126, 131
Murray, Lord Charles 112, 114, 128, 133, 138, 141–2, 148, 165, 179

Newcastle 6, 26, 29, 31–41, 44, 46, 52, 90, 96, 122, 143, 183, 190
Nicolson, William, Bishop of Carlisle 13–14, 23, 56, 60, 63, 67–9, 73–4, 76, 79, 107, 160, 180–81
Northumberland 4, 29–33, 39, 42–4, 46, 56, 58, 60, 65, 69, 73, 79–80, 85, 95, 97, 99, 109–10, 122, 128, 141, 180, 186, 189

Ormonde, Duke of 16, 24, 26, 30, 27, 58, 61, 84, 104
Owen, Charles 73–4, 82, 90, 163
Oxburgh, Colonel Henry 31, 110, 144–7, 162

Patten, Rev. Robert 4, 7, 9, 31, 35, 40, 42, 44–5, 48, 71, 74, 76–8, 81–2, 84–5, 91, 101, 106–7, 109–11, 115, 125, 128–9, 131–2, 134–5, 137–42, 144, 147, 149, 151, 154–5, 157
Pelham, Henry 119, 188
Penrith 23, 63, 68, 72–3, 75–6, 78–9, 96, 107, 141, 161, 187
Peploe, Rev. Samuel 6, 23, 57, 88, 107–8, 156, 161–3, 168, 182–3, 186–7, 223
Perth 26, 51, 157–9, 190
posse 5, 35, 72–8, 96, 108, 122, 141
Prescott, Henry 15–18, 20–21, 24, 26, 60–61, 92–3, 95, 104, 143, 150, 160–61, 163–4, 166, 171, 176, 178–82, 184
Preston 6–7, 9, 17, 24, 57, 61, 65, 72, 79, 82, 85–92, 95, 98–102, 104, 106–8,

114, 116, 120, 123–5, 128–30, 134, 143, 145, 147–8, 152–3, 157, 159–62, 164–5, 167–72, 181–3, 187, 198–214
Preston, battle of 1, 3, 8, 99, 111, 116, 118, 124, 182, 189, 190–92, 219–20
   preliminaries 125–30
   first day 130–43
   second day 143–50
   third day 150–53
   results of outcome 157–8
   damage to civilians/property 140, 152–3, 156, 221–7
   escapes, 140, 152
prisoners 9, 101, 151–2, 156–7, 159, 165–82, 184–5, 197–215,
   see also discharges, escapes, executions, transportation and trials
Pulteney, William 22, 33, 36, 91, 120, 157, 165–6

regiments
   Churchill's Dragoons 36, 120, 144
   Cobham's Dragoons 22, 36–7, 44, 118, 120–21, 144
   Dormer's Dragoons 91, 120, 126, 135, 139, 174, 217–29
   Fane's Foot 52, 91, 120, 127
   Honeywood's Dragoons 52, 90–91, 120–11, 126, 134, 154, 166, 217–18
   Hotham's Foot 35–6, 120
   Molesworth's Dragoons 36, 120, 144
   Munden's Dragoons 90–91, 120, 126, 135, 154, 217–18
   Newton's Dragoons 52, 91, 120, 158
   Pitt's Horse 52, 90–91, 118, 120, 126, 135, 143, 154–5, 217–19
   Preston's Foot 52, 90–91, 118, 120, 123–4, 126–7, 131, 134–8, 154–5, 217–20
   Sabine's Foot 52, 91, 120, 127
   Stanhope's Dragoons 82, 85, 90, 120, 126, 136, 139, 141, 158, 217–19
   Wynn's Dragoons 52, 90–91, 120, 126, 135–6, 154, 217–19

Ryder, Dudley 72–4, 82, 85, 90, 104

Scarborough, Earl of 33, 36–7
Sheriffmuir 3, 110, 114, 127, 149, 157–8, 160–61, 190–91
Sheriffs 13, 15, 37, 61, 73–4, 89, 107, 122, 167, 171,
   see also Johnson, John
Stanhope, James 16, 27, 118, 166, 173
Stanwix, Brigadier Thomas 51, 63, 67–9, 76, 107, 161
Stirling 26, 43–4, 47, 159–60
Stout, William 14, 84, 88, 95, 160, 164, 178
Sydall, Thomas 20, 22–3, 84, 99, 103–4, 152, 168, 170–72, 188, 193, 210
Symson, Joseph 13, 16–17, 23, 64, 73, 76–7, 79–80, 106, 108, 160, 179–80, 186

Tories 6–7, 12–13, 16–18, 21, 24, 30, 37–8, 57–8, 61, 66–7, 78, 84–5, 90, 104, 106, 159, 163, 182
Towneley, Richard 55, 80, 87–9, 98–9, 102, 103, 166, 173, 182, 188, 212
Townshend, Charles, Viscount 16, 18, 22–3, 26–7, 33, 36, 56, 65, 67–9, 76, 80, 82, 92, 94, 121, 129, 155–7, 163
transportation 172–5, 180–86, 198–201, 204–5, 207–10, 213–14
trials 23, 125, 145–6, 165, 167–70, 172–3, 180, 185, 198–204, 206–7, 209–13
Tyldesely, John 83, 89, 166, 173, 212

Westmorland 7, 23, 55, 57, 59, 61–3, 65, 67, 73, 76–8, 80, 84, 98, 100, 103, 105, 107, 182, 214
Whigs 6, 12–13, 15–18, 20–21, 24, 26, 35–8, 40, 51, 56–7, 59, 61, 67, 72, 101, 105, 107–8, 122, 159–60, 162–4, 179–180, 183, 185–6
Widdrington, William, Earl of 33–4, 55, 80, 99, 111, 125, 140, 144–5, 147–8, 166
William III, King of Great Britain 11–12, 31, 93, 106–8, 161

Wills, Major General Charles 2, 52, 85, 90–92, 96, 117–20, 123, 125–7, 129–32, 134, 139, 141–7, 150–51, 153–7, 161, 165–6, 173, 187, 190–91

criticism of 123, 141, 154

York 21, 35, 73, 166

Yorkshire 20, 35, 40, 62, 76, 90, 92, 99, 124, 180, 184